COPING
WITH
JOYCE

Woodcut by Sid Chafetz, 1978.

COPING
WITH
JOYCE

Essays from the Copenhagen Symposium

Edited by
MORRIS BEJA
and
SHARI BENSTOCK

Ohio State University Press
Columbus

ACKNOWLEDGMENT

The editors wish to thank Dennis Bingham for his help before the Copenhagen Symposium, and in the preparation of this volume.

LIBRARY OF CONGRESS
Library of Congress Cataloging-in-Publication Data

Coping with Joyce: essays from the Copenhagen symposium / edited by Morris Beja and Shari Benstock.
    p. cm.
   Essays from the Tenth International James Joyce Symposium held in Copenhagen in 1986.
   Includes index.
   ISBN 0-8142-0467-8
   1. Joyce, James, 1882-1941—Criticism and interpretation—Congresses.
I. Beja, Morris. II. Benstock, Shari, 1944-   . III. International James Joyce Symposium (10th : 1986 : Copenhagen, Denmark)
PR6019.O9Z52734 1989   88-21843
823'.912—dc19   CIP

Printed in the U.S.A.

For
Ellen
and for
Berni

CONTENTS

Introduction   ix

Abbreviations   xvii

MAJOR ADDRESS

1. Joyce's Heliotrope
   Margot Norris   3

2. Joyce the Verb
   Fritz Senn   25

3. The Joycead
   Colbert Kearney   55

4. Inscribing James Joyce's Tombstone
   Bernard Benstock   73

5. Joyce and Modernist Ideology
   Robert Scholes   91

CRITICAL STUDIES

6. Farrington the Scrivener: A Story of Dame Street
   Morris Beja   111

7. The Language of *Exiles*
   Clive Hart   123

8. And the Music Goes Round and Round: A Couple of
   New Approaches to Joyce's Uses of Music in *Ulysses*
   Zack Bowen   137

9. "Roll Away the Reel World, the Reel World":
   "Circe" and Cinema
   Austin Briggs   145

10. Images of the Lacanian Gaze in *Ulysses*
    Sheldon Brivic   157

11. Jellyfish and Treacle: Lewis, Joyce, Gender,
    and Modernism
    Bonnie Kime Scott   168

12. The Letter Selfpenned to One's Other: Joyce's Writing,
     Deconstruction, Feminism
     Ellen Carol Jones   180

13. Simulation, Pluralism, and the Politics of Everyday Life
     Jules David Law   195

14. Joyce's Pedagogy: *Ulysses* and *Finnegans Wake*
     as Theory
     Patrick McGee   206

15. From Catechism to Catachresis: Aspects of Joycean
     Pedagogy in *Ulysses* and *Finnegans Wake*
     Lorraine Weir   220

16. ALP's Final Monologue in *Finnegans Wake*: The
     Dialectical Logic of Joyce's Dream Text
     Kimberly Devlin   232

17. Shahrazade, Turko the Terrible, and Shem:
     The Reader as Voyeur in *Finnegans Wake*
     Henriette Lazaridis Power   248

18. The *Wake*'s Confounded Language
     Derek Attridge   262

Contributors   269

Index   273

INTRODUCTION

A couple of decades ago, some scholars and critics had the idea of gathering people together in one spot, for a few days, to talk about a writer whom many people regard as either the greatest writer of the twentieth century, or the most influential, or both. With a touch of veneration (more on that later), they wanted for James Joyce what Simon Dedalus calls in *Ulysses* "a symposium all his own"—and, as he also puts it, the devil wouldn't stop them.

They went to Dublin that first year, and for a long time the James Joyce Foundation, which sponsors and runs what came to be called the International James Joyce Symposia, kept to the tradition of holding them only in cities in which Joyce himself had lived for an extended period of time. Given Joyce's comparatively nomadic life, that would seem to provide a goodly number of choices. Even so, it obviously became unnecessarily or even pedantically limiting.

So the tradition was broken; and when the invitation to hold a Symposium in Copenhaghen in 1986 was issued, it was eagerly accepted. Certainly the timing was right: for the conference, always held around Bloomsday, came within a few weeks, as well, of the fiftieth anniversary of Joyce's own visit to Copenhagen.

There was also a more general appropriateness in the conference being held in the capital city of the Danes who founded the capital city of Ireland in the first place: for to Joyce, Ireland itself seemed a sort of offshoot of Scandinavia. As he wrote in "Ireland, Island of Saints and Sages" in 1907, the original Scandinavians did not leave Ireland, "but were gradually assimilated into the community, a fact we must keep in mind if we want to understand the curious character of the modern Irishman."

At the very start of his literary career, Joyce made clear the importance to him of Scandinavian literature—and especially of Henrik Ibsen. His first notable publication was, after all, on "Ibsen's New Drama," *When We Dead Awaken*. But even before that he had written about Ibsen in his "epiphanies," in one of which Ibsen is called "the greatest man in the world." Later, in 1907, Stanislaus Joyce recorded in his diary that "Jim told me that he is going to expand his story 'Ulysses' into a short book and make a Dublin

ix

'Peer Gynt' of it.'' And in *Finnegans Wake* we have numerous ''peers and gints, quaysirs and gallyliers, fresk letties from the say and stale headygabblers, gaingangers and dudder wagoners, pullars off societies and pushers on rothmere's homes.''

So Joyce's connection with what the ''Ballad of Persse O'Reilly'' calls ''Scandiknavery'' has long been acknowledged. For decades, scholars—especially, of course, Scandinavian scholars, displaying what the *Wake* more positively calls ''domfine norsemanship''—have also chronicled the influence of Joyce on later Nordic writers. All that kept coming up, again and again, during the week-long gathering in the city the *Wake* calls ''the cope of heaven.''

To have reached the milestone of a *Tenth* International James Joyce Symposium also means that we have passed through a succession of James Joyces along the way. As Fritz Senn implies in his provocative address ''named'' ''Joyce the Verb,'' there are as many meanings to the word Joyce, the name Joyce, as there are to that strange word ''Joycean.'' As a community of Joyceans (scholars and readers, teachers and students, translators and enthusiasts) have redefined themselves in various ways over the past two decades of coming together internationally, ''coping'' with Joyce has come to have a meaning beyond the wordplay that associates it with Copenhagen.

Three distinct approaches have previously been apparent to many who have attended these Symposia and the many other Joyce conferences and seminars that have proliferated across the world during the 1970s and 1980s. ''Venerating'' Joyce has long been in evidence, and can still be noticed on occasion: it has made Joyce an insurmountable obstacle, a totem for adulation, which if it has not actually impeded interpretation has at least set the first and forming condition, that Joyce was a genius and in such full control of his material and techniques that his intentions could only be surmised. Veneration has met with skepticism by the younger generation of Joyceans, some of whom have even avoided the name Joycean for fear that it implies unquestioning adulation. In addition, recent theoretical assumptions that all authors lack the authority that resides either in the text or with the reader have made veneration—even of Joyce—uncomfortable. Nonetheless, all of those who approach the Joyce texts find themselves having to contend with the redoubtable *presence* of James Joyce.

Joyceans have also had to face charges of ''exploiting'' Joyce, a concern recently brought forward (at the Symposia and in the media) by Joyce's grandson, Stephen Joyce. The institutionalization of what has been called The Joyce Industry has been responsible for the vast amount of scholarship and criticism filling library shelves, the organizational self-propagation through a series of periodicals—two or three seem always to be in circulation—and the self-identification of a Joycean community made most noticeable by the biannual International Symposia. Stephen Joyce has been particularly offended by the selling of blue-and-white neckties and other such paraphernalia at the Joyce Museum in Sandycove, a "commercialization" of James Joyce that after all was intended to help keep a small and unique museum in operation. That James Joyce was in danger of becoming a commodity in which speculative shares were being bought and sold has bothered Joyceans and others not immediately related to Joyce himself. Yet, since most Joyceans work in the academic marketplace— whose companies rarely appear in the Blue Chips board and where the stakes are usually embarrassingly low—the idea of Joycean academics getting rich on their investments is easily dismissed. But the idea of exploiting Joyce in less obvious ways, of living Joyce's life vicariously, has caused some degree of unease within the community. The mere specter of exploitation, however, has had the effect of reevaluating the scholar's relationship to the subject—and especially the motivations of those who have elected to involve themselves with so prominent a subject.

Perhaps the most audacious approach to that subject over the years has been the intention of "mastering" Joyce, of viewing the texts as capable of yielding up their secrets to the overpowering ingenuity of highly skilled practitioners of the Joycean craft. This *conquistadore* attitude made itself apparent fairly early, long before the first of the Joyce Symposia brought a working community together. It has its touch of Faustian audacity, each alchemist working alone and almost in secret to find the touchstone that would open up the formidable door, each cryptographer intent on breaking the code. Rumors circulated that certain scholars had found the central motif of *Finnegans Wake,* that the "grand design" would soon be disclosed, that a central thesis would be expounded. Others guarded their findings jealously, hinting at what they now knew but refusing to be specific for fear of having their discoveries appropriated. The coming together of a Joycean grouping in regular attendance at the Symposia has done much to dissipate the incipient paranoia, although it has also occasionally contributed to the heady atmosphere in which

Joyceans felt all the more assured of the inevitability (or at least the possibility) of mastering Joyce. Concentrated assault, under a corps of generals, replaced more individualistic forays, and the pooling of knowledge made for a more democratic campaign. Joyce has withstood the onslaught and has no more been mastered than has Nature, and as with Nature, neither exploitation nor veneration has contributed to mastery, an unlocking of secrets. Instead, we have come to the realization that ''coping'' with Joyce remains viable and productive—and perhaps even valuable.

Diversity and complexity, therefore, characterize the eighteen essays in this volume, representative of the numerous presentations and the prevalent ambiance of the Tenth International James Joyce Symposium. Describing them, much less classifying them, proves to be difficult, although arranging them in a reading order suggested itself very easily. The first five essays were major addresses at the Symposium, and, characteristic of such addresses, they all assume some sort of overview of the Joyce texts or of the Joycean perspective. The litany of these perspectives is almost in itself Joycean (or at least Shakespearean): historical, biographical, cultural, thematic, linguistic, textual, sexual—a plethora of Joyces (venerators would have said a ''pantheon of Joyces'')—with whom to cope. Thereafter, the chronology of the Joyce texts determines the order, from *Dubliners* to *Exiles* and then very rapidly to *Ulysses* and *Finnegans Wake*. The aspects of diversity/complexity, however, make discreet classifications at times impossible, since it has become increasingly apparent that Joyce's texts interleaf with each other, depend on each other, complement each other, extend each other. Margot Norris's opening essay establishes the intricacy and significance of that intertextuality: she reads the *Wake* ''through'' the other Joyce works and reads it as an organic text with the generating powers of a flower, Joyce's designated heliotrope. The answer to the riddle of desire in the *Wake*'s ''mime,'' and the narrative structure of the riddle, reside in the thematic heliotrope that derives from Nausicaa and ''The Dead,'' coloring each of the texts, turning toward each of the texts.

The quest for Joyce takes Colbert Kearney to Cork and Robert Scholes to Italy, has Bernard Benstock investigating plaques, street signs, and tombstones, and Fritz Senn investigating Greek and Latin grammar. Kearney locates Joyce among the Joyces of Cork, the father, grandfather, great-grandfather, as well as the marriage to an O'Connell, the building up of a *Joycead* that James Joyce contributed to in the history of his fiction. If Kearney exhumes the ancestors, Scholes exhumes Joyce's contemporaries, those involved as Joyce was with European socialism, and the divergent paths youthful socialism took for Joyce and others at the beginning of the twentieth century, as well as the cross-currents of politics and aesthetics. Each identifies a complex Joyce within the diversification and complexity of human history. Benstock carries that reading of history into the human family, determining landmarks noted by Joyce as he read the runic indicators to the history of the race in the individual. And Senn sifts through Joyce's own runes, deciding on the Joycean process of naming, the use of active and passive voices and the finding of a mediating way, a middle voice, between the fixity of nouns and the activity of verbs. Senn's concept of such mediation should in turn be read against Scholes's notation of Joyce's middle road between naturalism and aestheticism. As Norris reads the old stories as providing structures to make new ones, the other four authors of major addresses read the old stories of family and influences, linguistic and epigrammatic structures underlying Joyce's contributions.

A discernible change in Joyce studies, reflected in this collection of essays, is not only the concentration on *Ulysses* and *Finnegans Wake,* but especially the concern with that latter text. What some have suspected for a long time has now become a widely accepted view: that ignoring the *Wake* when coping with Joyce seriously limits the range of Joycean perspectives. New theoretical approaches in particular have paid prominent attention to *Finnegans Wake,* a text that is at least as challenging as the complexities and diversities of critical theories. Perhaps the suspension of the awe with which Joyce has too often been surrounded, the veneration of genius that kept the *Wake* as a sacred book to be honored but not approached, as well as the suspension of the notion that it is a text that must be mastered and rendered up to explication, have opened *Finnegans Wake* for new considerations. And frequently one finds that a coupling of *Ulysses* and the *Wake* within the same essay makes for a kind of double reading, the "easier" text providing an entry into the more difficult one, the earlier text providing a quite different perspective on some obscure activity of the later text.

Identifying the diverse/complex James Joyce in his various guises and in his various capacities highlights *Coping with Joyce* as a group of divergent essays. Historically, Joyce emerges as a product of his genetic world, an early movie-goer whose retina recorded the flickering of screen images allowing for a translation of that new and awkward medium into the magical transformations and quick changes of the Circe chapter. Politically he presents himself as a victim of a colonial policy toward his native land that colors his socialist ideals and causes him to espouse Irish nationalism while rejecting the theocratic state it has engendered. Culturally he is viewed as a central figure of a male modernism with which he was uncomfortable, preferring to move outside the masculine vortex that proves to be politically reactionary as well, and the Joyce now identifiable as the "womanly man" also has claims as a feminist opposed to the masculine modernist hegemony.

Correspondingly, Joyce has never lost his identity as the consummate artist, but new facets of his artistry have become apparent under recent examinations, especially with new materials of examination. Joyce as a creator of systems magnified the proportions of his ambitious range, and new credence is given to his role as rival to the god of creation, an anti-Babelist, for example, creating a "mediating" language rather than mediating between languages, repeating in the *Wake* the dispersal of linguistic controls that challenges "mastery." Often it is in his diachronic role, manipulating the words as well as the music under his specific signature, that the dualistic powers of creativity become established: condemned by his earliest and most severe critic as a "schoolmaster," he shows himself as a pedagogue of self-instruction, providing the means by which his readers teach themselves how to read the texts. As a worker in language, he can work the formal and fixed forms of speech in active relationship with colloquial and spontaneous modes of human expression. And as a writer credited with being the chronicler of everyday life in *Ulysses*, he simultaneously demonstrates his power as a mythmaker and esotericist, producing in *Ulysses* a perfectly heterogeneous text.

The essays collected in this volume not only mark a certain moment in the history of "coping" with Joyce but raise some new questions about the terms of that coping. The resulting volume is symptomatic of Joycean concerns: 1) reading the effects of Joyce's presence and participation in a Modernism that is itself being reread and revised through various lenses—socialist, feminist, deconstructionist, psychoanalytic; 2) defining both the aesthetics and ideologies of Modernism in terms of Joyce; 3) reading Joyce's texts through each other, with new interest in organic metaphors of Joycean textual construction and with particular attention to the ways in which the individual works, taken together, form a textual fabric—overlapped, interwoven, seamed, signed by knots and marked by holes; 4) being aware of Joycean pedagogy, a study of all facets of the notion of the pedagogic, both within and outside of the texts proper; 5) creating (or recognizing) rhetorical and grammatical readings of Joyce's texts that focus on the ruptures in textual logic. What is evident in this collection, and was in evidence in Copenhagen as well, is that the Joyce "industry" is caught in a moment of self-evaluation, a heliotropic turn to questioning the contexts in which we have for so long situated Joyce's texts, with a backward glance reflected in both irony and nostalgia at a time when our mutual goal was easily defined but difficult to reach: that is, to "master" the Joycean *oeuvre*. We have conceded the game, but—in a kind of wily, polytropic gesture—refused to admit defeat. Like Leopold Bloom, and Odysseus before him, we cope.

ABBREVIATIONS

The following abbreviations—those also used in the *James Joyce Quarterly*—have been used throughout this volume to indicate standard editions of Joyce's works and important secondary texts. No additional references to these works have been given in individual bibliographies.

CP   Joyce, James. *Collected Poems.* New York: Viking Press, 1957.

CW   Joyce, James. *The Critical Writings of James Joyce,* edited by Ellsworth Mason and Richard Ellmann. New York: Viking Press, 1959.

D   Joyce, James. *Dubliners,* edited by Robert Scholes in consultation with Richard Ellmann. New York: Viking Press, 1967.

     Joyce, James. *"Dubliners": Text, Criticism, and Notes,* edited by Robert Scholes and A. Walton Litz. New York: Viking Press, 1969.

E   Joyce, James. *Exiles.* New York: Viking Press, 1951.

FW   Joyce, James. *Finnegans Wake.* New York: Viking Press, 1939; London: Faber & Faber, 1939.

GJ   Joyce, James. *Giacomo Joyce,* edited by Richard Ellmann. New York: Viking Press, 1968.

JJI   Ellmann, Richard. *James Joyce.* New York: Oxford University Press, 1959.

JJII   Ellmann, Richard. *James Joyce.* New York: Oxford University Press, 1982.

Letters I, II, III   Joyce, James. *Letters of James Joyce.* Vol. I, edited by Stuart Gilbert. New York: Viking Press, 1957; reissued with corrections 1966. Vols. II and III, edited by Richard Ellmann. New York: Viking Press, 1966.

P   Joyce, James. *A Portrait of the Artist as a Young Man.*
        The definitive text corrected from Dublin
        Holograph by Chester G. Anderson and edited
        by Richard Ellmann. New York: Viking Press,
        1964.

        Joyce, James. *A Portrait of the Artist as a Young Man:
        Text, Criticism, and Notes,* edited by Chester G.
        Anderson. New York: Viking Press, 1968.

SH   Joyce, James. *Stephen Hero,* edited by John J. Slocum
        and Herbert Cahoon. New York: New Directions,
        1944, 1963.

SL   Joyce, James. *Selected Letters of James Joyce,* edited
        by Richard Ellmann. New York: Viking Press,
        1975.

U   Joyce, James. *Ulysses.* New York: Random House, 1934
        ed., reset and corrected 1961.

U-G   Joyce, James. *Ulysses: A Critical and Synoptic Edition,*
        edited by Hans Walter Gable et al. New York
        and London: Garland Publishing, 1984.

U-GP   Joyce, James. *Ulysses.* New York: Random House,
        1986: London: Bodley Head and Penguin, 1986.
        These editions have identical pagination.

MAJOR
ADDRESSES

1

Joyce's Heliotrope

MARGOT NORRIS

Heliotrope, the answer to the riddle of desire in *Finnegans Wake,* is a privileged figure in Joyce's work. It is an overdetermined figure, a word that means many things at once and yet points to only one thing: desire. A heliotrope is any flower that assumes a desirous attitude, that turns toward the sun, like a marigold or a sunflower. But it is also a specific flower, a fragrant, purple annual called heliotrope, whose sweet scent draws people toward it in a desirous movement. As parts of its whole, heliotrope is the light purple or reddish lavender color of the heliotrope, and, of course, its perfume, the desirable parts of the desirable whole. Heliotrope is another name for the gem with the oxymoronic alternative name of bloodstone. Heliotropism is a gesture of turning toward the sun—a gesture whose form is a dance or a movement in a desirous ballet. As a gesture or a signal, heliotrope is implicated in nonverbal language or pantomime, for it functions as a signal that refers us to acts and gestures rather than speech—including speech acts rather than the semantic content of discourse. A heliotrope is a signaling device using mirrors to reflect the rays of the sun: a semiological technique reflected in Joyce's works when its heliotropic references and gestures mirror and reflect each other in a thematics of desire. In all these ways, heliotrope functions as a trope, a metaphor or figure of the movement of longing, reaching, turning, communicating, and dancing that signifies desire. As all these things, in the plenitude of its overdetermination, and with its significatory function, heliotrope is the answer to the riddle of desire not only in "The Mime of Mick, Nick, and the Maggies" in *Finnegans Wake*, but in Joyce's *oeuvres* as a whole.

By serving as the answer to a riddle, heliotrope functions as an intellectual paradigm and suggests a model of reading Joyce's work that is unconventional both in its procedures and its goals, for a heliotropic reading of Joyce keeps its eye on the pantomime (rather than its ear on the speech) and works to decipher nonverbal semiologies. It is a Shaunian rather than a Shemian mode of reading—not surprisingly, since Shaun (or Chuff, the angel in the "Mime") successfully solves the riddle of desire, while Shem (the devil, Glugg) fails. The basis of "The Mime of Mick, Nick, and the Maggies" is a children's guessing game called "Angels and Devils or colours," that Joyce described to Harriet Shaw Weaver like this: "The Angels, girls, are grouped behind the Angel, Shawn, and the Devil has to come over three times and ask for a colour, if the colour he asks for has been chosen by any girl she has to run and he tries to catch her. As far as I have written he has come twice and been twice baffled."[1] Since clues to the answer of the riddle are embedded in gestures, flowers, colors, dances, charades, and the like, guessing the answer requires talent at reading the signs of nonverbal languages—the reason, presumably, why the spirit of Marcel Jousse hovers over the chapter (Weir). It was James Atherton who suggested that Joyce intended the Pantomime as a metaphor for *Finnegans Wake* as a whole, and indeed, if one thinks of the pantomime as a carnival of nonsense, of discredited, devalued, partial, truncated language whose subtraction of sense is designed to produce delight and pleasure, one has a fair description of the text of *Finnegans Wake*. As the product of an intellectual knot or puzzle, may heliotrope not reveal something hidden and disregarded—perhaps the desirous or libidinal aspect ("Angelinas, hide from light those hues that your sin beau may bring to light! [*FW* 233.5]) of intellectual activity? Is there not in the act of reading *Finnegans Wake*, in our desire for intellectual intimacy, our movement toward intellectual closure, our longing to possess its meaning, something of a heliotropic motion?

Joyce adds to the children's guessing game a small erotic twist. It is not only the little girls' colors, but the colors of their panties the boy angels must guess. The game thereby becomes a ritual of courtship and seduction, and the operatic analogues Joyce introduces into the "Mime"'s texture—the religious quest of *Parsifal* and the dangerous guessing game of *Turandot* (Hodgart)—serve to elevate the sense of the stakes in the riddle of desire, and to illuminate the logic of the repressions that produce its frustration. Perhaps this is what makes my claims for the heliotropism of the Joycean text seem so heretical. The best authorities have denied or denounced its pleasure: Judge Woolsey, who legally and officially denied the aphrodisiac quality of *Ulysses*, and Stephen Dedalus, who terms the kinetic response to art pornographic, when it incites desire. The desirous nature of reading, the amorous or erotic relationship with the Joycean text, has been primordially tabooed. For Stephen, indeed, the aesthetic text is like a Freudian primal scene, that is, a view of the parental copulation or of the mother's body, that mandates the denial and repression of desire, and thereby becomes the site of misreading. Stephen philosophically interrogates his origin in the parental copulation—"They clasped and sundered, did the coupler's will" (3.47)—but by subtracting from his imaginings all feeling, all libido, all pleasure, his theories of love remain as sterile as his theories of aesthetics, from which he likewise amputates the kinetic, the vital, the libidinal, the erotic element. It is Stephen, I believe, who is parodied in the "Homework" chapter of *Finnegans Wake,* as one of the little boys who study the "whome" of their "eternal geomater," the mother's genitalia (whose veiled and infantile form were the colored panties) armed with surveyor's equipment, diagrams, and mathematical calculations. They may indeed succeed in mapping her geometrical surface (Solomon, Brown)—but at the risk of missing the erotic point. The "Homework" chapter of *Finnegans Wake* serves as a caveat to the reader of the Joycean text, and especially to the reader of *Finnegans Wake*. Approaching that work with theories, diagrams, numerology, and other systems, may yield much information, but at the price of missing the pleasure of the text.

Because it is apt to be disconcerting to find ourselves heliotropically reflected in the signaling mirror of criticism as pleasure-seeking readers, I chose an unconventional form for exploring the riddle of desire in Joyce's work. Instead of a scholarly anatomy or a theoretical dissection of desirous reading, I chose to do a dramatization. I transformed the Joycean text into a valentine for Joyce lovers: a romantic collage of hearts, flowers, candy, and cupids—sentimental and decorative, insipid and intellectually retrograde—with the bland wit and easy puzzling that Bloom (kinetic poet), the master of the valentine, sent to Miss Marion (Molly) Tweedy on the 14 February 1888—

> Poets oft have sung in rhyme
> Of music sweet their praise divine.
> Let them hymn it nine times nine.
> Dearer far than song or wine.

You are mine. The world is mine.

(17.410—16)

It is offered with affection and a twinkle of the eye in the hope of
seducing readers to the fond delusions woven into the more somber
naturalistic hues of the Joycean text. If Joycean women suffer brutal
lives of "commonplace sacrifices closing in final craziness" ("Eveline"
40; Bauerle, Devlin), they also have their heliotropic moments: "So
she had had that romance in her life: a man had died for her sake"
("The Dead" 222). These pleasures and gratifications are virtually
always retrospective and textualized, represented as tender moments
from the past encoded as personal myth and nostalgic history. These
romantic fictions are no more and no less emotionally authentic and
significant than women's suffering, and their retrieval is a legitimate
critical enterprise even when, as in this instance, it elides their dark
frame. The Joycean text can be wielded in many ways and with many
intentions by critics, and *Finnegans Wake,* especially, is easily flourished cruelly, as a punishment to teach the confident reader humility
and diffidence before the indomitable text. I choose to flourish it
like a fan, or a bouquet, in the hope of charming the reader with
the text's poesy. If this retrieval of the discredited feminine—both in
my critical gesture and in the feminization to which I plan to subject
the text—seems hopelessly regressive, I would suggest that it is not
only the male writer and thinker who may appropriate the figure of
"woman" and the disguise of the "feminine" to explore transpor-
tations into states of "otherness" (Jardine, Spivak). I intend it, in
this instance, only as a momentary and playful masquerade, and I
ask readers to remember that my subject, the heliotrope, is, after all,
embedded in a Pantomime.

I begin my floral rehabilitation of *Finnegans Wake* by suggesting
the flower as an alternative to the architectural and geometrical
metaphors that have historically dominated our thinking about its
structure. Implicit in the hope of finding a "skeleton key" to
Finnegans Wake (Campbell and Robinson), for example, is not only
its depiction as a chamber or a building whose entry would ensure
intelligibility. This architectural notion also tends to imply a logical
and systematic construction on Joyce's part, from which a coherent
aesthetic and narrative structure can be deduced. This model further
produces such ancillary structural concepts as the architectural hier-
archization of textual effects: the illusion that one can separate
structure and embellishment.[2] As an alternative to this mode of

thinking the Wake architecturally, I suggest the flower as a textual model that is organic and generational. Flowers are not designed by a mind or constructed by hand, but grow out of other flowers, and their structure is therefore neither logical nor systematic, but evolutionary, created unconsciously out of others of their kind, under the sway of the exigencies of necessity in the interest of survival. Even if our study of the production techniques of *Finnegans Wake* were to show that Joyce indeed worked rationally and systematically at its construction, I would argue that the text represents not his mind, the actual working author's mind, but a different mind, an intuitively and emotionally remembering mind absorbed in its history, and impelled not by architectural ambitions but by the psychological necessities of desire. Flowers grow out of other flowers, and if we picture *Finnegans Wake* as stories that grow organically, unconsciously, out of older stories, stories already contained in the earlier Joycean texts, we can see its structure as floral: petals enfolding other petals—invaginated (Derrida)—to use the botanical term that preserves the female resonance, the erotic allusion. The amorous undertone of this structural metaphor is quite helpful for illuminating the emotional gesture implicit in the remembering of old stories, particularly the preservation and enfolding of old stories, as constituting a kind of narrative embrace, a textual act of love. Figuratively, *Finnegans Wake* is a flower or a bouquet embedded in a female imagination.[3] Joyce gives us an image of such an invaginated text representing a female imagination in Molly Bloom's soliloquy, which is a bouquet of love stories that enfolds the tales of many flowers, rhododendrons on Howth Hill, poppies for her birthday, a wish for a room swimming in roses, and the most precious of all, a poetic flower of the mountain, remembered and enfolded in Molly's heart.

How does one read a floral text, particularly a lush and bountiful garden, like ''The Mime of Mick, Nick, and the Maggies'' in *Finnegans Wake*? One reads not only *about* a pantomime riddle, but one begins to interpret the silent gestures and signs themselves in their overdetermined multiplicity. Because the languages acted out in the chapter are children's languages, primitive verbal and musical languages full of rhymes and rhythms and preverbal visual and symbolic languages, they require a sensual interpretive mode. Reading the language of perfume or flowers or color in the ''Mime'' is less a matter of decoding them according to some conventional archaic system, a scholarly foray into arcane flower symbolisms, than the exercise of an intuitive aesthetic response armed with a finely tuned sense memory for hues of color, redolence of perfume, delicacy of texture, and a gift for recapturing the pleasures they produce. The reader of the "Mime" must, I believe, cultivate an erotic hermeneutics. Such an enterprise requires access to the workings of infantile logic—whose best model is still supplied by the theories of Freudian psychoanalysis. For the purpose of pursuing the heliotrope in Joyce's work, I will borrow only one of its procedures: free association. It functions both rhetorically and hermeneutically in the *Wake*, I believe, as symbolic codes are created by free association, and its exercise by the reader makes their interpretation possible. In practical terms, it is, of course, not a private free association that the reader practices (of what colors and fragrances and flavors remind *us*) but a literary free association, a remembrance of the remembrances of Joycean figures in *their* experiences with the aesthetics of love and seduction.

We could, of course, learn all this from Molly Bloom as well as Freud. For if a floral text works like a woman's mind—a woman's mind, that is, when occupied with the figurations of her emotional life—then its technique of free association is simply a way of remembering that is impelled by desire, and a way of selecting and combining that is motivated by pleasure. When Molly moves from hill to hill, from man to man, from kiss to kiss in her imagination, she constructs neither a system, nor a lesson, nor a linear narrative, but a floral gyre of amorous experience that signifies no more and no less than does the language of a flower, whose heliotropism bespeaks only the subtle rhythms of its own vitality. Insofar as Joyce's heliotrope is my lure, the riddle of desire I hope to solve and the object of desire that leads me along a trail of amorous musings in Joycean characters, I inscribe a critical heliotropism in my text. My procedure becomes as overdetermined and multiplicitous as heliotrope itself, as the trail crosses over characterological and textual boundaries—like the word "heliotrope" transgressing semantic boundaries to live, like desire itself, in a space of indeterminacy. I pursue heliotrope along a concentric journey into the old love stories of Joycean figures, on a route that leads from "The Mime of Mick, Nick, and the Maggies" to "Nausicaa," and from there on to "The Dead"—then back again from the "Mime" to an elided moment in *Portrait*. Only then does the invagination of the "Mime"'s structure become clearly visible, as an experience from Stephen's childhood that was repressed and forgotten, a moment absolutely interiorized, becomes dramatized and exteriorized, outer, in the pantomimic forms of the "Mime."

I'll begin my heliotropic pursuit of heliotrope with its fragrance, because it signifies the insubstantiality of heliotrope that seems so disproportional to its emotional power, its status as a kind of "trace," an effaced sign always there and yet not there, mysterious and elusive, invested in hints and suggestions like the word "heliotrope" in the "Mime." I first follow its redolent trail to an imaginary appearance in "Nausicaa," where it surfaces embedded in a riddle with three guesses, ostensibly as a wrong guess. "Wait. Hm. Hm. Yes. That's her perfume," Bloom thinks, as he catches a whiff of Gerty MacDowell's sachet. "What is it? Heliotrope? No. Hyacinth? Hm. Roses, I think." (13.1007). Gerty's perfume ambushes Bloom at a critical moment, as he speculates on the secret of desire in what seems like his usual, casual, pseudoscientific way—that yet masks the personal anxiety and painful urgency of the new cuckold who fears he has lost it. Gerty's perfume diverts Bloom from a fruitless foray into the positivism of physics, explaining sexual attraction as molecular magnetism ("Fork and steel. Molly, he" [13.993]), and puts him on the right track by putting him on the scent of the scent, as it were. Bloom's empirical models are inadequate to the mystery of desire because desire is premised on a lack and structured around a palpable absence. Once he leaves off science and follows the subjective colorations of his aesthetic imagination, he begins to explain the chemistry of perfume and of female fragrance in diaphanous imagery that oscillates between presence and absence: "Tell you what it is. It's like a fine fine veil or web they have all over the skin, fine like what do you call it gossamer, and they're always spinning it out of them, fine as anything, like rainbow colours without knowing it" (13.1019). Bloom comes much closer here to solving the riddle of desire than does little Glugg or Shem in the "Mime," for he understands the synesthetic ambiguities of eroticism, the sensuous response to essences as evanescent as the fragrances of flowers, the prismatic colors of the rainbow, the impalpable textures of gossamer— the whole range of responses to beauties on the edge of substantiality that prefigures the overdetermination of "heliotrope" in the "Mime"—suspended as it is between color, fragrance, substance, and gesture.

It is ironic that the heliotropic gestures of other women—Gerty opening to him and revealing her "roses," as it were—stimulate Blooms' own heliotropism toward Molly. This mirroring effect of desire that generates many displaced versions, and demonstrates that, even if he is a Flower, one woman's sun (her object of desire) can be another woman's Bloom (or desiring subject), enacts the sense of heliotrope as a reflecting solar signaling device. It is Martha Clifford who produces a heliotropic trope in the rhetorical gesture of her own desire amid the forced erotic verbal postures in her letter to Bloom: "I have never felt myself so much drawn to a man as you" (5.249). Here too heliotropism expresses itself in the erotic semiology of perfume, "P.S. Do tell me what kind of perfume does your wife use. I want to know" (5.258). This would be a very funny question if Martha Clifford were a funny woman—a little joke asking Henry Flower how Mrs. Flower smells—but we must assume she betrays here a highly conventional romantic desire. Her question is aimed at discovering the secret of Bloom's desire by eliciting the nature of his aphrodisiac. But the swift and clear certainty with which Bloom answers this question in his imagination holds out little hope for Martha Clifford's aspirations: "Why Molly likes opoponax. Suits her, with a little jessamine mixed" (13.1010). For Molly is to Bloom a very fragrant bloom indeed, as he demonstrates how intimacy is the fulfillment of desire because it abolishes the distance, the separation, at the heart of desire. In his imagination the thought of her fragrance lures him back to their bedroom strewn with Molly's redolent things, "Clings to everything she takes off. Vamp of her stockings. Warm shoe. Stays. Drawers... Also the cat likes to sniff in her shift on the bed. Know her smell in a thousand" (13.1022). In his imagination he follows her fragrance to its source in the "holes and corners" of her body, "Wonder where it is really. There or the armpits or under the neck. Because you get it out of all holes and corners" (13.1025). Desire is constituted of absence and distance that inaugurates a motion of yearning, a heliotropic odyssey toward the closure of intimacy, that transforms Bloom into a kind of bee following the lure of women's fragrance from flower to flower, from Gerty's cheap perfume, to Martha Clifford's "no smell flower" pinned to her letter, and onto Molly's scent that he knows "in a thousand."

As a movement toward the sun, as a desirous motion, heliotropism enacts a romantic ballet or a seductive dance. If we strip from "Nausicaa" the seductive language of the narration, that urges us to believe its flattery of Gerty and tempts us to assume the admiring posture of the hypothetical suitors she wishes for but never possesses, we are left with a nearly silent pantomime or dance that can be recognized as a model for "The Mime of Mick, Nick, and the Maggies." For the scene consists of three girls dancing to attract the attention of Bloom: Edy to a lesser extent, but Cissy's leaps and gambols are choreographed, if comically, like a ballet, and Gerty in her stationary high-kicking does indeed, like the flower girls of the "Mime," show Bloom the colors of her drawers. As a Pantomime, "Nausicaa" functions like the adolescent screen memory that is replicated in an infantile retrieval in "The Mime of Mick, Nick, and the Maggies": Bloom is Chuff, the angel who is the object of the flower girls' heliolatry; Gerty, Cissy, and Edy are the seductive flower girls; and Tommy Caffrey is Glugg, the little devil who is rejected and rebuffed by the girls in favor of his rival—Bloom. The verbal echoes that make the tripartite riddle of Glugg ("—Haps thee jaoneofergs?—Nao" [*FW* 233.21]) a replay of Tommy Caffrey's own tripartite riddle ("Is Cissy your sweetheart?—Nao, tearful Tommy said" [13.66])[4] make the figures of the two little boys analogues as failed riddlers and rejected suitors. This echo in the "Mime," of the infantile riddle of desire, obliges us to interrogate the function of the children in "Nausicaa" as *Ulysses* does not. Why did Joyce add the children, the twin boys and the baby, to "Nausicaa," when they are absent from the Homeric narrative? They serve virtually no plot function in the chapter, and could be omitted without altering the erotic dynamic of Bloom and the girls. Did Joyce plan to have the children's perspective, occluded in *Ulysses*, become retrospectively important through its retrieval in the "Mime"? Does the "Mime" oblige us to reread "Nausicaa" from Tommy Caffrey's point of view? Does Tommy come close to tears because the delay of the teasing sweetheart riddle nearly causes him to wet his pants (as the riddle in the "Mime" does Glugg)? Or does Tommy Caffrey have a sweetheart after all, and is he sweet on Gerty, or even his sister Cissy, as Glugg is sweet on his sister Issy? Does the sweetheart riddle therefore sexually excite him and create in him the infantile version of an erection, which a child could construe only as a need to urinate? Did he feel rejected and rebuffed when the girls teased and titillated him with their sweetheart riddle, but then gave their real attention, their adoration, to his rival, Bloom? I would argue that the children's game in the "Mime" reenacts a hidden childish love story concealed in "Nausicaa" of a little boy who feels teased and excited by a bevy of girls, and who watches in baffled frustration as they caper and gesture their pantomimic seduction of a lucky rival, a victorious other, who appears to possess the answer to the riddle of desire.

This structural reversal, of foregrounding occluded perspectives from the earlier works in *Finnegans Wake,* allows the later dream work to retrieve infantile experience and feeling. Once Tommy Caffrey is recognized as a prototype for Glugg, the little devil of the "Mime," other verbal echoes become audible in the "Mime" that confirm its organic generation from the thematic structures of "Nausicaa."[5] The infantile equation of love and sweet food is one such structure. We learn in "Nausicaa" that "Tommy Caffrey could never be got to take his castor oil unless it was Cissy Caffrey that held his nose and promised him the scatty heel of the loaf or brown bread with golden syrup on" (13.30). In the "Mime" the golden syrup is embedded in the formal structure of a children's game that mimics courtship and marriage while preserving the connection of love and food as parallel forms of gratification and frustration—

> As Rigagnolina to Mountagnone,
> what she meaned he could not can.
> All she meaned was golten sylvup,
> all she meaned was some Knight's ploung jamn.
> (*FW* 225.15; rhyme structure added)

McHugh (225) and Rose and O'Hanlon (129) provide much useful information about this game, including the original rhyme:

> There stands a lady on a mountain,
> Who she is I do not know.
> All she wants is gold and silver;
> All she wants is a nice young man.

We see here the technique of invagination, as the inchoate feelings of an interiorized, infantile trauma are translated into the exteriorized, public, conventional form of the game, play, ritual, and song. This game, titled "Lady on a Mountain," is an infantile parody of romantic and worldly desires that acts out infantile fears of rejection and hunger through the form of a courtship ritual. In the game, the little boy's marriage proposal, "Madam, will you marry me?" is turned down with a resounding "No!" and his request for breakfast, "What's for breakfast, love?" is answered with an increasingly repulsive menu, degenerating from "Bread and butter, watercress" to "Squashed flies and blackbeetles" (Rose and O'Hanlon 129). Glugg presumably fails to guess that the lady wants golden syrup and nice plum jam (the infantile versions of gold and silver and a nice young man). He gets neither castor oil nor golden syrup to alleviate his gripes, nor even bread and butter. His breakfast is first "breath and bother and whatarcurss," degenerating into "no breath no bother but worrawarrawurms." Infantile rejection and lovelessness is figured as a diet of bread and water and curses, or a Diet of Worms, or a diet of nothing at all, like Baby Boardman, who is given an empty nipple to suck. Bloom predicts that this deprivation will produce a colicky baby—"Oughtn't to have given that child an empty teat to suck. Fill it up with wind" (13.958) and, indeed, a devilish or Mephistophelian stomachache, a "muffinstuffinaches" afflicts the little devil, Glugg. The "Mime" aggravates the significance of this deprivation even further by having the little girls promise Chuff, the Shaunlike angel, a sort of gustatory Bloomusalem, an infantile *Schlaraffenland* or *Good Ship Lollypop*, in which sweet foods are personified and elevated into an accommodating aristocracy of sweet figures—

> Lady Marmela Shortbred will walk in for supper with her marchpane switch on, her necklace of almonds and her poirette Sundae dress with bracelets of honey and her cochineal hose with the caramel dancings.... And the Prince Le Monade has been graciously pleased. His six chocolate pages will run bugling before him and Cococream toddle after with his sticksword in a pink cushion." (*FW* 235.32–236.5)

Although "Lady on a Mountain" belongs to a large repertoire of children's games in "The Mime of Mick, Nick, and the Maggies,"[6] it describes—in its social and spatial elevation of the unattainable object of desire—the psychological abyss of the rejected suitor. In *Beyond the Pleasure Principle*, Freud explains the function of this type of children's game by arguing that children will often repeat unpleasurable experiences in their games in order to acquire mastery over their own painful feelings and fears. Once cued to its figure and its function, we can see the typology of "Lady on a Mountain" occurring earlier in "Nausicaa" where its meaning shifts with the relative position of the suitor. If beautiful Gerty MacDowell sitting on her rock on Sandymount strand were indeed an unattainable Lady on a Mountain to little Tommy Caffrey, she is no more than a girl on the rocks to Bloom, who has his own Lady on a Mountain: the beautiful Marion Tweedy of the Rock of Gibraltar, who many years ago, on another mountain, or hill, the Hill of Howth, answered his implicit proposal, "Madam, will you marry me?" with her breathless

embraces it, and imaginatively returns his gift. Heliotrope as a trope, a rhetorical figure, has the power of sealing the temporal and naturalistic chasm that the years of marriage, childbearing, poverty, and death open between lovers.

This is what Gabriel Conroy believes and desires ("Their children, his writing, her household cares had not quenched all their souls' tender fire" [*D* 214]) but cannot achieve. Curiously, it is an antonomastic failure that symbolizes Gabriel's marital failure. His gift to Gretta is not a verbal embrace, a poetic translation of her name, but its opposite: a refusal and inability to rename her in words of love. He gives Gretta a poetic negative, an image of his own self-consciousness as a poet that effaces her altogether from his words:

> In one letter that he had written to her then he had said: *Why is it that words like these seem to me so dull and cold? Is it because there is no word tender enough to be your name?"* (*D* 214)

The artifice of the rhetorical question betrays his total negation of her even as his addressee, for it makes the question one she could never properly answer except by appreciating the litotic intention, and thereby admiring his poetizing more than his ardor. His language transforms her from love object to audience, and effects that subtle egotistical boomerang by which attention putatively paid to her is diverted back upon himself. Because he has given Gretta no verbal gift of love, Gabriel gets none back. The night of the Morkan's party, when Gabriel desires desire, he tries to close the distance between himself and his wife by writing in his imagination a heliotropic script for her to enact:

> When the others had gone away, when he and she were in their room in the hotel, then they would be alone together. He would call her softly:
> —Gretta!
> Perhaps she would not hear at once: she would be undressing. Then something in his voice would strike her. She would turn and look at him . . ." (*D* 214)

In the ellipsis that follows, Gretta's heliotropic gesture is proleptically inscribed. She is to turn toward him like a flower to the sun. But, of course, she turns instead to the memory of a man who gave her a gift of love, a song, a devotion, a life. Unlike Joyce's other lovers, Gabriel cannot receive from Gretta the rhetorical keepsake the other wives can return to their husbands, enriched with their own loving remembrance. The auto-eroticism of his enamourment with his own language, his own poetizing, leaves him with nothing to quote but his own cold love letters, in which he tells his beloved that he has no metaphors, no tropes, no love name to give her. One of the bitter secrets of desire that Gabriel learns late in his life, and late in his marriage, is that the object of one's desire is also a desiring subject, and can therefore be both coveted and won by a rival. Bloom even knows that the same lure that excites him works in the same way on his rivals, as he remembers being enticed by Molly's perfume on the very night she meets Boylan: "At the dance night she met him, dance of the hours. Heat brought it out. She was wearing her black and it had the perfume of the time before" (13. 1011). Joyce structures the romantic fates of Gabriel Conroy and Leopold Bloom as precise opposites. Gabriel desires his wife in the present, but is defeated by a rival from the past; Bloom appears to be vanquished by a rival in the present, but remains the successful suitor from her past. With respect to the secret of desire, Gabriel is Glugg or Shem, the poet who fails; Bloom is Chuff or Shaun, the angel who succeeds—like Michael Furey, the Archangel Michael, the Mick of "The Mime of Mick, Nick, and the Maggies." The ability to collapse adult and infantile rivalries as versions of one another, to see the triangles of Glugg, Issy, and Chuff as homologous and analogous to those of Gabriel, Gretta, and Michael Furey, or Tommy Caffrey, Gerty MacDowell, and Bloom, or Stephen, Emma Clery, and Father Moran, bespeaks the organic and floral structure of psychic life. Psychoanalytically, the adult still enfolds the child he or she once was, and adult erotic behavior reenacts infantile erotic desires.

This leads me to the final love story that I find embedded in *Finnegans Wake*'s "The Mime of Mick, Nick, and the Maggies." It accounts, I believe, for its most aesthetically and erotically appealing features: the wonderful concatenation of flowers, girls, games, and desire in the magic childhood garden of the "Mime." The "Mime" enfolds "Nausicaa" with its infantile and adult games of desire, yet "Nausicaa" itself already enfolds another such memory of a lovely springtime garden party that was the setting for adolescent, and perhaps also infantile, love. "Mat Dillon and his bevy of daughters: Tiny, Atty, Floey, Maimy, Louy, Hetty, Molly too. Eightyseven that was" (13.1106). This is Bloom's heliotropic memory, and he turns toward it frequently, for it offers him the gratifying image of flowers and girls conflating into a seductive beauty that opened itself to him. "But it's the evening influence. They feel all that. Open like flowers, know their hours, sunflowers, Jerusalem artichokes, in ball-rooms, chandeliers, avenues under the lamps. Nightstock in Mat Dillon's garden where I kissed her shoulder" (13.1088). Mat Dillon's bevy of six daughters, who together with Molly form a group of seven so pretty they rival the flowers in loveliness, prefigure the dancing, seductive flower girls of the "Mime"—now named "Winnie, Olive and Beatrice, Nelly and Ida, Amy and Rue. Here they come back, all the gay pack, for they are the florals, from foncey and pansey to papavere's blush, foresake-me-nought, while there's leaf there's hope, with primtim's ruse and marrymay's blossom, all the flowers of the ancelles' garden" (*FW* 227.14–18).[7]

In Bloom's memory, Mat Dillon's Maytime garden party held at Roundtown in 1887, is remembered as a triumph. There he first met and wooed Molly, his future wife. But there is an infantile witness to their meeting: Stephen Dedalus—and, indeed, all three principals of *Ulysses* possibly all meet there for the first time: Bloom at twenty-one, Molly at sixteen, and Stephen at five.[8] There, at the very dawn of their story, they play a game of desire and form a romantic triangle, no less intense for its incongruous configuration. Since Stephen was there, Mat Dillon's garden party ought, hypo-thetically, to be an event in *Portrait* where it would have occurred just prior to Stephen's entry into Clongowes; but it is elided and thereby serves to remind us how partial and selective the strokes of *Portrait*'s portrait are. In *Ulysses* Mat Dillon's party emerges as a collection of memory fragments, distorted and colored by desire. It is not until the "Mime" that the event's repressed and emotional residues are exteriorized and dramatized as a Pantomime that replays this springtime festival from the emotional perspective of its youngest guest, the five-year-old Stephen. I will now reconstruct Mat Dillon's garden party, not as history—*for we can never know what happened*—but as a fable of the experience of an overstimulated little boy who, intoxicated by the perfume of spring flowers and dazzled by the glamour of a bevy of beautiful young girls, is heartbroken when they turn heliotropically toward the dashing older man who becomes his successful rival—the twenty-one-year-old Leopold Bloom.

The setting is Mat Dillon's opulent villa in Roundtown, a grand house whose gorgeous implements of hospitality are remembered by the Blooms as including a solid silver coffee service on the mahogany sideboard, fine cigars, and "Tantalus glasses" (6.1008; 18.723). The spacious grounds include a lilac grove and a green on which bowls could be played on a warm May evening. Leopold Bloom and the law student John Henry Menton are among the players, and they are highly self-conscious of being watched in their game by the pretty young girls:

> A shaven space of lawn one soft May evening, the well-remembered grove of lilacs at Roundtown, purple and white, fragrant slender spectators of the game but with much real interest in the pellets...And yonder about that grey urn where the water moves at times in thoughtful irrigation you saw another as fragrant sisterhood, Floey, Atty, Tiny and their darker friend with I know not what of arresting in her pose..." (14.1362)

Their "darker friend" is the buxom and exotic looking daughter recently brought back from Gibraltar by Major Brian Tweedy, who is partial to his drop of spirits, and who is friendly with his host, the kindly ("Heart of gold really" [6.1010]) and jovial Mat Dillon. The darling little boy Marion Tweedy and her girl friends are holding aloft on an urn over the pool, like a little Cupid, is Stephen Dedalus, who is there with his mother. "A lad of four or five in linsey-woolsey...is standing on the urn secured by that circle of girlish fond hands" (14.1371).

What happened at this garden party? Very little, probably, except perhaps some small romantic dramas that were never forgotten and never forgiven. Bloom's ball sails inside Menton's during the game of bowls, and Menton treats Bloom contemptuously seventeen years later at a funeral. There were parlor games and entertainments, but the outcome was not only a tie at musical chairs, but marriage and a daughter and a son mourned. Yet on this evening Molly Tweedy still distributes her favors among her rivals, dancing with John Henry Menton, but letting Bloom turn the pages for her when she sings the song *Waiting*, at the piano perhaps gallantly offered by the kindly Mat Dillon, "her father was an awfully nice man he was near seventy always goodhumored well now Miss Tweedy or Miss Gillespie theres the piannyer" (18.721). Later, on a walk in the garden scented by the opening nightstock, Bloom kissed her shoulder. How much of this does Stephen take in and see? Did the girls show him the flowers still furled in their buds and ask him to guess what their colors were? Did he, dazzled by their gossamer, tissue-thin dresses, confound the girls and the flowers, and find himself stupidly

unable to answer the question because it had become for him a
sexual question, and a sudden inhibition[9] made his myopic eyes
erotically blind? Did his spectacles become the true ''Tantalus
glasses''—proffering objects of irresistible desire that he could not
grasp? Was he smitten by one of the girls, perhaps the dark one
with the Spanish eyes and the cherries hung like earrings on her
ears? Molly seems to think so, ''I suppose hes a man now by this
time he was an innocent boy then and a darling little fellow in his
lord Fauntleroy suit and curly hair like a prince on the stage when
I saw him at Mat Dillons he liked me too I remember they all do''
(18.1310). Was little Stephen first titillated, and then heartbroken,
when his flower girls abandoned him to give their attention heliotropically to another? And did he then despair of ever guessing the
riddle of desire?[10]

Of course, I am speculating a great deal here. But my aim is
to show how easily and naturally this romantic garden party could
have become the dream of ''The Mime of Mick, Nick, and the
Maggies.'' The first erotic experience of a five-year-old, presenting
to him the mystery of sexuality in the images of flowers and courting
couples, of music, dances, games, and riddles, could in later years
have resurfaced in a dream—perhaps on the very night he encountered
again the very same romantic couple, Leopold Bloom and Molly
Tweedy, now long married and living in prosaic domesticity on Eccles
street. Stephen could have dreamt Mat Dillon's garden party again
as his private *Paradise Lost*, enhanced with the glamour of Boxing
Day pantomimes and the music of opera, the half-remembered
nursery rhymes and children's games, the flower girls from *Parsifal*
merging into the Dillon girls, the worrisome questions they asked
him taking on the danger of the naming riddle from *Turandot*,
Ophelia's flower speech from *Hamlet* echoing from his library lecture,
and the celestial battle of Lucifer and Michael restaged not over the
theological issues that Stephen claims as the motive of his *non
serviam,* but over love. Stephen, like Bloom after *his* heliotropic
experience, could have dreamt a pantomime, and where Bloom
dreamt the mime of his imago, *Sinbad the Sailor,* at the end of
''Nausicaa,'' Stephen might have dreamt the mime of ''Mick, Nick,
and the Maggies.''

Joyce, with a psychoanalyst's respect for the significance of
childhood experience, cues us in the ''Mime'' to the historiographic
functions of the retrieval of children's memories. The dreams of a

Stephen, who in his waking hours teaches history and hallucinates its apocalyptic end, may well offer, as Freudian wish-fulfillment, a benign dream of organic history figured as floral pollination, regeneration, and perpetuation. Joyce wove into the *Wake* the sentence from Edgar Quinet that he loved, and that imagines the continuity of natural life in the universal and eternal endurance of wildflowers:

> Today, as in the time of Pliny & Columella, the hyacinth disports in Wales, the periwinkle in Illyria, the daisy on the ruins of Numantia; & while around them the cities have changed masters & names, while some have ceased to exist, while the civilisations have collided with one another & smashed, their peaceful generations have passed through the ages & have come up to us, fresh & laughing as on the days of battles. (McHugh 281)

This is the submerged reassurance that eludes Stephen's waking nightmare eschatology of history culminating in toppled masonry and shattered glass—and that appears to become available in dream only as the vision he cannot glimpse, the truth he cannot guess. The secret of desire, the mystery of sexuality, offers not only the personal salvation of regeneration and propagation, but it offers a saving historical perspective as well, a vision of perdurable organic life surviving repeated colonizations with vigor and joy. Floral history is the dream antidote to an apocalyptic cultural history, and in it sexuality is history in the making, a ballet of pollination and procreation—

> Just so stylled with the nattes are their flowerheads now and each of all has a lovestalk onto herself and the tot of all the tits of their understamens is as open as he can posably she and is tournesoled straightcut or sidewaist, accourdant to the coursets of things feminite, towooerds him in heliolatry...(*FW* 236.33–237.1)

The flower girls, the angels, dance around Chuff, Mick, Bloom the heliotropic dance of the flowers, their version of the dance of the hours, the organic dance of history. Because the "Mime" 's floral history is a vital, erotic, kinetic history, Joyce emphasizes its heliotropic momentum by retelling Quinet's sentence in the "Mime" as the eternal history of dance (*FW* 236.19–32), of stately pavanes giving way to lively waltzes in the suburban streets of Dublin, Miss McCloud's Reel ("mismy cloudy")—the same to which the Donnelly children danced in "Clay"—is tripped daintily by Issy's "hercourt," and rigadoons and modern ragtime lead to zany cancans ("cancanzanies'') of the kind Gerty imitates in her high-kicking for Bloom. But in the end, it is the female imagination in Joyce's text that intuitively grasps, in waking thought, this floral philosophy which may elude Stephen even in dream. Perhaps you have to be a Bloom to understand the cosmic significance of flowers, and to intuit Quinet and encode his floral philosophy as a kind of religion. "I love flowers," thinks Molly.

> Id love to have the whole place swimming in roses God of heaven theres nothing like nature the wild mountains then the sea and the waves rushing then the beautiful country with the fields of oats and wheat and all kinds of things and all the fine cattle going about that would do your heart good to see rivers and lakes and flowers all sorts of shapes and smells and colours springing up even out of the ditches primroses and violets nature it is as for them saying theres no God I wouldnt give a snap of my two fingers for all their learning'' (18.1557).

NOTES

1. Letter to Harriet Shaw Weaver, 22 November 1930 (355).

2. See Derek Attridge's "The Backbone of *Finnegans Wake*" for an interesting discussion of this issue.

3. I am not suggesting here that the "dreamer" of *Finnegans Wake* is female, but that the dreaming mind, insofar as it can be thought of as enfolding the old stories of its history, acts like a female imagination.

4. Although I had mentioned this echo in my *Decentered Universe of* Finnegans Wake, (135–36), John Gordon recently pointed out to me that Adaline Glasheen had mentioned it even earlier in "A Riddle Not Answered." *A Wake Newslitter* IV/5 (1967):100–101.

5. The draft evidence for this chapter (*II*.1) is interesting, because it indicates that the "Nausicaa" references, while not belonging to the very earliest draft, were added soon after, as if to deliberately cue readers to the similarity. See MS 47477–64, for example, where Glugg's answered "Now" and "Nowhowhow" is changed to "Nao" and "Naohaohao," or MS 47477–10, where "All she meaned was multimoney, all she meaned was a nyums nyum nyam" was changed to "All she meaned was golten sylvup, all she meaned was some knight's ploung jamn."

6. Grace Eckley's *Children's Lore in* Finnegans Wake is the only book length study of children's games in the *Wake*, but it neither mentions nor discusses the role of "Lady on a Mountain" in the "Mime."

7. Vincent Cheng points out that this is one of many versions of Ophelia's disbursement of flowers in the *Wake* (67–68). Its appearance in the "Mime" is especially motivated by the complex role of *Hamlet* motifs in the children's games: an incongruence softened by remembering that the "low art" of the Pantomime readily assimilated popular bits and pieces from the "high arts." Insofar as this spreads a dark lining under the flower motifs in the "Mime," it may well allude to more tragic female fates, for example the martyrdom of Issy's prototype Isabel in *Stephen Hero*, following her banishment to a nunnery, or ALP's shedding all of

her leaves (or leafies) but one, as her death approaches and she *leaves* (Rose and O'Hanlon 328).

8. Molly does some of this arithmetic herself in "Penelope": "I wonder is he too young hes about wait 88 I was married 88 Milly is 15 yesterday 89 what age was he then at Dillons 5 or 6 about 88 I suppose hes 20" (18.1326).

9. One can readily make guesses about the nature of this inhibition. My own best inference is that Mat Dillon's garden party might serve as a screen memory for another kind of infantile scopophilia: the desire to see the mother's body that is dramatized in the next chapter, the "Homework" chapter. This may also have been the transgression censored in *Portrait*, for which Stephen is threatened with the ocular punishment of blindness. The larger consequence of such an infantile trauma might be a taboo on any kind of desirous seeing, a fear whose adult rationalization might be found in Stephen's promotion of a static response to art over the more dangerous and culpable kinetic response to beauty. That not only Stephen's, but Joyce's, constitution as artist is reworked in the serious Shem parodies of *Finnegans Wake* is an important theme in Bernard Benstock's *Joyce-Again's Wake*.

10. Patrick McCarthy points out the similarity between Glugg and Stephen in that, even though they themselves pose riddles, they are unable to solve others (141).

WORKS CITED

Atherton, J.S. "*Finnegans Wake*: 'The Gist of the Pantomime'." *Accent* 15 (1955): 14–26.

Attridge, Derek. "The Backbone of *Finnegans Wake*." *Genre* 17 (1984): 375–400.

Bauerle, Ruth. "Date Rape/ Mate Rape in Joyce's 'The Dead'." Paper presented at the Philadelphia Joyce Symposium, June 1985.

Benstock, Bernard. *Joyce-Again's Wake: An Analysis of Finnegans Wake.*" Seattle: University of Washington Press, 1965.

Brown, Richard. *James Joyce and Sexuality*. Cambridge: Cambridge University Press, 1985.

Campbell, Joseph, and Henry Morton Robinson. *A Skeleton Key to* Finnegans Wake. New York: Viking Press, 1969.

Cheng, Vincent John. *Shakespeare and Joyce: A Study of* Finnegans Wake. University Park: Pennsylvania State University Press, 1984.

Derrida, Jacques. "Living On." In *Deconstruction and Criticism,* edited by Harold Bloom et al., 216–19. London: Routledge & Kegan Paul, 1979.

Devlin, Kimberly. "ALP's Final Monologue in *Finnegans Wake*: The Dialectical Logic of Joyce's Dream Text." Paper presented at the Tenth International James Joyce Symposium in Copenhagen, Denmark, June 1986.

Eckley, Grace. *Children's Lore in* Finnegans Wake. Syracuse: Syracuse University Press, 1985.

Freud, Sigmund. *Beyond the Pleasure Principle,* edited and translated by James Strachey. New York: W.W. Norton, 1961.

Glasheen, Adaline. "A Riddle Not Answered." *A Wake Newslitter* 4 (1967): 100–101.

Hodgart, Matthew. "Music and the Mime of Mick, Nick, and the Maggies." In *A Conceptual Guide to* Finnegans Wake, edited by Michael H. Begnal and Fritz Senn, 83–92. University Park: Pennsylvania State University Press, 1974.

Jardine, Alice. *Gynesis: Configurations of Woman and Modernity*. Ithaca: Cornell University Press, 1985.

Joyce, James. *Dubliners*. New York: The Modern Library, 1969.

The James Joyce Archive, edited by Michael Groden. *Finnegans Wake Book II, Chapter 1: A Facsimile of Drafts, Typescripts, & Proofs*. Pref. David Hayman, Arr. Danis Rose. New York: Garland, 1977.

McCarthy, Patrick A. *The Riddles of* Finnegans Wake. Rutherford: Associated University Presses, 1980.

McHugh, Roland. *Annotations to* Finnegans Wake. Baltimore: Johns Hopkins University Press, 1980.

Norris, Margot. *The Decentered Universe of* Finnegans Wake. Baltimore: Johns Hopkins University Press, 1976.

Rose, Danis, and John O'Hanlon. *Understanding* Finnegans Wake. New York: Garland, 1982.

Solomon, Margaret. *Eternal Geomater: The Sexual Universe of* Finnegans Wake. Carbondale: Southern Illinois University Press, 1969.

Spivak, Gayatri Chakravorty. "Displacement and the Discourse of Woman." In *Displacement: Derrida and After*, edited by Mark Krupnik. Bloomington: Indiana University Press, 1983.

Weir, Lorraine. "The Choreography of Gesture: Marcel Jousse and *Finnegans Wake.*" *James Joyce Quarterly* 14 (1977), 313–25.

2

Joyce the Verb

FRITZ SENN

in the muddle was the sounddance

(*FW* 378.29)

I begin with a few sample quotations. These are not for your applause or disagreement, but merely in order to probe and appreciate the semantic variety of the one recurrent word, "Joyce":

Joyce was born in 1882. —The Tenth International James Joyce Symposium. —Joyce was conscious of his control of English and other languages. —This book enters Joyce's life to reflect his complex, incessant joining of event and composition. —From his late adolescence onward, James Joyce intended to be a writer. — The sacred is at the heart of Joyce's writing experience. —Joyce insists that man's will is free, that it can be exercised for good or evil, and that the state of the world's affairs will vary with the quality of leadership. —What does Joyce assert or imply about guilt in *Ulysses*? —Joyce is disgusted by sexual impulses regarded as normal by most standards of behavior. —Joyce's mind was at all times engaged in the search for truth. —When I first met Joyce in 1901 or 1902, he was beginning to emerge as a Dublin "character." —Joyce was too scrupulous a writer to tolerate even minor flaws. —Joyce spent his life playing parts, and his works swarm with shadow selves. —Joyce's laughter is free and spontaneous. —Joyce wrote not for literature, but for personal revenge. —Jim Joyce devoted a whole big novel to the day on which I was seduced. —Joyce is writing the book of himself.

There needn't be any contradiction at all, but meanings differ. It is equally true to say "Joyce has been dead for 45 years," as to claim "Joyce is alive." "Joyce" does not equal "Joyce": What is the statue of Joyce in the Fluntern cemetery of Zurich a statue of? Joyce Symposia, among other events, give partial answers.

The question will not be pursued here. It is the name, noun, *nomen*, "Joyce," that interests. It epiphanizes a bewildering diversity of meanings, semantic differences that we, the professional differen-

25

tiators, do not always notice. The diversity at first sight would appear
odd, for names, of all words, ought to distinguish persons; it is their
function. They often fulfill it. Reading Joyce (you see, we use the
name but don't mean the person), we might learn about the chanciness
of easy identification by nominal labels. Insofar as names are for
things, the distinctions work reasonably well. But even so, undoubtedly
concrete objects like keys or bowls are not just objects. Keys can open
or lock, they are for entering, for excluding, for taking along, for
forgetting, for being handed over, for ruling or usurping. Bowls are
for carrying (or "bearing"), for holding aloft, for shaving, for mocking, they may play the roles of chalices at times, and chalices, we
have read, may contain wine, or be empty, even "idle," can be
broken—or not broken. Such objects, many at the beginning of
Ulysses, are for actions, or acting.

Those privileged and, usually, capitalized nouns, however, that
have no general referent, the names, serve to keep persons apart for
convenient identification. Not unconditionally. You may remember
Kitty O'Shea, the one that, Molly says, had a "magnificent head of
hair down to her waist tossing it back," and who lived "in Grantham
street" (*U* 18.478). This name then has different reverberations for
a reader who (a) knows no Irish history at all, for one who (b) knows
a little, and for one who (c) is an expert. It is the knowledge we
bring to bear on the name that makes the difference. But even a
historian well versed in late nineteenth-century Irish affairs will have
to match Molly's acquaintance, at least for a fleeting instant, against
the bad woman "who brought Parnell low," and then decide against
an attractive identification. A name translates into knowing, or not
knowing. Walter W. Skeat, the English etymologist, makes one of
his infrequent negative remarks in the entry on "NAME": this work
and its Latin cousin *nomen* are "not allied to 'know.' " The two
word families are not related, but in practice they work together. The
cognates of "know," however, are allied to that one item in the
much-quoted triad of strange words at the opening of "The Sisters"—
"*gnomon*" (*D* 9). And this gnomon merely sounds like, but has
nothing to do with, Latin *nomen*, though it happens to be one; the
similarity is deceptive and ominous.

The platitudinous pay-off of all this, predictably, is that in
identifying we are *doing* something. All the meanings we concede,
knowingly or not, to the term "Joyce" imply some kind of activity.
At one extreme the word does duty for a life lived in various cities

in the course of almost sixty years; at the other possible ends of the scales it suggests writing, thinking, creating, developing, intending—you name it, and you name it appropriately by verbs. Such verbs also become our panels and lectures and animated disputes. Aware of such dynamisms, some of us have quite independently—when this could still be done with impunity and even self-respect—coined the verb REJOYCE or REJOYCING.

Even the adjective "Joycean" predominantly means not some stable quality, but rather what Joyce actively provoked and what, conspiratorially, we now do in turn and with considerable energy. None of us may be able to define "Joycean" adequately, but we vaguely sense that it connotes some heterogeneous, but characteristic hyperactivity: words seem to be charged, or else we readers charge the words, somehow, it seems, beyond the norm. Ask anyone in Dublin.

To simplify the foregoing, names, for all their accepted substantiality, soon dissolve into doings, into the verbs from which grammar distinguishes them, at least in Indo-European languages. If at this point you nod facile assent and find, rightly, that I am kicking oudated horses and dismiss notions long out of date—or that someone has already put all this into a system of trendy abstractions—then just look at most of our practical applications. Look at how we, commentators or critics, seem often at pains to re-reify all that elusive work in progress, to freeze it into solid theses, symbols, parallels, discourses, or even "puns," things that we can categorize and administer.

Joyce might be the antidote. His works release the processes out of the nouns, nouns which are so much easier to handle than events or doings. The pioneering etymologists who drew up a set of language origins of common Indo-European ancestry, usually tabulated roots that tended to be verbs of action. Joyce seems to descend to such origins. The roots of the two cultures that he revived bear this out as well.

Dominenamine (U 6.595)

Once the God of the Old Testament had spoken light into being and approved of it, he went on and "called the light Day" (Gen. 1:4). Genesis follows the birth of the world right away with the birth of the first noun. Somehow Joyce celebrated this pristine noun thus generated in his secondary creation; we in turn now also use "Blooms-

day.'' God then, soon after, shaped a being that was called ''man.''
His personal name emerges first in the midst of another naming
process:

> The Lord brought [the beasts of the field] unto Adam, to see
> what he would call them [and we find an almost Joycean sort of
> divine curiosity]: and whatsoever Adam called every living crea-
> ture, that was the name thereof. (Gen. 2:19)

Calling (''quod vocavit,'' as the Vulgate has it) precedes the name
(''ipsum est nomen eius''). And Adam, the first-named, started giving
the animals around him names; he also decided that the outgrowth
of his rib shall

> be called Woman, because she was taken out of man. (Gen.
> 2:23)

Adam is the object of naming and becomes its prolific active
subject right away. Creator and first creature are both protonomastic,
not only the first namers around, but also those who start with naming
before almost anything else they do on the record. The names, of
course, allow the record to be written. Conversely, the calling of
names in the upward direction, towards the divinity, might be tabooed. Potent naming and ineffability go together. Naming is potent,
and so is knowing or uttering a name. Adam's powerful prerogative
is shared by writers of fiction.

The Hellenic version differs in conception and idiom, but the
Greek epics, oldest witnesses, work the naming of some of their heroes
into their tales. In the most famous digression in literature, Odysseus
is named in what appears the most arbitrary and whimsical way, in
almost Saussurean fashion, and yet the random signifier becomes
potently ominous. Since grandfather Autolykos passing by at the birth
happened to be ''odyssamenos,'' the child was called, ''epony-
mously,'' ''Odysseus.'' The participle form ''odyssamenos'' is either
''made angry'' or else ''making angry'' (reductive philologists, like
their Joycean counterparts, may disagree); it suggests a man connected
with wrath or odium, and it came to signify both a wrath inflicted
and a wrath suffered.

So naming has been around, from the beginning. Joyce, the
Namer, is well within a tradition that allowed for metamorphotic
scope. A central name ''Bloom'' coincides with a common noun,
offshoot of a verb BHLO (cf. *florere*, blühen, etc.), but a noun for
some live process, blossoming, growing, changing, withering, radi-

ating, smelling, all astir with poetical echoes. When Miss Marion Tweedy adopts it by patriarchal custom through marriage, her rivals inevitably joke: "youre looking blooming" (*U* 18.843). The verbal connection offers an appropriate flourish for the central onomastic cluster. Names, necessary social designations, arise out of, and turn again into, verbal energies, long before *Finnegans Wake*.

Joyce the Writer set off with almost no names, as suits lyrical poetry. *Chamber Music* can do, practically, without them. But not prose narrative; *Dubliners* has a wide range of appellative possibilities: full-fledged name (Ignatius Gallaher), last name only (Lenehan, Farrington), or first name alone (Maria, Lily), with or without a honorific (*Mr* James Duffy, *Mr* Duffy, but Corley), with a sprinkling of eponymous flourishes (Hoppy Holohan, Little Chandler). In all this diversity, the first three stories do not divulge what the protagonist narrator is (or the three narrators are) called. The technique of gnomonic elision or silence extends to names: one that is pointedly withheld seems to assume even more power than those known. But from now on there are names in abundance: a whole critical study (*Who's He When He's At Home?*[1]) can be devoted to them. Some were taken from Joyce's own background, some appropriated abroad, from printed sources, or invented, many synthesized. Perhaps the most outstanding example of imaginative naming is "Stephen Dedalus," in defiance of almost all realistic plausibility: it represents a soaring, mythical, high water mark of portentous naming—its growing significance is thematized in *A Portrait*. But more and more, especially from *Ulysses* onwards, personal names are shown to be problematic. In the final work, they have lost their discriminative graphic edges, and identification becomes our readers' necessity and pastime more than an overt concern of the work. It would be difficult to talk about the *Wake* if we had no nominal handles for its profusion. But its nominal blurrings would not be accepted by immigration officers on our passports, and our computers too would be obstinately uncooperative.

So we might roughly sketch a curve rising from pristine, lyrical anonymity to mythological ostentation, and down again towards a terminal pseudonymous fuzziness. But such a simplification would obscure the innate perplexity in between, the inherent riddling nature of names. But throughout, I submit, the naming is at least as important as the individual names used. Joyce's methods are often genetic. Ironically, the first occurrence of "name" in *Dubliners* is

connected, not with something coming into being, but with the loss
of the vital force. The reverberating term "paralysis" is introduced
as sounding strangely like the name of some maleficent and sinful
being (*D* 9), attached to a mortal activity, an action which means
the disablement *from* acting. Appropriately then, the priest's name
is not communicated to us until it is being read on his death notice,
when paralysis has done its fascinatingly "deadly work."

Before any one person in *A Portrait* has been identified, the
process of naming is put before us. The opening tale within a tale
features a "nicens little boy named baby tuckoo"—*named*. Named
by others, from outside, imposed from above. It will happen to the
main character soon "—O, Stephen will apologize," and whether
guided by the precedent of Genesis or simply by empirical common
sense, we take the name on trust ever after. Stephen hardly thinks
about it until others remark on its strangeness. Once the naming of
"baby tuckoo" has taken place, incidentally, the fairy story is
discontinued right away, as though it had now, the secret being out,
lost all further interest.

When real names do take over, we are not always helped. One
fully labeled "Betty Byrne" is never heard of again. Soon we will
come across a "Michael Davitt," but few readers nowadays could
tell, offhand, untutored, who he is; for all we know at first, it might
be a member of the family. (If you disagree, you are simply
substituting scholarly annotation for average knowledge.) One early
conspicuous name, "Dante," is flickeringly misleading. Most of us,
semi-erudite, will have to discard the nominal association of an Italian
poet who *will* be named, towards the end of the book. But the
person called Dante early on will later translate itself unexplained
into "Mrs Riordan." In life and in literature, we usually come to
terms with such confusion. Joyce exploits the confusions inherent in
naming. Coincidences and convergences will later facilitate the me-
chanistics of *Finnegans Wake*.

When Stephen's family name, commented on all along, is
linked to its mythological origin and import, it translates into such
actions as flying, soaring, falling, creating and, later on, estheticizing,
or forging. Most of these active revelations follow close upon the
mocking evocation of a Greek participle, "*Bous Stephanoumenos*,"
in which Stephen's Christian, very Christian, name is made to derive
not from crown, the object, but from a verb for crowning. The
fourth chapter, where all this happens, moves from a static beginning

of almost lifeless order and institutional clusters to an ecstasy of motion.

It would be idle to repeat how deceptively the first names come on in *Ulysses*, "Buck" and "Kinch." Commentators who claim that "Chrysostomos" in the earliest non-normative, one-word, sentence, "is" the name of some specific saint disregard the inherent process of naming through characterization, a process which may very well then lead to *one* particular saint. Stephen silently bestows an appelation on the usurper[2] who towers over him, one that fittingly singles out his most prominent organ. In some way this is Stephen's tacit hellenized tit for Mulligan's loudly voiced tat, "Kinch." *Ulysses* starts naming procedures even before the absurdity of "Dedalus" or the trippingness of "Malachi Mulligan" are remarked upon.

One whole chapter is notably given over to the bafflement of naming. It begins with "I," the polar opposite to individual verbal labels, a pronoun without a noun. Unique among words, its meaning changes with every speaker. As Stephen intimates in a passing "I, I and I. I." (*U* 9.212), the meaning may even change for any *one* person—through time; "I am other I now." The "Cyclops" chapter, whose governing saints are "S. Anonymous and S. Eponymous and S. Pseudonymous and S. Paronymous and S. Synonymous," contains *"Adonai!"* in its terminal paragraph (12.1915), a word that looks and functions like a name but pointedly is not. It is in fact a substitute for one that is unspeakable and prohibited. "Adonai" is making a nominal noise for a sacred onomastic absence.

One minor event in *Ulysses* is the devious misnaming of "M'Intosh" by a collusion of oral, written, and printed communication. The mystery surrounding this figure is mainly due to its being given a name that we know to be chancy. If there had been no newspaper reference and if Bloom had wondered, at the end of his day, who the *man in the* macintosh was, very little print would be expended on him. It is our knowledge of his pseudonymity that provokes so much curiosity. As naming, however, the procedure is true to universal type. What we wear can turn into what we become known by (Robin Hood may be a case in point; his sister Little Red Riding certainly is).

The misnomering integrated into the texture of *Ulysses* is intimately tied up with fiction, a process of feigning (or the invention of "figures"). As an obliging intermediary, Leopold Bloom assists in dissimulating the presence of M'Coy among the mourners (who

is neither present nor mourning). Newspaper fictions get M'Coy as
well as Stephen Dedalus B.A. into this second *Nekuyia*. In the midst
of what looks like the least questionable list of mere names some
fictions have intruded; we, in our superiority, translate the fictions
into complicated actions and dysfunctions of information. We still
don't know who "M'Intosh" is (some readers have thought they do,
others claim we never will; but knowing who he "is" would mean
substituting his wrong name by one that is considered circumstantially
plausible—a change of labels), but we recognize "M'Intosh" as a
series of mishappenings. Joe Hynes's misunderstanding also shows
the reporter's need for labels of that sort. As we do not know the
civil service data of the person who tells us what goes on in Barney
Kiernan's bar, we change this negative condition *into* a name and
refer to his as "The Nameless One," following a hint (*U* 15.1144).
Namelessness is unsettling. So that in *Finnegans Wake* we are striving
for identification tags to attach to the paronymous noncharacters,
and we co-create Earwickers and Porters, or pit Shems (in Hebrew
shem intriguingly *means* name) against Shauns even where these
configurations of letters do not occur, in the majority of cases, and
we treat them as though they were friends of the family we would
recognize anywhere.

   Naming confers power. The namer feels superior to the namee
(who is generally a helpless infant). Once a name is given, it tends
to stick. Only when we assume important positions, like Pope or
King, may we choose our own different names. Writers can do it
too. They can name themselves, or one of their figures, "Stephen
Daedalus" or "Dedalus." Or they can title a prose work about a
day in Dublin "*Ulysses*," and we realize the potency of this when
we consider what difference it would make if someone discovered
that Joyce's real intention had been something like "Henry Flower"
or "Love's Old Sweet Song," "Atonement," or "The Rose from
Gibraltar."

   if we look at it verbally
Naming, however, is just one of the many activities we find in
Joyce's cosmos, but a prominent one—of paradigmatic significance:
an action through words. My exemplification is simply a renewed
demonstration of a direction away from the stability of things or
persons towards movement, change. Verbs, which here represent
action, movement, processes, are less tractable than nouns (nouns

are ideal for catalogues or filing cards), less easy to pin down. Verbs have more flexibility, or *flexion*. They extend beyond the immediate present, or presence, into the past and the future; they are not restricted to what *is*, but can imply variant attitudes towards factuality, what *might be*. They have, in other words, *tenses, moods, aspects, voices*. At the present stage of ignorance it might be more profitable to phrase our views of literature in general, and Joyce in exemplary particular, in terms of inflexion and syntactic interaction than as an assembly of themes, ideas, messages. Physics in the twentieth century developed in a similar direction: things, bodies, mass, matter seemed to give way to motion, energies, speeds—nouns into verbs. Contemporary theories also tend towards verbal processes. I hope the simplistic way of putting it here is seen for what it is, a corrective convenience for illustration. As *Finnegans Wake* tries to spell out, "perhaps there is no true noun in active nature" (523.10).

   I am going to apply my figure of speech—taken from the *parts* of speech—to the newly edited text of *Ulysses* on the occasion of its first rebirth in a new dress, the paperback Blue Book of Errors Corrected. Some of the arguments of last year (1985) might have been controverted with more urbane understanding if the issues had not been treated as things, choices right or wrong, but had been seen as problems of the verbs that are implied. What the text of 1984 offered is not so much an object rectified in 5,000 instances and made reliably stable—or else, in an opposing view, a product wholly misconceived and faultily executed. It is, if anything, rectification in visible progress. The process is spread over the entire synoptic array on the dynamic left-hand page, down to footnotes, into the back of the book with textual notes, a historical collation, and a discursive afterword. The constant scuttling it demands of its users is troublesome, but essential, work in progress. The left-hand page activates us.

   One might say in metaphorical exaggeration that the left-hand page, the one with all the action, constitutes the verbs as against the deceptively stable nouns on the page that provides the final (not definite) results in undisturbed typography. By common, misleading, usage a text is called "established"—the Munich text emphasizes establish*ing*. Those sinistrous verbs have changing forms, have tenses (the page is diachronic), have moods, have voices. All the nonalphabetic features, those elevated diacritical irritations, are functional imperatives: they tell us what to do, where to go[3]—to the drafts, fair copies, proof sheets, and all the rest. They also actively report what Joyce did.

It is for us to translate the left page, which by itself does not make immediate sense, and not because of the editors' instinctive nastiness. The pages on the left are "genetic," they display *becoming*. Our own postcreative retracings match the author's creative bustling: an author who was indeed *auctor*, an "increaser," and an excreaser. To bone-set, after the act, excrescences that extended over three cities and seven years is a task to tax the best prepared of experts, almost beyond the reach of prescriptive principles. That the synoptic, left-hand page and the internal explications offered in the edition require conjugations that happen to surpass my own mental capacities does not detract from the necessity for conjugation, Joycean conjugations.

What we face, inevitably, is not a text freed from error (though this in itself was a worthwhile goal which resulted in a great number of unquestioned improvements), but a refined documentation of what an error might be. The apparatus shows how errors came about. The text, in its hazardous growth, was in itself erring all along (the drafts show abortive attempts and wrong starts). It, *Ulysses,* in its laborious progress from abandoned short story to no-longer novel, had its share of vicissitudes or, to borrow some quotations, it

> travelled far—was fated to roam—many a way wound—was harried for years on end—was driven far journeys—was made to stray—had a changeful course—*multum erravit.*

All these paraphrases refer, of course, to Odysseus, whose changeful course was due to force of circumstances *and* to his own nature. The text of *Ulysses*, similarly, was redirected at various points, on various pieces of paper.[4] It had to suffer countless injuries done to it from outside, but it also, in the nature of its being, caused many of its own predicaments. *Ulysses* was in need of reediting, not only because of the shortcomings of typists and printers, but because it is *as* it is.

So it is now for us to sort out the highroads and the deviations and to synopt. We know that some of our synoptions are chancy, many wayward itineraries of long ago remain irretrievable. The new edition strives to leave out scribal sins—what inattentive or meddle-some copyists had committed or omitted by faulty conjugation, departures that usually consist of words known to all men with the possible exception of French typesetters in Dijon. What all this implies, in practice, is that Joyce (here in the sense of someone writing, revising, adding, proofreading), actively engaged in new creations, was passively overlooking thousands of wrong turns, or gaps. Preoccupied with what lay still ahead, he was not undoing the doing of fallible mediators. The Munich team stepped in and did the close examination that Joyce was incapable of, had failed to carry out, and so they incurred, as one might telegrammatically put it, the immense debtorship of a thing done sixty years later.

From my given bias, I stress the verbal framework—Joyce actively composing the end of *Ulysses*, passively overlooking numerous misadventures of transmission. "Passive authorization" is a conventional technical contradiction of terms, the notion for a principle that is not valid for the new edition of *Ulysses*. The principle defines Joyce's oversights as failed actions, failures by inattention, which the approval of a *bon à tirer* does not authorize. If Joyce *had* noticed the errors, the assumption is, he *would* have interfered. You notice that an edition of *Ulysses* can hardly remain in the indicative mood; conditional[5] or subjunctive aspects (what would have been, or should have been) come into play.

The accomplicity long after the fact, which results in so many improvements, worries me all the same. How are we to deal rationally with what, by definition, is not a rational decision, is outside the normal range of conscious volition? A new psychology that was coterminous with Joyce's development and coincided with some of his insights, diagnosed overlooking—forgetting, lapsing, erring (and all parapractic varieties)—no longer as neutral, accidental blanks among business as usual, but as negative *actions*, as significant *not* looking, *not* recalling—as twisted, deviant, aberrant *doings* outside of consciousness. Psychomorphoses of that kind are, furthermore, vitally part of Joyce's realistically erroneous cosmos of words; the verb to err is integrated into Joyce's works (and I still believe that its concurrence in the first word of *Finnegans Wake* is significant: "Riv-*err*-un"). What is the meaning of *that* other world, the one thought to be outside of what our minds know they know? How are we to deal with those verbs below the surface of reason and, perhaps, an author's conscious control?

Or, to put it differently, if so much care was not taken by Joyce, as evidenced by the much touted number of 5,000 errors, would not this fact in its totality constitute a kind of vague cumulative volition? Authorization and will are related. "Which will" ("We are getting mixed," *U* 9.794)? Who was it again that was troubled

all day long about the correct voicing of—"voglio"—or is it perhaps
"vorrei"? (auxiliary verbs are tricky and ubiquitous). I have no
solution to offer for what the author's will may have been *when*.
This was an author fretted, harried, optically handicapped, oblivious
and, at that stage, not omniscient, certainly no longer scrupulous
over minor flaws, an author who missed hundreds of commas that
had been officiously introduced into the typescript of "Eumaeus."
We all have overlooked commas in our petty time, nothing is easier.
But can the wholesale sprinkling of them be missed? Does Joyce's
noninterference mean Will, Impotence, Carelessness, or Passive Resignation? If Joyce—"writing the mystery of himself" (*FW* 184.9),
"*lisant au livre de lui-même*" (*U* 9.114), that is rereading the proofs
of himself—so often forgot himself, which part of Joyce are we going
to call up in his stead? I, for one, do not have the strong verbs to
tackle such questions, and so commas will continue to haunt,
subjunctively, the Eumaean prose for me.

My phrasings have been hovering, in subtle confusion, between
activity and passivity in which author and transmitters shared. The
text was made, begotten, augmented, changed, it suffered damage,
neglect, was interfered with, but there is also a sense, much amplified
in current vogues, in which Joyce's texts seemed to have a will of
their own, appear to have written themselves, autogenetically. The
synopsis of the new *Ulysses*, writes Hans Walter Gabler, using a
reflexive form, displays "a text as it constituted itself in the process
of writing".[6] The works, moreover, tend to comment *on* themselves
in narcissistic self-preoccupation and internal reciprocality. Later texts
also look back, retrospectively, on the earlier ones. We now discover
more and more, and pontificate on, how *Ulysses* and *Finnegans
Wake* are self-reflexive.

reluctant to use the passive voiced (FW 523.8)

Now verbs can be used either actively or passively in our languages
(those that concern us here), and that seems to be all. But our Indo-
European dialect once expressed a third, in-between, possibility, with
separate forms. The Greek prototexture of a work entitled "Ulysses"
may permit a look into that language, a characteristic it had preserved
from its ancestors. The verbal system included what was called a
"middle *diathesis*" (disposition), in Latin grammar the *genus "medium,"* the so-called Middle Voice, partaking of the active *and* the
passive. It was an old, original part of its inflected system (in fact

the passive voice has been thought to derive from it). "But learn from that ancient tongue to be middle" (*FW* 270.17).

Nowadays the main use of the Middle Voice is to bewilder the student of Greek and the translators, but it once expressed, very sensibly, a most common involvement of the subject beyond its own grammatical confinement within the sentence. Definitions speak of "actions viewed as affecting the subject," which is a very general condition to which formal attention was paid long ago. The Middle Voice is an "intermediate between active and passive," or a voice which "normally expresses reflexive or reciprocal action." Another traditional way describes its function as "the voice of verb inflection in which the subject is represented as acting *on* or *for* itself." By chance this may almost sound like, and remind us of, Stephen's Shakespeare: "He acts and is acted on" (*U* 9.1021). A Greek writer might well have used one verbal form for this, and we would then wonder if the passive or the medial sense is dominant. The verb "act," Stephen's choice, is a good paradigm: it shows that verbs too play roles, roles that were distinguished and highlighted in Greek. "Epiphany," a favorite term of Joyce's youth, has much to do with the middle voice: "*epi-phainesthai*," "to manifest itself, appear, come into view"; it can also mean, of course, passively, "to *be* manifested." The Latin equivalents are the *Deponents*, verbs with passive forms but active function—hybrids. Joyce acknowledged them. A defendant in court becomes a "Deponent" (as a witness he would have to "depone"):

> the deponent...may have been (one is reluctant to use the passive voiced) may be been as much sinned against as sinning, for if we look at it verbally perhaps there is no true noun in active nature... (*FW* 523.7)

Anyone accused is likely to present himself not as an agent but as a passive victim; "more sinned against than sinning" is a moral medial position between the voices that grammar keeps apart. A deponent verb is passive ("sinned against") in looks but active ("sinning") in intent. Another court room situation also plays on the morality of the verb:

> no longer will I follow you oblique like through the inspired form of the third person singular and the moods and hesitensies of the deponent but address myself to you, with the empirative of my vendettative, provocative and out direct (*FW* 187.2)

Grammatical terms reappear:

> And egg she active or spoon she passive, all them fine clauses...
> never braught the participle of a present to a desponent horta-
> trixy, vindicatively...(*FW* 269.29)

The verb contained in "hortatrixy" is a well-known paradigm for
the deponent, *hortor* or *hortari*, passive in appearance, in the active
sense of exhort or incite.

Being "one of those mixed middlings" and volatile, unstable,
formally not always distinguished from the passive, the Middle Voice
tended to disappear as a separate category, not, however, as an
inherent assignment in language. If we want to express medial
participation in English, we usually choose a form in which the
subject finds itself at either end of the inflected verb. My sentence
just did that: "the subject finds itself...." Characteristic is a bending
(*flectere*) back (*re-*) upon the agent, so we call it "re-flexive."

Stephen's theory can be rephrased in grammatical metaphor.
One of its cornerstones is the report that Shakespeare the actor took
the part of King Hamlet's ghost. A premise is that Shakespeare
played, acted, himself in this role, and from this a whole algebra
of equations is then extrapolated. Of Shakespeare, named Will, the
"unremitting intellect is...Iago ceaselessly willing that the moor in
him shall suffer" (*U* 9.1023). This is the activity and passivity of
suffering.[7] Shakespeare's errors are "volitional"; yet he is pained
because he was "overborne in a cornfield" (9.456) by Anne who
"hath a way" over others' will. So—always according to Stephen's
self-projections—Shakespeare, partly driven, in varied reiteration wills
himself into his writing. Hamlet is, in Mallarme's phrasing, "*lisant
au livre de lui-même*, don't you know, reading the book of himself."
He does this, we are told, walking—in reflexive French: "*il se
promène*" (9.114).

Stephen may vary his views in terms of scholastic actuality and
possibility: "He found in the world without as actual what was in
his world within as possible," and he adduces a saying of Maeterlinck's
"If Socrates leave his house today he will find the sage seated on
his doorstep" (9.1041). The "sage," reciprocally, is Socrates, the
subject. We walk through ourselves, meeting many people along the
road, but always, in fateful fulfillment, meeting ourselves.

The Shakespeare posited by Stephen is that of a compulsive
and highly versatile auto-bio-grapher of enigmatic genius. Psychologically, the life acted and suffered and partly self-determined, can
hardly help writing itself out into the plays. Autobiography is

tautologically medial. So is a basic assumption of a writer's biography: the personality must be reflected, repeated, modified, conjugated, "worked off," in the work. The consubstantiality of any writer's life and writings looks like a medial truism. Whitman's "One's self I sing" could be seen as the traditional epic invocation translated into the Middle Voice and into English near-reflexivity.

In the following presentation I will deflect the Middle Voice (often using the Latin term medium) as an analogy or descriptive handle for Joycean features that are already well known, in what I hope will be mainly quick illustrative flashes.

"What would grammar matter?" (D 66)

"The Boarding House" may serve as a convenient sample. Consider dominant Mrs. Mooney, who manipulates two lives with a firm hand, as almost exclusively expressed in the active voice, with purposeful active verbs. And isn't her voice active! She even does the speaking for others, her own last word is on behalf of Doran: "Mr. Doran wants to speak to you" (D 69). Mr. Doran, in the role of victim (as he would see himself), is largely and momentously passive, in behavior and in grammar: he is being sent for and being decided on, even his "wants" are expressed *for* him: "he was being had" (D 66). Polly Mooney, the strategic intermediary, conducts herself a good deal in the middle voice: "She knew she was being watched... She would put an end to herself." In her own little scene towards the end, "she dried her eyes...refreshed her eyes...She looked at herself in the mirror." She falls into a revery, withdraws into her own memories and visions. When her story is continued into *Ulysses*, the brief sketch of "the sleepwalking bitch...the bumbailiff's daughter," retains its typical quasi-reflexive syntax even in hyperbole: "without a stitch on her, exposing her person" (12.401).

Bob Doran finds fault with Polly's vulgar grammar: "sometimes she said 'I seen'" (D 66). What she means is, actively, I have seen, but her wording is passive, as though she were using a Latin deponent. Her "being seen," of course, is literally an ingredient in the seduction (a scene mainly hidden from us). Seduction, as active strategy, passive entrapment, or some medial involvement, of the main persons, is one of the story's themes. Up to a point, the grammatical distribution works; if taken too far into a system, it would become as absurd and constrictive as all such attempts.

Stephanoumenos

We also find the detached artist-God in Stephen's esthetic proclamation on either side of the verb:

> The artist, like the God of the creation, remains within or
> behind or beyond or above his handiwork....(*P* 215)

and no matter how refined out of existence, or indifferent,the pose expressive of such indifference is manifested by the type of verbal form which in Greek grammar is always instanced as typical middle voice (*louomai bous podas*: I wash my feet = myself): "paring his fingernails" (*P* 215); which becomes, naturally, a reflexive form in French: ("*en train de se limer les ongles*").

The would-be artist who thinks like that is to declare, programmatically: "I will not serve that in which I no longer believe...and I will try to express myself in some mode of life or art as freely as I can and as wholly as I can" (*P* 224). Our stress is on "myself." The triad of arms to be used in defense ends on "cunning," and it is oddly fitting that the Greek prototype name Daidalos translates into "cunning." Dedalus using cunning (the skill of being daidalos) is a piece of philological reflexivity.

One of the classmates' appellations, *"Bous Stephanoumenos,"* will be repeated and remembered in *Ulysses*, where it leads to another Greek participle of echoing ending and like form, "Autontimoroumenos" (9.939). The latter is close to the title of a play that Terence adapted from Menander. The title is conspicuously reflexive: it moves the self into the accusative case: *auton-*; the "Self-Tormentor," as it is translated. The Greek participle written into *Ulysses is* in the middle voice. Tormenting and being tormented: so is Stephen. The verb *timoreo* (active), originally did not mean torment, but "to help" and then "to revenge." In this collection we also see a change rung on the *Hamlet* theme. Prince Hamlet and Stephen do take revenge, but in part *on* themselves; an unvoiced middle participle brings this out.

Stephen's entry into *Ulysses* is revealing. He is first an object when Mulligan catches sight of him and goes into a mimetic routine of exorcism. Then the perspective changes:

> Stephen Dedalus, displeased and sleepy, leaned his arms on the
> top of the staircase.

He leans part of himself (or, in reflexive French: "*il s'inclina*") onto the world outside. Soon after he will "lean his palm against his brow" (1.100). In "Eveline" such leaning had a strongly passive air, here it expresses a more in-between stage. Notice what Stephen is: "displeased." No doubt the overbearing Mulligan displeases him, perhaps also the raving Englishman in the tower; but the word mainly expresses an internal disposition. In translation such medial forms usually come out twofold: passive (as in "*contrarie*" or "*contrariato*"), or in partial self-inducement: "*malhumorado–mis-slaunig–med mishag.*" In *A Portrait* Stephen had been characterized twice as "displeased"—one of his habitual moods. It is hard to imagine him pleased. The opening beat, "displeased," is in the right medium. The epithet relates him to Telemachos, who was beset by afflictions from outside, and it also differentiates him from the Greek role and prepares the way, psychologically and grammatically, for *Autontimoroumenos*.

Psychogrammar

On a much grander scale, we may redescribe what has been Bloom's affliction. He suffers his wife's adultery, is being injured and victimized, yet he also co-determines this state of the affair, he connives and goes out of his way to make it possible. All of this is, in the characterization of the middle voice, action also "for himself." The hyperballistics of the Circean mode transform such attitudes into large stage action and passion. In a climactic scene Bloom watches and applauds Boylan's copulation with his wife through a keyhole in twisted enjoyment of cockoldry, being "bawd and cuckold" (9.1021). The situation leads right into the vision of Shakespeare's face in the mirror: the optical multiplicity involves Stephen and Bloom and, in widening perspective, the creator of the scene and its voyeuristic readers. It is an interreflective node of voices and visions, a muddle of reciprocity.

Bloom's medial actions do not always, as we recall with divergent evaluations, conform to the stereotypes of sexism. It is on record that the male has predominantly been equated with active action, the female with passive submission. Something of this sexual grammar is mediated in an Ithacan passage

> the natural grammatical transition by inversion involving no alteration of sense of an aorist preterite proposition (parsed as masculine subject, monosyllabic onomatopoetic transitive verb

with direct feminine object) from the active voice into its
correlative aorist preterite proposition (parsed as feminine subject,
auxiliary verb and quasimonosyllabic onomatopoetic past participle with complementary masculine agent) in the passive voice
(*U* 17.2217)

Into such a system, which Dublin society at the turn of the
century would no doubt uphold, Joyce inserted a middle way which
manifests itself first, mildly, in Bloom's sympathy, or compassion,
for women: he can put himself in their position. This makes him
an outsider, particularly in the male congregation of the maternity
hospital. In a transitive sense, Bloom is not very active. Activity is
the role of the Boylans and the Mulligans who in turn are not too
sensitive and, on the whole, lack empathy. When critics, superior
by self-appointment, judge Bloom a failure or decree, for instance,
that throughout his day he takes the "wrong choices" (not going
home to assert a possessive masculinity), it is generally done within
a transitive patriarchal framework.

Bloom, the reproach goes, is "one of those mixed middlings...
Lying up in the hotel...once a month with a headache like a totty
with her courses" (12.1658). In "Circe" such traits are externalized
and Bloom is turned into yet another paradigm, "a finished example
of the new womanly man" (15.1798). This puts him midway between
the "manly man" of Gerty MacDowell's imagination, and how very
soon after she views herself as a "womanly woman" (13.210,435).
There is then, as Bloom asserts in one of his defense speeches, "a
medium in all things" (15.878). He is not explaining Greek grammar
by a Latin term, but echoing Horace's familiar *"est modus in rebus"*
("there is a measure in all things"), and asking for moderation. But
medium he is, all the same, also between male and female.

Circean androgyny enables the newly generated finished example
to finish the example by giving birth to eight male children. It so
happens that the number eight is also that of Molly Bloom's
"sentences" in her chapter, eight verbal units generated by the
book's representative woman: there may be a numerical correspondence. Bloom's children are "respectably dressed and wellconducted"
(15.1824): both epithets are in the middle voice, in particular
"wellconducted": it can be construed as active or medio-passive.

Androgynous features animate *Finnegans Wake* and extend
across genders or religions to appellations like:

> In the name of Annah the Almaziful, the Everliving, the Bringer
> of Plurabilities, haloed be her eve, her singtime sung, her rill
> be run, unhemmed as it is uneven (*FW* 104.1)

in which august divinities are feminized and brought into line with
Eve, or in which Moslem and Christian prayer become assimilated
to the beginning of *Finnegans Wake* itself, with "rill be run"
echoing "riverrun." The equation of Annah, ALP, Eve, with Allah
and the Lord looks like a cosmogenetic middle voice. All of this ties
in with the observation that in Latin grammar verbs as well as nouns
have *genus*, gender. Active, passive, and medium, are *"genera."*

Medial Monologue

The interior monologue once seemed the most striking feature of
Ulysses, the one that once attracted most of the serious attention. It
is a kind of speech not addressed to an outside object; the subject,
as it were, is talking to and often about itself. In a very loose and
yet coincidentally precise sense, Bloom, Stephen, and Molly become
reflexive verbs. They mirror the outside world but also, and at times
exclusively, their own selves, "bend back" (re-flect) on themselves.
In Homeric diction "thinking" is often expressed by a person
addressing his (her) heart, or breast, or mind: "I think" is "I said
to myself." By a definition that is almost grammatical and, again,
tautological, everything thus expressed is "subjective." What is
perceived is subjected to the perceiver's nature. One of the narrative
advantages is the economy of such characterization that is two-
directed: towards the world without *and* within: "She understands
all she wants to. Vindictive too. Cruel. Her nature. Curious mice
never squeal. Seem to like it" (4.27). This tells us something about
cats, and mice, but even more about Bloom (at a later stage we may
find, moreover, that some of Bloom's attitude towards his wife is
already caught in this observation). We can move, in other words,
towards the thing said (thought) and towards the sayer (thinker).
We generally recognize the reflector, can tell Bloom from Stephen
or, by extrapolation, deduce the author himself who, biographically,
is all to all, Bloom and Stephen and Molly and Lenehan. All the
works are, truistically, *pièce de Joyce*.

The internal middle voice appears in a very brief flash on the
first page: "Chrysostomos." Insofar as it is a naming (see above), it
characterizes the person named as well as the namer, indicates

something about his erudition as well as his state of mind. The interior monologue's official initiation takes place fittingly at the moment when, looking at the mirror held out to him, Stephen begins internally to speak to himself: "As he and others see me" (1.136). At this point perspective, pronouns, tenses, all have changed. The reflexion is optical, psychological and grammatical. The self seen in the mirror reflects back: "Who chose this face for me?...It asks me too": the face that is being addressed reciprocally asks back. Interestingly enough, Stephen sees himself when he "bent forward"; bending forward is the mirror reflexion of bending (*flectere*) backward.

Gerty MacDowell, whose thoughts are presented more indirectly, also "bent forward quickly," after "being bent so far back" (13.742,728); but her physical action is described more as leaning: "she leaned back" we read several times (13.695,715, "ever so far," 717,941), or she "had to lean back" (744). We know that this enables her, medio-passively, to be seen in a particular way. Reciprocally, however, Bloom in his turn "was leaning back," he "coloured like a girl," also reciprocally (13.743). All these bendings and leanings are not connected with the thinking that goes on but with the chapter's activities which are more solitary (or "ipsoerelative") than other-directed (or "aliorelative," as in 17.1350).

Physically, the associations of the middle voice can be extended to masturbation. Whether through necessity or fastidiousness, the subject also becomes its own object. In the "Nausicaa" chapter, the arena for such economy or auto-reciprocity, Gerty and Bloom are not so much transitive verbs with each other as objects, at least not each other's direct objects, except visually. Something as erotic and tactile as "the quick hot touch of his handsome lips" occurs only in Gerty's imagination (13.708). Bloom wets and stains himself. Even his watch has stopped. In Greek such intransitive stopping would be in the middle voice (*pauesthai* as against an active *pauein*, to stop): "Funny my watch stopped at half past four" (13.846); the watch, clearly, ceased its activity, it "stopped itself"; what Bloom considers "funny" seems to be that whatever went on at home had some enigmatic influence and, actively, stopped it. In this view or superstition, the watch, like Bloom, acts and is acted on.

Both Gerty and Bloom, reflect, often in reciprocal convergences. Nothing is passed across but looks, and "a kind of language between them." Gerty MacDowell, "lost in thought" or "wrapped in thought," as the medial phrases have it, acts, in terms of the grammatical descriptions indicated before, mainly "on herself or for herself." She is conscious of her effects on others, admiration that turns back on her. With the rest of humanity she shares the delight in the "lovely reflection which the mirror gave back to her" (13.162). Her circumambient style shows her as the victim of forces that have shaped her. They range from society's conventions and imperatives to the injunctions of advertising and the illusions of compensatory literature. But she is also their subject and, in her own conditioned turn, now regenerates the same attitudes in cosmetic circularity. She reshapes life in the style that shaped her. Lest this sound too condescending, let me add that I believe such medial conditioning holds true for most of us in all culture contexts. Stephen, for example, is similarly co-determined by the catholicism he projects in his very efforts of rejection. I can't answer for any of you out there, but for me, Gerty MacDowell "*c'est moi.*"

The chapter's events are set off against the "voice of prayer" emanating from the nearby church, and the refrain of the litany, "pray for us," is woven into the foreground. Prayer is a model for the middle voice; in practice it often amounts to wishing something for oneself: *ora pro nobis*. The Greek verb was naturally medial: *euchesthai*, both in Homer and in the New Testament. Bloom notes the repetition of "Pray for us. And pray for us. And pray for us" and links it to his profession: "Same things with ads. Buy from us. And buy from us" (13.1122). Advertisements proclaim themselves; what Catesby's Cork Lino or Plumtree's Potted Meat spell out is, above all, "Buy me!"

Middler the Holy Ghost

The economy of heaven, androgyny, and a masturbatory Everyman Immorality Play are combined with gusto by Bullocky Mulligan at the end of "Scylla and Charybdis." But we have never been far from the consubstantial intricacies that obsess Stephen. His silent creed looks like a travesty of a Divine Middle Voice

> He Who Himself begot middler the Holy Ghost and Himself sent Himself, Agenbuyer, between Himself and others...sitteth on the right hand of his Own Self...(9.493)

("on the right hand of His Own Self" has come true of the synoptic text of *Ulysses*). All of the middling has been transposed to patristic, Sabellian absurdity and incestuous economy. Unmistakable are the mocking reflexivity and the trailing, echoing Selves. "Middler the

the first old wugger of himself in the flesh'' (79.2)[8]

The "old wugger" incarnates "himself in the flesh." The reflexive duplication of "wuggering"—offsetting the rather sterile act of buggery implied—is similar to the *Wake*'s first clearly medial verb, the "rocks" that "exaggerated themselse" and went "doublin their mumper" (3.7). Part of the activity of exaggerating is directed towards others ("-else"), part bends back on the subject ("themsel[ves]").

laughing-like to himself

I have wuggered myself into a hyper-emphasis of a grammatical ploy, what the Greek called the middle *diathesis*, the Romans the *genus medium*. The whole point could have been made, more briefly, by focusing on Joyce's first and last work. In "The Sisters" a declining priest wants to reshape an impressionable boy in his own likeness; perhaps he obliquely tries to continue himself through the disciple. Professionally he listens to the confession of others, yet in the boy's dream and a reversal of roles, the priest seems to be confessing. In confession we say something to someone about ourselves; appropriately the Latin word for it is a deponent again, a medio-passive *confiteor* (the word is repeated in the partly auto-confessional *Portrait*: 78.9, 82.17, 143.31). *Confieri* (infinitive form) is derived from *fari* (to speak) of which it is a special, retroactive, variant. "The Sisters" is a story in which the same boy later retells the events. Our last glimpse is of Father Flynn "sitting up by himself in the dark of his confessionbox, wide-awake and laughing-like softly to himself" (*D* 18). The distortive confession is repeated, as if for emphasis: "Wide-awake and laughing-like to himself" towards the end, and we know that "there was something wrong with him".

Sitting, laughing to himself—that is one of Nora's reports of her husband composing *Finnegans Wake*, which has also been considered a twisted confession where much has gone wrong. It contains a "convulsion box," a "confisieur" and "confussion" (261.F3, 531.2, 353.25). It is a work that repeatedly speaks about itself, to itself, or tangentially admits that it is "a letter selfpenned to one's other" (489.33). This also ties in with the dream analogy of the Wake (which, to some of its commentators, who seem to know what a dream is, achieves axiomatic status). Most interpreters of dreams agree that whatever they contain, the dreamer is also voicing him/herself in intricate guises and that dreams are a tortuous kind of confession.

Revoicings

With considerable metaphorical latitude I have been applying a grammatical analogy in free and easy dispersion. Analogy is what Joyce works with. On a small scale his Revoicings take the form of all those evocations of prior phrasings, often the most memorable ones of literature, sometimes the tritest of ready-made stereotypes. They may be formulas, clearly marked "quotations," or the most evanescent of "allusions." There is a medial sense in them, insofar as only a portion of their semantic energies are directed toward external actuality. The rest bends back, or retroflects, on their origin or the fashion of their articulation. The ghosts of former texts are called up, called up for readers in proportion to their familiarity with them. Some attention then turns back on the source, literary or otherwise. In *Ulysses* the method is heralded by Buck Mulligan who exhibits, from the start, remarkable mimetic and recitative skills. One reason why some of our initial effort is required to figure out the external setting is that most of Mulligan's second (perhaps golden-) mouthed pronouncements deflect our attention away from what referential direction they have. A ceremoniously intoned "*introibo ad altare Dei*" tells us less about what is really going on than about the history and proper context of the words quoted. A tension is set up between the two.

Quotations brought to bear upon "reality" also detract from it. This is in the nature of the title "Ulysses," or of an entire chapter like "Oxen of the Sun," where indeed the literary parading so far has engaged most of our critical endeavors. Each Revoicing (which here subsumes all evocations of prior texts) contains a feature of the middle voice, standing midway between what is being pointed out and its own peculiar manner of pointing. Each quotation in part epiphanizes itself. "*Thalatta! Thalatta!*" (*U* 1.80) refers to the visible sea, but also to a speaker who flaunts classical knowledge: it looks forward to an object, and backwards towards a secondary quoter (Mulligan) and beyond to a primary author (Xenophon), and, from another angle, to one more adventurous journey with a return, analogous to the one of Odysseus. When Bloom enters his back garden in the morning and we read

> No sound. Perhaps hanging clothes out to dry. The maid was
> in the garden. Fine morning. (4.472),

he is taking stock of what he sees and hears. But "The maid was
in the garden" does not belong to this order. At least to a majority
of those initiated (having a nursery rhyme in their ears), this is not
a comment on a maid's presence. The maid leads a mere fictional,
evocative existence "in the garden," she is in another grammatical
mood, a subjunctive wish-fulfillment. The quotation—if recognized—
displays itself as a medium. It refers back to a cultural thesaurus
and applies one of its items to an analogous occasion. If we do not
know the sentence as an echo we may misread the situation. "The
maid was in the garden" means, if anything, its own opposite: a
conspicuous, frustrating absence. The quotation fills the vacuum of
"No sound." It utters mainly its existence as language re-used.

In this allusive function, language still transitively refers to
something outside: there is a possible transition to an actual situation.
In its self-expressive, autophanic, effects, however, it moves closer to
the middle voice. Semantic energies are divided as well as multiplied.
Language itself, and by extension Literature, can be said to have a
middle voice, mediating between an external objective, and a preening
self-consciousness. Joyce, as usual, carries both functions—referential
potency and the retroflection of utterance—to extremes.

Nominal Shorthand

In my confession I have said nothing that might not have been
known before. Do not write this statement off as modesty—the same
claim could be made about *Finnegans Wake*. I just tried to use a
point of view (taken from classical languages) to subsume a variety
of Joycean features that might otherwise have little in common. The
terminology chosen tried to do more justice to Joyce's kinetics than
what nominal stability might describe. There are, naturally, excellent
reasons for still resorting to the fixation that nouns tend to indicate.
Certain situations require classification or a provisional foothold. We
need reassuring support as we need the solidity of a verifiable city
of Dublin of 1904 to get our bearings and as a backdrop for the
elusive narrative processes in *Ulysses*. The format of Notes or Annotations, of brief glosses, allows for little else. Nominal shorthand
saves time and space. The discursive articulation of verbal motion is
laborious and hardly ever completed: a Protean sense of not-quite-
thereness always remains.

As long as we know about the necessity for convenient simplification, the danger is minimal. Take the practical requirement for
a concise commentary on *Finnegans Wake*. As an example we hold
up for inspection the first word in the text that is clearly not English:

by a commodius vicus of recirculation (3.2)

Annotations says (and must say, reductively): "Vico." We have a
right to expect this sort of information, not to give it would be
wrong. But the abbreviated near-truth is less justified when we deal
with credulous novices. In a first learning process such premature
labeling (nothing but the name "Vico") is unhelpful or even
impedimental. For "vicus" (lower case) should be treated in its own
right, or else brought back into the contextual currency (the English
language) from which it sets itself off. In its *prima facie* inassimil-
ability it acts as an imperative for transformation: translate me! (or
else, it leads us to different environs). A Latin dictionary would offer
several interconnected meanings: "district of a town, village, neigh-
borhood, street, hamlet." Out of this spectrum, "street" or "road"
seems to fit best, for we are casting about for something to move
in ("brings us back"). But even so, we have to discard—or hold in
suspense—all the other possible meanings: this is already semantic
work in progress. A diachronic view of language as growth through
time (remember "past Eve and Adam's") would assemble cognates
like English "wick" (in the sense of hamlet, village, mostly in place
names) and, in particular, Greek "*oikos*" (house), and it would lead
us back to an original root, deduced from existing words, which in
this case would sound, of all things, like WEIK—very close to how
we pronounce (Finnegans) *Wake*. Such a phonetic coincidence need
not be belabored as part of an intended meaning, but some readers
might be intrigued that an early non-normative word can recirculate
to an element of the book's title. What an etymological excursion
into history reveals is that development, becoming, time, are involved.
That oddity "vicus" acts like a signpost and takes us elsewhere (and
perhaps back to the context).

Going along the road of wakeful meanings, we will, in the
course of further input, also arrive at Giambattista Vico, eighteenth-
century Italian philosopher estimated by Joyce. For the initiated the
click may set in as early as "recirculation." At some stage and time,
recognition *turns* "vicus" *into* "vico" as a plausible matching. Once
this has occurred, supportive hindsight evidence then may become

overwhelming (with the stress again on becoming): It was words of
the type and ending like *"vic-us"* that tended to turn into Italian
words like *"vic-o"* (though this one does not exist, Latin *commodus*,
on the other hand, became *comodo*). We may recall that the
philosopher of temporal patternings used Roman history and Latin
etymologies to illustrate recurrencies and changes. *Finnegans Wake*
anachronistically inverts the process. We can retranslate, by a similar
leap across languages, *"riverrun"* into a favorite Viconian term,
ricorso (the flowing back, run, of a river, with the phoneme *ri*—as
an external common link). Many additional roads can be traveled
towards the particular goal. One is Vico road in Dalkey, obligingly
incurvated, a parochial accident to be exploited by Joyce on further
occasions. An instrumental preposition like *"by* a commodius vicus"
would properly take the ablative case in Latin and change to "vico"—
but this would be our doing. "Vico" in fact originates through our
cooperation: the textual irritations prompt us into hermeneutic
activity.

If you insist that, all right, many semantic manipulations may
be necessary to construe an Italian name out of a Latin noun, but
once that is done, on all recirculatory readings there will be an
instant identification, and no further quibblings, then you simply
neglect how much "vicus" on all occasions also visibly protests against
such violation. Wakean vital gestures towards dissociation are disregarded a trifle too complacently. "Vicus," in other words, may well
strive to collide with "Vico," but with equal validity it aims to
escape from the restriction. Neither turn should be ignored in our
scope, nor the awareness that it is a matter of turning, of conversion.
Vico, as a reductive name, is a valid and poor interpretation of
"vicus" (among other things simply because it leaves out "us"),
but it is an excellent verb to conjugate the Wake.

•

Nothing new has been said, nothing for which external sources,
protographs, archetypes had to be called in, not even a smattering
of little Latin and less Greek: other catalysts would have done just
as well. Nothing has been put forward that might not have been
noticed from immediate observation, unaided, by verbal communication with the text.

The most programmatically pertinent verb of them all may be
reading. We know from experience it is both transitive and self-

reflexive. What we gather, select, recognize, rearrange, construe, from the alphabetical configurations, we remake in our own likeness. It is no secret that some likenesses are more rewarding and conveyable than others, and, for better or worse, at a Symposium most likenesses are speaking, are our vocal confessions, with a fair proportion of self-display. Leopold Bloom exemplifies one of the pitfalls when he hastily projects his own name into a word that for a few letters looks alike:

> Bloo...Me? No.
> Blood[9] of the Lamb.

> (*U* 8.8)

In his zeal and inclination—misreading the throwaway of himself—he has forestalled us all. It is to his credit that he corrects himself in time. We don't always. That is one reason why we depend on each other's self-pennings. And one reason why I have argued in favor of interactions, at our conferences, against long, monologous, medial, "major" addresses, with all the tedium between active oral pontification and passive auditive suffering.

In the beginning, we have learned, was the joy. The enjoyment that makes life, perhaps, almost worth reading.. It is a reading, also, of ourselves; but the selves may become a bit more aware, or refined, or sensitive, in the process, in all those processes that, when old is said in one, have gathered us here together and will continue to bring us back to Joyce—the Verb.

NOTES

1. Benstock, Shari and Bernard. *Who's He When He's at Home: A James Joyce Directory.* Urbana, Chicago, London: University of Illinois Press, 1980.
2. "Usurper" (as in *U* 1.744) derives from a verb *usurpare*, one of whose meanings is "to call names."
3. One of the abbreviations used in the footnotes "*STET*" in the old code of the typesetters is an injunction "Let it stand!"
4. Such documents are called "witnesses," not just passive products of writing or printing, but live persons actively making statements that have to hold up to cross-examination.
5. The conditional nature of the text that has been established is well in evidence in Richard Ellmann's wording: "What Gabler aims at is an ideal text, such as Joyce would have constructed in ideal conditions." "Preface" to *Ulysses: The Corrected Text* (see next note), p.x.
6. "Afterword." In *Ulysses: The Corrected Text,* edited by Hans Walter Gabler with Wolfhard Steppe, p. 649. New York: Random House, 1986.
7. The verb "to suffer," active in form, is medio-passive. "Stephen suffered [Mulligan] to pull out and hold up on show by its corner a dirty crumpled

hankerchief'' (*U* 1.70). The transitivity is deceptive and reciprocal: something is done to Stephen and he suffers from it, he also suffers it. But there is self-involvement in the action. The Latin for suffering, *pati, patior,* is naturally a deponent; its derivatives are *passio* and our "passive," the name for the *genus* which translated Greek "*pathetikos,*" from *pathos* or a verb *paschein,* in whose system active and medio-passive forms intermingle.

8. Atherton, James S. *The Books at the Wake.* London: Faber & Faber, 1959, p. 196.

9. Walter W. Skeat with some reservation ("doubtfully") mentions the root BLOW for "blood," which would connect it to "bloom." *An Etymological Dictionary of the English Language,* Oxford (1909).

3

The Joycead

COLBERT KEARNEY

Every Irish schoolboy and schoolgirl—and consequently every serious Joycean—has heard of the Battle of Clontarf: how, in the year 1014 at the place called the Meadow of the Bulls, the saintly Irish King Brian Boru drove the heathen Danes into the sea, and how King Brian was surprised at prayer and killed by the cowardly Bruadar. Like a good deal of what every Irish schoolboy and schoolgirl—and every serious Joycean—knows, this account is somewhat wide of what might loosely be termed *the truth*. In fact, it is part of a propaganda campaign run by Brian's supporters, the chieftains of Munster, to assert the primacy of the southern province over the rest of Ireland. The actual situation was more complicated. You must understand *Dane* to mean not merely an inhabitant of Denmark but any of the Scandinavian adventurers who tried his luck in Ireland. You must understand *Irish* to mean not all the people of Ireland but only those who were allies of Brian of Munster. The people of Dublin sided with the Danes which is not really surprising because Dublin, like all the major Irish towns, was a Scandinavian foundation. And the Danes were not expelled from Ireland: a large Scandinavian element remained, became assimilated with the locals and fought side by side with them when the next wave of invaders—the Normans—arrived in the twelfth century.

This essay is concerned with another piece of Munster propaganda which every Joycean is familiar with and which, given the constant increase in the popularity of Joyce's writings, every Irish schoolboy and schoolgirl may know before long.

In January 1932, shortly after the death of his father, Joyce wrote to Harriet Weaver:

> He thought and talked of me up to his last breath. I was very fond of him always, being a sinner myself, and even liked his faults. Hundreds of pages and scores of characters in my books

came from him. . . . I got from him his portraits, a waistcoat, a
good tenor voice, and an extravagant licentious disposition (out
of which, however, the greater part of any talent I may have
springs) but, apart from these, something else I cannot define.
(*JJII* 643)

I want to take as my topic those portraits which are now in
Buffalo and, more especially, the purple hunting waistcoat in the
Joyce Museum in Sandycove. This garment was made by Ellen Joyce
for her son, John Joyce, who gave it to his son, James Joyce. Its
fictional form figures in "The Dead" when Gabriel remembers that

one year his mother had worked for him as a birthday present a
waistcoat of purple tabinet, with little foxes' heads upon it, lined
with brown satin and having round mulberry buttons. (*D* 186)

Associated with this waistcoat is a tale of two cities, Dublin, the
capital of Ireland, and Cork, on the south coast, the capital of Munster,
both of them originally Scandinavian settlements and both of them
crucial to any account of the life and writings of James Joyce.

•

Though he loved his father dearly Joyce would not return to
Dublin to see him. He kept him

constantly under the illusion that I would come and was always
in correspondence with him but an instinct I believed in held
me back from going, much as I longed to. (*JJII* 643)

Joyce often expressed a fearful unwillingness to put himself in
the hands of those in Dublin who had proved so treacherous and
malignant in the past and this may be the *instinct* he refers to.
However, like much that seems strange in the career of James Joyce,
his failure to make an appearance at the death-bed of his beloved
father is not quite so strange when seen in the context of his family
history. John Joyce, it would seem, was also absent from the death-
bed of his father.

At the time of his father's death, Joyce was living comfortably
in Paris, the hero of the literary *avant garde*. Many were taken by an
apparent contradiction between James Joyce, the daring apostle of
literary freedom, and Mr. Joyce, the formal man who frowned on any
references to sex, who loved to dress up for the Opera and who was
surprised by the effect he had on some people:

My habit of addressing people I have just met for the first time
as "Monsieur" earned for me the reputation of a *tout petit*

bourgeois while others consider what I intend for politeness as most offensive. (*JJII* 510)

Had these people known Joyce's family background or had they read his writings more carefully they would have recognized his social demeanor as yet another aspect of his paternal inheritance.

John Joyce was born in Cork in 1849 and died in Dublin in 1931 at the age of eighty-two. Though he spent most of his life in Dublin—having moved there in his mid-twenties—he remained a Corkman all his life, and his son recognized this when he had his gravestone inscribed in memory of *John Stanislaus Joyce of Cork.*

Among the many remarkable things about John Joyce is that, having lost his job in the Rates Office in 1891—at the age of forty—he never again reaped the benefits or bore the strain of full-time employment. His life divides neatly in two. Before 1891 he was a man of means, albeit of diminishing means, who had inherited a considerable amount of property in Cork; not long after 1891 he had mortgaged his properties away and was the unemployed father irresponsible for the welfare of a wife and ten children. John Joyce was a spectacularly inadequate breadwinner. He earned little by a series of occasional jobs but his social pleasures seem to have taken precedence over his domestic obligations. He abused his children physically and verbally and he made several attempts to inflict grievous bodily harm on his wife. Here is the opinion of one who knew him well:

> He was a man of unparalleled vituperative power, a virtuoso in speech with unique control of the vernacular, his language often coarse and blasphemous to a degree of which, in the long run, he could hardly himself have been conscious. . .[His] stories would be of a perfectly drawing-room character till suddenly, as if taken unawares, he would slip into the coarse vein and another side of his nature and vocabulary would be revealed. (Curran 69f.)

And yet—and this is not the least remarkable aspect of the man—despite the humiliations of poverty, despite the loss of employment, property, and social status, and despite his ignominious flights from angry landlords—John Joyce retained an invincible sense of himself as a *gentleman* and he sought to transmit that consciousness to his eldest son. At bay before a Clongowes bully whose father is a magistrate, Stephen maintains that *his* father is a gentleman. Even as he loses the last of the Cork properties, Mr. Dedalus clings to his hopes for a well-bred future:

> —When you kick out for yourself, Stephen—as I daresay you will one of these days—remember, whatever you do, to mix

> with gentlemen. When I was a young fellow I tell you I enjoyed
> myself. I mixed with fine decent fellows...we were all gentlemen,
> Stephen—at least I hope we were—and bloody good honest
> Irishmen too. (P 91)

Though like all fathers and sons they had their little disagreements,
John Joyce always had hopes for James, and James, as he grew older,
saw himself increasingly as his father's son. Just as John Joyce combined
"a perfectly drawing room character" with what his son euphemized
as "an extravagant licentious disposition," so too James Joyce, having
scandalized the western world with his writings, could put on his
evening clothes and appear at the opera as a model of bourgeois
propriety.

Stanislaus Joyce, who hated his father and his native land with
a religious passion, wrote as follows in *My Brother's Keeper:*

> The two dominant passions of my brother's life were to be love
> of father and of fatherland...love of his country, or rather of
> his city, that was to reject him and his work; love of his father,
> who was like a mill-stone round his neck. (238)

Throughout his many wanderings James Joyce carried his family
portraits as *pius Aeneas* bore his household gods. These portraits were
the icons of a family cult, an oral history which transcended genealogy
and attained the status of a foundation myth or an epic. We may
refer to it as *The Joycead* in order to emphasize the conventions which
govern it and to distinguish it from more orthodox history. The full
text was lost, as it were, with the last breath of John Joyce, who was
the principal author of this epic, but it is possible to reconstruct *The
Joycead* by conflating the derivative versions found in the writings of
his sons, James and Stanislaus. It is then possible to deconstruct this
reconstruction by relating it to the historical circumstances and to
contemporary records of people and events mentioned in *The Joycead*.
The fact is that, despite the impression given in *The Joycead*, the
Joyces made no lasting mark on Cork: their only existence is in the
dusty obscurity of public records, legal documents, rates valuations,
and commercial directories. John Joyce's attitude was more histrionic
than historical. His pride in the Joyces was matched only by his scorn
for the families of those women—including his wife and his mother—
who married Joyces and thus—at least in the eyes of the world—
contributed an equal share to the genetic pool.

Although *The Joycead* does not stress the far distant past, we
may assume that Joyces were Scandinavians who settled in what is

now northwestern France and later on, in the twelfth century, took part in the Norman invasion of Ireland. In Ireland they have always been associated with a part of a western county, Galway, which is known as The Joyce Country. What we think of as traditional Norman virtues—urban development and regulation—do not appear to have found much expression on the western seaboard but the Joyces were not utterly lost in the Celtic ethos of Connemara: one strain moved south and into the Irish historical record at the end of the eighteenth century as builders. (They may have been connected with the marble quarries of Connemara where Joyces are still working.) They settled around the town of Fermoy in East Cork, the only part of Cork where the name is still reasonably popular. To this day the Joyces of East Cork preserve a tribal memory of their Galway ancestry and they believe, with justification, that they are descended from masons who came south in search of work. They prospered but at some stage they excited the envy or the disdain of their neighbors who composed a saying which still survives: *never trust a Joyce, or Rice or a Quirke.*

In many ways the history of the Joyces is the history of the Catholic middle class in Ireland. During the eighteenth century Irish Catholics suffered under a system of penal legislation which was designed to bar any Catholic from social advancement. During the nineteenth century, thanks to a series of measures which culminated in the Catholic Emancipation Act of 1829, middle-class Catholics came to dominate most aspects of Irish life. This social adjustment did not take place without a great deal of pushing and shoving as middle-class Catholics and Protestants sought to claim or maintain what they believed was exclusively theirs. Against the Protestant claim that the Catholics were treacherous and ignorant bog-trotters, the Catholics maintained that they were every bit as honest, as intelligent, and as cultured as the Protestants—in other words, the Catholic was just as much a gentleman as the Protestant.

The Joycead, in true epic style, launches forth *in medias res* with the Joyces established in the forefront of Catholic society. It does not inquire too deeply into the manner in which they achieved their social status but the fact is that the Joyces, like Tim Finnegan, rose in the world by carrying a hod. They made bricks with which they made houses with which they made money.

The move from manual labor to property development coincides with the move from the town of Fermoy into the city of Cork around 1800 and is associated with James Joyce, "manufacturer and chapman of salt and lime." Though it seems an unlikely combination today, salt and lime were essential commodities in the economy of Cork at the time. Lime was used in the making of building bricks and mortar and also as a fertilizer; salt was always in great demand in a city which was the center of the British butter trade. Various dependable documents—legal records, rates valuations, trade directories—establish James Joyce in the city of Cork as the owner of a brick-building business, of a salt and lime business, and of property.

In *The Joycead* this primal James Joyce functions as a cultural hero whose exploits hover between mythological and academic history. If we recall that in this form he is the creation of John Joyce, we shall not be surprised if he epitomizes the virtues which his creator would claim as quintessentially Joycean. Here he is in *A Portrait of the Artist*:

> He was a good Irishman when there was no money in the job. He was condemned to death as a whiteboy. But he had a saying about our clerical friends, that he would never let one of them put his two feet under his mahogany. (38)

In other words: James Joyce was the model of a spirited Irish gentleman. The Whiteboys were a clandestine agrarian terror society and were active around Fermoy in the late eighteenth century but the name was often used to indicate any secret society which used extreme methods on behalf of Catholics. The episode suggests that the Joyces, like many ambitious Catholics, resented the advantages, commercial and social, enjoyed by their Protestant competitors. This would have made them sympathetic to secret societies and, consequently, brought them into conflict with the Catholic clergy whose official position was in support of the *status quo*. Nationalism and anticlericalism are intertwining threads of *The Joycead* and of Irish political history.

James Joyce's unexplained reprieve may seem odd unless we remember we are dealing with a myth which is not constrained by the conventions of realism. The mythic element is more obvious in the case of James' son, James Augustine, who was born in 1827 in Rose Cottage, just outside Fermoy and quite close to several limestone quarries. The road between Rose Cottage and the main road to Mallow was known into our own time as *Joyce's Boreen*. In *The Joycead* James Augustine is the most obviously superhuman of the Joyces: almost everything about him suggests a quasi-divine status. He was "the handsomest man in Cork" and, most tellingly, a man of "angelic temper" (*My Brother's Keeper* 21, 23). Even his physical position is on high: in the pageant of the past he rides along, aloft on his horse, resplendent in his red hunting jacket, the admiration of all who gaze up at him (*P* 94). He was also above vulgar commerce with such mundane materials as salt and lime—he went bankrupt at least once—but before alluding to his human imperfections it is necessary to say something about his marriage.

In *My Brother's Keeper,* Stanislaus, presumably repeating his father, writes that James Augustine

> married a woman of some means, an O'Connell, one of a family
> of nineteen, the daughter of the proprietor of one of the largest
> general stores in Cork. Some of the nineteen became priests and
> nuns. (22)

John Joyce was the only child of an only child and his own domestic circumstances did not encourage him to admire large families. He had little to say in favor of the O'Connells who figure in *The Joycead* as the antitheses of the Joyces: graceless, superstitious and, despite their commercial success, peasants. He may even have blamed his own prolific paternity on the O'Connells.[1]

James Augustine's father-in-law, the polyphiloprogenitive shop-keeper, was also a representative figure of Irish life in the early nineteenth century. John O'Connell was a successful draper who had served in local politics. His political beliefs may be deduced from his claimed relationship with Daniel O'Connell, the Liberator of Irish Catholics by means of constitutional agitation and clerical support, and an uncompromising denouncer of political violence. I have been able to trace only five O'Connell children, four of whom answered the call to the religious life. One of these was Ellen O'Connell who followed her sister, Alicia, into the South Presentation Convent in Cork in October 1836. Ellen left the convent after four months.[2] Ten years later she was still unmarried but her patience was to be rewarded with a proposal from "the handsomest man in Cork." They were married in 1848, an exceptionally unhappy year for Ireland which was being ravaged by the Great Famine. In July 1849 their only child was born, John Stanislaus, the father of James and Stanislaus and the main author of *The Joycead*: a child of the Famine, he was to prove himself a great survivor.

The documentary history of the marriage is mainly legal. A deed of settlement records the merging of assets: the Joyces contributed house property close to their own town residence and the

O'Connells gave land and quarries close to the Joyce brick-building business outside the city in Ballinlough. Stanislaus suspected that the parents looked to the mature Ellen to temper the extravagance of James Augustine and teach him the sober virtues of the O'Connells. Not the least of Ellen's attractions was the equivalent of $100,000 she brought in hard cash but hopes of a successful merger were vain: four years later James Augustine was bankrupt. In retrospect it is clear that the angelic James Augustine frittered the family fortune. Before his early death in 1866 he had lost the family interests in brickmaking, building, and the sale of salt and lime. His death certificate describes him as Inspector of Hackney Coaches—almost certainly a sinecure in the gift of the O'Connells.[3]

The mythological history of the union is much more interesting and is concerned with the nature of James Augustine, the nature of Ellen O'Connell, the nature of the marriage, the naming of the child, and finally, the amazing survival of the child. As usual the sordid commercial details are more or less dismissed as vulgar and beneath the notice of gentlemen.

The story of James Augustine and Ellen may be seen as a parody of the Adonis theme, with James Augustine as Adonis and Ellen as a dull peasant Persephone; there is even in *My Brother's Keeper* the suggestion of occasional visits to Aphrodite (23). James Augustine was young, exceptionally handsome and "of angelic temper"; no longer young, Ellen was plain and shrewish. Nor would Ellen's defection from the convent have added to her attractions in a society which branded young men who left the seminary as "spoiled priests."

Here, to change terms, was a Dido whom James Augustine should have loved and left. What prevented him? What else except the malign influence of the priest-ridden O'Connells? At least that is how it was in *The Joycead* as reported in *My Brother's Keeper* (23). No doubt the O'Connells blamed the failure of the marriage—carnal and commercial—on the fecklessness of the ill-disciplined and licentious Joyces, but the Joyces saw things in a different light. The marriage was a loveless and grotesque conjunction contrived by the O'Connells and their clerical mentors as a last ditch effort to marry Ellen off to the angelically ingenuous James Augustine.

The most farcical of the mythological episodes was that of the naming of the only son. According to *The Joycead* it was intended to christen the son James but, thanks to the bungling of a drunken parish clerk, the baby was named John. It is infinitely more likely that John was named after his maternal grandfather, the irreproach-able John O'Connell. The story of the drunken clerk was a Joycean denial of the O'Connell heritage, a heritage which teemed with scheming clerics.

One can only guess as to which Joyce was responsible for this tale. Its garrulous form suggests John Joyce but perhaps it originated as James Augustine's apology for not protecting his son more effectively from the O'Connells. More than likely, both men had a hand in it for they were unusually close to each other, "more like brothers than father and son." John Stanislaus had been a weak child and had suffered from typhus, the disease which would later kill James Augustine. He was saved by James Augustine in a manner which would not have been out of place in a more ancient myth: James Augustine arranged for his son to go out in the pilot boats and the fresh salt air of Cork Harbour not only cured him of childish illness but enabled him to live to the age of eighty-two.

John Joyce remembered his twenty-five years in Cork as a sort of paradise. Wanting for nothing, assured of everything, innocent of the harder facts of life, free from the inconvenience of work, he set out to emulate his father: he excelled at outdoor pursuits—riding, sailing, rowing, bowling, athletics—and, spoiled with money, an engaging manner, a good voice, and a talent for mimicry, he was equally successful as a young man-about-town. Even the early death of his angelic father does not seem to have interrupted the blissful tone of his youth. The story is that James Augustine, as he lay dying, urged his son to go to the Opera House (*My Brother's Keeper* 23). The death of James Augustine left John Joyce alone among the O'Connells. He went up to Queen's College, now University College, to study medicine in order to consolidate his social status by earning a living as a professional gentleman; but it was his Joycean spirits that won out and he dedicated himself so assiduously to athletics and dramatics that there was no time for studies and he abandoned his attempt to become a professional gentleman, preferring to live the life of a gentleman of leisure. One presumes that the O'Connells tried to point out the weakness of his position—that his inheritance was not unlimited, that he was living off his capital while creating none; at any rate, his relations with his mother and her people may be gauged from another episode of *The Joycead*.

The story goes that in his early twenties John Joyce made two efforts to join violent organizations, the French Army and the Fenian Brotherhood. In the first case he was frustrated by his mother who followed him to London and dragged him home; to extricate him from the Fenians his mother took him to Dublin where she hoped he would find some respectable and profitable expression for his political energies. Ellen O'Connell appears here as typically O'Connell, dull, constitutional, and bent on repressing the extravagant disposition of the Joyces. As a man of property John Joyce should not have sympathized with the Fenians but he needed some outlet for the colorfully rebellious streak he had inherited from his father's people. Soon he was to find a cause which would allow him to become involved in radically nationalist politics without prejudicing his position as an Irish Catholic gentleman. Charles Stewart Parnell united almost all strands of Irish nationalism behind him: a Protestant landlord who was as anti-English as any Catholic peasant, Parnell seemed set to deliver a new Ireland in which men like John Joyce would come into their own. John Joyce became his fanatical supporter.

Though removed from his southern paradise, John Joyce continued on the primrose path. Against the wishes of their parents, he married May Murray and in 1882 their son was born and christened James Augustine: there was no bungling this time. John Joyce took his family to live in Bray—on the coast just south of Dublin—where he resumed the water-sports he had excelled in while in Cork. There were danger signs but spotting them had never been a Joyce forte. The series of only boys was broken and then gradually shattered as May Murray showed herself to be the equal of any O'Connell when it came to bearing children. John Joyce must have known that he was living beyond his means but if he did, he took no corrective measures. As a gentleman of means he sent his son James to Clongowes, a prestigious and expensive school run by the Jesuits for the sons of Catholic gentlemen.

And here endeth the first part of *The Joycead*.

•

The child James Joyce was nourished on this family myth and within it he found his role: he was *Sunny Jim*, first in line to the solar throne which had been occupied by the immortal James I whom even a sentence of death could not kill, by the angelic James Augustine whose brief life shed sunshine on all around him (with the possible exception of his wife and his creditors), and by his own father. John Joyce was not the least superhuman of these Joyces: the only begotten son of a heavenly father and an all-too-earthly-mother, he had grown up in the distant paradise that was called Cork and he would establish his beloved Jim in the promised land into which Mr. Parnell was about to lead all the people of Ireland. At the same time young Jim was being nourished—some would say force-fed—on another myth: "Dante" was instructing him in the Roman Catholic religion.

The central episode of the second part of *The Joycead* was the loss of paradise: this fall from graciousness was not due to the sin of any Joycean father but to the meanminded treachery of the Irish people. A less creative account would point out that the Joyces had been living beyond their means for two generations and that James Augustine's commercial ineptitude had only been disguised by his alliance with the O'Connells. John Joyce had failed either to earn enough money or to marry a sufficiently rich woman to finance his life of genteel leisure. It was only a matter of time before he fell into debts which could not be sustained.

John Joyce had begun to mortgage his property ten years before the fall of Parnell but according to *The Joycead* the fall of John Joyce was part of the greater fall of Parnell. Both men had been betrayed and deserted in their hours of need by the uncouth Irish rabble encouraged and directed by their masters, the Catholic bishops and priests. It was probably at this juncture, c. 1891, that the family myth assumed its final form, which I have called *The Joycead* and which, for John Joyce, provided an acceptably coherent account of the fate of the Joyce family. The Joyces were gentlemen and not to be confused with the peasants who marveled at them as the Joyces rode past. The Joyces were good Catholics and good Irishmen but they were contemptuous of the Irish Catholic clergy whose bullying of the Irish was matched only by their subservience to the English. The Joyces were men of spirit who had sported in paradise until they were trapped into marriage with the O'Connells, a dull priest-ridden family whose only achievement was the breeding of priests and nuns, the same priests and nuns who had organized the peasants against Parnell and thereby thrown away the future of Ireland.

Joyce had been removed from Clongowes in June 1891. *A Portrait of the Artist* suggests that hints of John Joyce's troubles had begun to filter through beforehand: Stephen is upset by the aggressive snobbery of Nasty Roche and the mean behavior of Athy whose father owned horses and was probably, thinks Stephen, another magistrate.

> [Stephen] thought of his own father, of how he sang songs while
> his mother played and of how he always gave him a shilling
> when he asked for sixpence and he felt sorry for him that he
> was not a magistrate like the other boys' fathers. Then why was
> he sent to that place with them? But his father had told him
> that he would be no stranger there because his granduncle had
> presented an address to the liberator there fifty years before.
> (26)

If he was not a magistrate, that is, if he could not afford to
send his son to Clongowes, why had he sent him there? John Joyce's
reassurance is a reference to *The Joycead:* Clongowes was for young
Catholic gentlemen and James' status was assured because an an-
cestor—for once the O'Connells proved useful—had presented an
address to Daniel O'Connell there. But such references would not
satisfy a bursar and young James did not return to Clongowes after
the summer vacation of 1891.

Perhaps the most amusing testimony to the power of *The
Joycead* is Joyce's implicit denial—in *A Portrait*—of his attendance
at North Richmond Street Christian Brothers School. While Stephen
enjoys what is termed a "long spell of leisure and liberty" (71)
between Clongowes and Belvedere, it is almost certain that James
Joyce spent the corresponding period with the Christian Brothers.
The writer who would become notorious for his relentless honesty
drew the line at subjecting his fictional self to the tender mercies of
the Christian Brothers. His fictional father would have agreed:

> —Christian Brothers be damned! said Mr Dedalus. Is it
> with Paddy Stink and Micky Mud? No, let him stick to the
> jesuits in God's name since he began with them. They'll be of
> service to him in after years. (*P* 71)

The Jesuits were the teachers of young gentlemen, the Christian
Brothers of the lower orders, the peasants and urban proletariat. The
Christian Brothers were members of the gang which had betrayed
Parnell—and Ireland—in the name of Catholic morality. They would
therefore have been allies of that uncouth and meanminded clergy
which had always been the traditional enemy of the Joyces.

Although the Jesuits retained their access to the more exclusive
corridors of power, the Christian Brothers were more overtly influential
in the post-Parnell era. They were associated with the popular wave
of cultural nationalism which was organized by the Gaelic League
and was eventually taken over by the revolutionaries who would
beget the Irish Free State in 1923. Despite the passionate nationalism

that was a family tradition, John Joyce took no part in these developments: he remained on the sideline, utterly contemptuous.

John Joyce withdrew from active political involvement partly because he could no longer afford to contribute as he had done and partly because, having identified so completely with Parnell, there was no way he could join with those who had, in his opinion, betrayed him: Irish history was—and would always be—a series of great men betrayed, a view which he impressed on his favorite son. Why did he not lend his support—even his verbal support—to the "hillsiders and fenians" who, despite the threats of the bishops, were plotting to bring about an independent Ireland? After all, his grandfather was reputed to have been involved with the precursors of the Fenians and he himself had flirted with the Fenians in Cork: why not support the new Fenians? Because the Gaelic League had transformed nationalist politics. The ideal of the Gaelic League was a new Ireland which sought its inspiration not in British Victorian society but in the Gaelic culture of Ireland's past, a culture which had only survived in the remotest parts of the country and especially along the western seaboard. This did not appeal at all to people like John Joyce who in the course of the nineteenth century had established themselves as *gentlemen* by distancing themselves from the hovels and the peasants which the English satirists associated with Irish separatism. And yet the members of the Gaelic League—like Miss Ivors in "The Dead"—saw these peasants as cultural heroes of the new Ireland they hoped to bring about. The Joyces were among those who were intensely proud of the fact that they had made their way from the hovel to the city, from scratching a living to making a fortune, from rags to hunting waistcoats. Though they had come a long way, they were still too close to their rural origins to relish any idea of return: for them the cult of the Irish-speaking peasant was a relapse into barbaric isolation.

Like almost everybody else, James Joyce was attracted by the excitement which the Gaelic League generated but he resisted the cult of the peasant which Yeats and Synge and Lady Gregory had made fashionable. In his journal for April 14, Stephen mocks this fashion but the tone changes from mockery to something more complex when he imagines the face of the peasant:

> I fear him. I fear his red-rimmed horny eyes. It is with him I must struggle all through this night till day come, till he or I

lie dead, gripping him by the sinewy throat till...Till what?
Till he yield to me? No, I mean no harm. (*P* 252)

Like Gabriel Conroy, Joyce came to accept his relations with
the Irish past but, like his ancestors, he preferred to look to the
future and head for the city. And that future would be outside
Ireland altogether. Joyce lived through the achievement of an Irish
Free State but, despite the traditional nationalism of his family, he
was always careful to avoid any remark or gesture that could be
understood to imply his approval of the new Ireland.

In far-off Trieste in 1907 Joyce decided to recast his autobiographical novel into a fictional account of his development as an
artist. The opening section is dominated by his memories of the row
which spoiled the Christmas dinner at 1 Martello Terrace, Bray, in
1891. In his clash with Mrs. Conway, John Joyce was supported by
Mr. John Kelly from Tralee who had been imprisoned on several
occasions for his political activities and who was, according to
Stanislaus, "of peasant stock" (13). Of Mrs. Conway Stanislaus says,
vaguely, that "she seems to have been some distant relative of my
father's" (7). Given Stanislaus' attitude to Mrs. Conway and his
attitude to his O'Connell relations, one must assume that he was
unable to accuse Mrs. Conway of being related to John Joyce's mother
rather than his father: if there was even a hint that Mrs. Conway
was of the tribe of the O'Connells, we can be sure that Stanislaus
would have mentioned it for Dante embodies all that *The Joycead*
mocks as typical of the O'Connells—even to her spell in the convent
and her romantic ineptitude—*plus* an extravagant aggression.

Uncle Charles is based on William O'Connell who came to live
with the Joyces shortly after the death of his wife on August 4,
1881. Though very much an O'Connell—quiet and religious—he is
somebody who understands Simon Dedalus' references to Cork. On
their Sunday walks Stephen absorbs details of *The Joycead* as Uncle
Charles and his father speak constantly

> of the subjects nearer their hearts, of Irish politics, of Munster
> and of the legends of their own family, to all of which Stephen
> lent an avid ear. (*P* 62)

But why should John Joyce welcome an O'Connell into his
home, particularly an O'Connell who had a son and grandchildren
in Cork? Perhaps it was a case of simple generosity; perhaps a clue
is to be found in the marriage settlement of James Augustine and

Ellen back in 1848. Among the Joyce contributions was property in White Street where, according to Griffith's *Rates Valuation*, James Joyce is listed as the owner of number 17—*house, offices and yard*—and of Joyce's Alley (also known as Joyce's Court), a lane of seven small houses which survived into the 1930s. In 1852—the year in which Griffith's *Valuation* was published and thus some time after the actual research—James Joyce went bankrupt. A *Rates Assessment* of 1854 confirms that he lost the White Street property which was then owned by one William O'Connell. It is hard to avoid the suspicion that, faced with the inevitability of bankruptcy, James Joyce "sold" this property to William O'Connell who somehow "donated" it back to the Joyces; at any rate, it is among the properties which John Joyce mortgaged and finally sold in 1894. If Uncle William had indeed been so considerate in the Joyces' hour of need, he would have been a welcome guest in their home when he, having lost both his money (*P* 62) and his wife, fell on hard times. Shortly after the Christmas Dinner of 1891, when it became clear that John Joyce was in financial difficulties, Uncle William returned to Cork: there is a death certificate for a William O'Connell, draper, who died of heart failure on August 31, 1892.

Two years later John Joyce brought James to Cork to see where the episodes of *The Joycead* had taken place and to be present at the sale of the last of the ancestral properties—including that in White Street which Uncle William may have "minded" for them in the past. His eyes unmoistened by alcohol, young James did not see Cork as the paradisal scene of his father's narratives but as a fallen world of booze and bombast where people preferred to live pseudo-heroic roles from the mythical past rather than face the facts of contemporary life.

There is no allusion in *A Portrait* to any meeting with relatives in Cork. Ellmann reports that they heard an O'Connell cousin sing for them when they visited the Presentation Convent in Crosshaven, a nearby seaside resort (37). This was May O'Connell, a granddaughter of William O'Connell, who was a student at the convent and who went on to become a Presentation nun, Sr. Mary Ita O'Connell. The visit to the convent was an embarrassing failure and yet another indication of how the Joyce stock had fallen. According to *The Joycead* the convent in Crosshaven had been planned and paid for by Alicia O'Connell—daughter of John O'Connell and sister of Ellen and William—who had been inspired by a dream "that she was standing on a hill overlooking the sea, succouring children" (*JJII* 13).[4] In 1894 John Joyce had come to ask that what he thought of as more or less a family foundation should take two of his daughters as boarders at reduced rates. He was not pleased when his request was refused by the principal, Mother Teresa, whose version of the founding of the convent differed from that given in *The Joycead*.

Alicia O'Connell entered the South Presentation Convent in Cork city in 1836 and became Sr. Mary Francis Xavier. While it is likely that she had—with or without the assistance of dreams—taken part in the planning of the convent in Crosshaven and had given or raised money for the project, she died of liver disease in 1872, four years before the foundation of the convent. The money which enabled the nuns to open it was donated by a former student who married a rich American and who is buried in the convent.[5] The adjacent grave is that of Mother Teresa, "our beloved foundress." Although Mother Xavier is remembered with affection and respect by the Presentation nuns she does not, in their records, figure quite as prominently as she does in *The Joycead*.

It is a commonplace of criticism that in *A Portrait* Joyce used the visit to Cork to dramatize Stephen's emerging individuality; it is likely that this was inspired by his own experience in Cork where he became aware of the gulf between the world his father lived in and the world he himself inhabited, between the romance of *The Joycead* and the facts of his own circumstances. Unlike his father, he could not close his eyes to the grim reality. His revised role in *The Joycead* could be understood by reference to another myth—the myth which he had first heard about from Dante and which was the theme on which the Jesuits had constructed their rich and subtle intellectual structures: because of the sins of our first—and only— parents, we had been deprived of the paradise which might so easily have been ours. If there is one central theme in his work from the earliest verse on Parnell up to *Finnegans Wake* it is that of the fall. He had been born Sunny Jim, heir to the solar throne, but he soon preferred to make a virtue of his fall and see himself as Lucifer, splendidly rebellious and spectacularly fallen. Because of the sins of his father he had been deprived of the cricket fields of Clongowes, of the elegant houses and big gardens south of the river, of the privileges and prospects of a gentleman's son; he found himself living among the navvies and assorted commoners of the northern suburbs where the little back gardens reeked of ashpits.

There was not return to paradise in this life but there was one obvious way back to the world of Clongowes and elegant culture: to accept the invitation of the Jesuits and become The Reverend James Joyce, S.J. But he resisted the temptation of the order and went home:

> The faint sour stink of rotted cabbages came towards him from the kitchen gardens on the rising ground above the river. He smiled to think that it was this disorder, the misrule and confusion of his father's house and the stagnation of vegetable life, which was to win the day in his soul. (*P* 162)

In contrast to the saintly namesake who had written of the city of God, he would dedicate his life to the city of fallen man. He would accept the facts of his life and would celebrate the common people who walked the mean streets rather than the blustering heroes of ancient glories. He would not, as his father did, actually believe in the account of the personal, familial or racial past or present which he found in *The Joycead* but neither would he, as his brother did, dismiss the extravagances of *The Joycead* with contempt; rather, with an extraordinarily sane generosity, he would understand why and how human beings tell each other stories to pass the time outside paradise.

Prompted to some extent by genetic pressure he became a maker, a word-mason, a masterbuilder, erecting the most famous city of modern literature, the Dublin of *Ulysses*, a city which has survived better than the city on which it was based, thanks to the new Homeric scaffolding system which he invented and patented. He would not have been displeased to be described as a builder. His work was construction, putting his city together brick by brick, using words rather than the bricks and mortar the earlier Joyces had used. While others lauded his powers of imagination, he claimed it was simply memory (*JJII* 661). As he followed the tradition of his ancestors by traveling as a wandering craftsman from Dublin to Trieste to Zurich to Paris he came to treasure what his father had given him, not least the purple hunting waistcoat made by Ellen, the wife of the earlier James Augustine Joyce, a genuine relic of the world of *The Joycead*, the world of his father's tales which he himself had quarried and refined as his ancestors had quarried and refined the limestone of Cork.

NOTES

1. John Joyce, after his fashion, treated James as if he *was* an only child and in his will made him sole benefactor. Despite his low opinion of his father, Stanislaus too believed that the O'Connells were genetically inferior to the Joyces. See Healy 21, 37, 72.

2. The convent records show that Ellen followed her sister's example and entered the convent in October 1836. The records have this to say about her when she left: *It was a matter of her own choosing. She became nervously and unnecessarily anxious about her health, which was not, in reality bad. She had just finished the fourth month of her Postulant ship. She was a nice, amiable and good girl*—too good, *to encounter the rough sea of this world; where, she can scarcely escape the meeting of many a rock and many a breaker—but, little as her religious training has been, may she have learned in her short Noviciate, to look up only to the* one eye, *that steadily and securely guides, each bark of this uncertain life.* Her brother Charles (1826–1872) attended Maynooth, spent seven years in West Cork and then thirteen as a curate in Carrignavar. Ellmann reports the rumor that he had been silenced for refusing to accept offerings from his poor parishioners. The fact that no mention of this is made in his death notice in the *Cork Examiner* is by no means a disproof, and it is not impossible to imagine a rich priest sparing his parishioners in time of Famine, but it would be typical of *The Joycead* to mitigate the existence of a priestly relation by having him incur the wrath of a bishop. At Charles' funeral was his brother, Fr. O'Connell CM, of Castleknock, about whom I could discover nothing else.

3. For details of the settlement see *JJII* 747. There were many O'Connells—a popular name in Cork—in the hackney business and James Augustine's office was in a boarding house owned by a Miss Hannah O'Connell. One of the taxi firms in Cork today is called *Joycecabs;* the eponymous owners do not claim any connection with the late inspector and rest their claim to fame on the prowess of their sons in international amateur boxing.

4. See *JJII* 13. Though the Joyces were not overly impressed by her singing in 1894, Sr. Mary Ita retained her interest in music—and in literature—throughout her life. Though typically O'Connell in her vocation, Sr. Mary Ita is said to have been a passionate nationalist who offered the sanctuary of the convent to several guerillas during The Troubles. For this and for other kindnesses some older people in Cork still speak warmly of her. Born on February 2, 1883, May O'Connell shared a birthday with James Joyce but even this connection did not earn her a mention in Joyce's fiction. Although she did not wish to be publicly associated with Joyce, she spoke privately of her relationship and her meetings with him. Her attitude to Joyce softened as a result of her correspondence with his sister, Margaret, who became a nun and lived in New Zealand.

5. The orthodox history is quite as romantic in its own way: a former student of the South Presentation Convent in Cork went to America where she was wooed by a wealthy Jew whom she accepted on condition that he become a Catholic. She used some of her newly acquired wealth to endow the Crosshaven project.

WORKS CITED

Curran, C.P. *James Joyce Remembered.* London: Oxford University Press, 1968
Healey, George H. *The Complete Dublin Diary of Stanislaus Joyce.* Ithaca:
        Cornell University Press, 1971.
Joyce, Stanislaus. *My Brother's Keeper.* New York: Viking Press, 1958.

4

Inscribing James Joyce's Tombstone

BERNARD BENSTOCK

Preamble

A reexamination of literary modernism, and Joyce's role as a modernist, might well concern itself with the relationship between *in*scription and *de*scription, between the spoken and the written word, the living and the dead, the voice and the written text. "Inscribing James Joyce's Tombstone" isolates the tombstone as a simulacrum of the literary artifact—both as claimed by the individual artist and as attributed by an external audience—and as a device for questioning the status of narrative voice as opposed to narration.

Modernists have been credited with opening up a new relationship with the past (Pound's MAKE IT NEW and Gertrude Stein's "continuous present" and Joyce's "continuous present tense" of "cyclewheeling history"), implying a rethought relationship between the past and the present, the ancient and the modern. Modernists were especially sensitive to the degree to which the present will soon fade into the past, the living voice (heard throughout all modernist texts) will soon be deadened into the written epitaph. In "The Preludes" T. S. Eliot isolated "grimy scraps / Of withered leaves about your feet / And newspapers from vacant lots," and in "East Coker" the same wind shakes "the tattered arras with a silent motto." Later in "East Coker," Eliot comments on "a lifetime burning in every moment / And not the lifetime of one man only / But of old stones that cannot be deciphered." I will be turning over old stones and attempting to read silent mottoes, employing Joyce as a test case of the ways in which writing emerges in modernist works as both subject matter and writing practice, and investigating differences in status between various kinds of written texts within the larger text: postcards, letters, newspaper notices, tombstones.

Inscribing James Joyce's Tombstone

We are all aware that James Joyce has had the honor of having been buried twice, the first time as a pauper, the second as a celebrity. It is that first flat, embedded tombstone that interests me at the moment, a small, simple rectangle that marked his burial in Fluntern cemetery on 15 January 1941, with the laconic inscription: JAMES JOYCE 1882–1941. So terse a commentary seems hardly worthy of so overwhelmingly verbal a writer, who himself scratched endless additions on galleys and placards of his endlessly extendable *Ulysses*. How disproportionate compared to the commemorative awarded a totally insignificant Dubliner in *Ulysses*, who is granted a whole quatrain:

> *It is now a month since dear Henry fled*
> *To his home up above in the sky*
> *While his family weeps and mourns his loss*
> *Hoping some day to meet him on high.*
>
> (*U* 91)

Dear Henry's epitaph, however, is not that which had been engraved in stone, but merely set in type on the pages of the *Freeman's Journal*, and in this meandering quest for the perfect Joyce inscription, I will be gravitating between the printed and the engraved, the scriptural and the sepulchral. The easy modulation between the two was apparent within a year of Joyce's death, when Louis Gillet published *Stèle pour James Joyce*, the Grecian stele-stone serving as prototype for the book title—a book itself structured along the lines of a stele. Where the context shows itself to be indeterminate—as in the list of Finnian characteristics in the riddles chapter of *Finnegans Wake*—the gap between print and embossing diminishes: "his birth proved accidental shows death its grave mistake" (*FW* 134.20–21). Here the succinctness and the subject matter conspire to make this grave statement as apt as the dates 1882 and 1941, the boundaries of the message clearly set.

Nowhere has the potency of a tombstone inscription been as sanctified (and simultaneously derided) as in William Faulkner's *Absalom, Absalom!*, where Mr. Compson comments about the family of mourners, noting that "to them their funerals and graves, the puny affirmations of spurious immortality set above the slumber, are of incalculable importance." Puny affirmations are apparent to Bloom as he glances at the *Freeman's Journal*, noting the pathos of "dear Henry fled." The obituary verse, that printed remembrance a month after the funeral, seems pathetically transitory to Bloom: "Inked characters fast fading on the frayed breaking paper'' (*U* 91), he comments. From paper then to stone: soon after, the funeral carriage that carries Bloom and the other mourners nears the cemetery, and he muses:

> The stonecutter's yard on the right. Last lap. Crowded on the spit of land silent shapes appeared, white, sorrowful, holding out calm hands, knelt in grief, pointing. Fragments of shapes, hewn. In white silence: appealing. The best obtainable. Thos. M. Dennany, monumental building and sculptor. (*U* 99)

Puny affirmations have not as yet expressed themselves, since the unbought, unmarked stones are silent, awaiting the appropriate death, and there is no message there for Bloom to read. As an advertising canvasser, however, Bloom reads the message of the living, the self-advertisement of the monumental builder and sculptor Thos. H. Dennany, who is responsible for the sign that claims *The best available*. In his hyperbolic description Dennany emerges as an avatar of God— and of James Joyce the Creator, monumental builder and sculptor.

After the funeral service, the casual mourners ''moved away slowly, without aim, by devious paths, staying awhile to read a name on a tomb'' (*U* 112), Bloom among them. And he now allows himself some random thoughts on funeral literature, the writings on the stones:

> Who passed away. Who departed this life. As if they did it of their own accord. Got the shove, all of them. Who kicked the bucket. More interesting if they told you what they were. So and so, wheelwright. I travelled for cork lino. I paid five shillings in the pound. Or a woman's with her saucepan. I cooked good Irish stew. Eulogy in a country churchyard it ought to be that poem of whose is it Wordsworth or Thomas Campbell. Entered into rest the protestants put it. Old Dr Murren's. The great physician called him home. (*U* 113)

Bloom's botched attributions are themselves diagnostic: William Wordsworth may not have been responsible for Thomas Gray's ''Elegy Written in a Country Churchyard''—and neither was Thomas Campbell—but Wordsworth did indeed write an ''Essay on Epitaphs.'' Even more significantly, Bloom has shifted the emphasis from the elegiac to the eulogistic, and in the process domesticates the specific pieces of information.

Had Joyce sought a similar style of immortality for himself, he need only to have waited until the memorial plaques began appearing on the walls of his cities of residence and refuge, in Dublin on the houses where he was born and where Bloom lived (one of them at least probably the correct address) and on a park bench for himself and his father; and in Trieste, Rome, Zurich, and St. Gérand-le-Puy. A street staircase in Trieste, for example, was renamed Scala James Joyce, with the familiar opening and closing dates, but a bit more largesse than the pauperstone: "*Scrittore Irlandese*," it reads, which Bloom might translate as "He cooked good Irish stew." At one of his Triestine residences the information recorded is that he wrote the first chapter of *Ulysses* there (which *is* a start), while at the house in Rome where his brief odyssey had once taken him the plaque reports that Joyce evoked the story of Ulysses. Knowing as we do that "Not marble, nor the gilded monuments of princes, shall outlive this powerful rhyme," it is not surprising that the city of Zurich chose the most enduring of the eight Joyce residences there for the single plaque, what is now a dormitory for nurses and therefore least likely to be bulldozed for urban renewal. It was disappointing that no plaque was placed at Elsinore, during the Symposium, since the castle there also looked as if it might withstand the temptation for urban renewal.[1]

Tombstone literature provides a form of post-creation, a filling in of the blank, but within a restrictive space. Nietzsche's declaration that God is dead serves as an epitaph, neither elegiac nor eulogistic; Roland Barthes's contention that the author is dead (Joyce might have preferred "refined out of existence"), placed alongside Nietzsche's, neatly parallels God and the author, a parallel that already has a Joycean imprimatur. The ways in which the creation outlasts the creator—and even retrospectively mocks the Creator—are suggested at various instances and in various manners throughout the Joyce canon. When he sent *Chamber Music* from Trieste to Elkin Mathews, the live inspiration was in full force, yet when it was accepted for publication, Joyce regretted the death of that inspiration, and even considered cabling London to have the poems retracted, labeling them "dishonest," having essentially outlived them. The telegram, had it been sent, would have served as a death notice, or even a death warrant, but Joyce's ultimate revenge was already destined to be engraved on the cover of the book, the title having been chosen both for its suggestion of restrained lyricism and its allusion to chamber pot tinklings.

The history of the *Finnegans Wake* title, a title that spells the death of poor Finnegan (but not for long), is accepted as a commonplace by Joyceans, but can still cause a raised eyebrow when reported to normal people. During the sixteen years of composition that title, known only by its creator, was mysteriously and superstitiously withheld from public knowledge, until the tentatively titled *Work in Progress* was completed and the epitaphic statement was about to be embossed on the book. The hundreds of pages of galleys now in the Lucie and Paul Léon/James Joyce Collection at the University of Tulsa library indicate that even the printers in Glasgow thought that the ultimate title was *Work in Progress*: every signature page has its WiP. From 1923 to 1938 the hypothetical cover of the book was a blank, like Thomas Dennany's hewn stone, in white silence, awaiting completion, awaiting a death, for a lasting inscription.

No matter how minimal or condensed the memorial message may be, there is often the possibility that it says *more* than intended, or more than should have been intended. Triestine pride of place credits the city for being the site where Joyce began *Ulysses*, while the Roman plaque addresses Romans who may never have heard of the wandering Joyce, but certainly heard of the wandering Ulysses, the Latinized Odysseus. What would one expect, for instance, as an epitaph for the creator of as famous a literary personage as Sherlock Holmes, and what does his epitaph actually specify?

STEEL TRUE

BLADE STRAIGHT

ARTHUR CONAN DOYLE

KNIGHT

PATRIOT, PHYSICIAN & MAN OF LETTERS

A grateful nation had knighted him for his propagandistic pamphlet justifying the British action in the Boer War. At the tag end he is, however, remembered as a "man of letters."

With the same degree of calculation, James Joyce was himself quite skillful in writing the extended death notice, the overly informative but concise capsulization of a life. On the opening pages of his first story, an important message replaces the notice that appeared on "ordinary days... *Umbrellas Re-covered.*" Instead, the boy in "The Sisters" reads from "a card pinned on the crape":

JULY 1ST, 1985

THE REV. JAMES FLYNN

(FORMERLY OF S. CATHERINE'S CHURCH, MEATH STREET)

AGED SIXTY-FIVE YEARS

R.I.P.

(*D* 12)

The story of Father Flynn is the story of a man who has died twice: how absolute is that telltale "formerly of S. Catherine's," insisting on the first death, which the boy will only learn about after he has absorbed the message of the second death of a priest whose first coffin was a confession box.

Leopold Bloom spends his time at Glasnevin cemetery "reading" coffins, and hits upon a concept of post-creation that involves the recuperation of some aspect of the newly deceased, discovering the possibility of the *voice* as the medium of retaining the living experience by gramophonic re-creation:

> Have a gramophone in every grave or keep it in the house. After dinner on Sunday. Put on poor old greatgrandfather Kraahraark! Hellohellohello amawfullyglad kraark awfullyglada-seeragain hellohello amarawf kopthsth. Remind you of the voice like the photograph reminds you of the face. (*U* 114)

No such creaking recording exists for Bloom of any of his ancestors, and it is with alacrity that he transfers the "speaking eiptaph" out of the grave and places it in the home. In his own home, of course, he keeps various memorabilia of his dead father (whose speaking voice will pursue him later through Nighttown). The written record-ings of his father's words are retained in the old man's suicide note that Bloom retrieves (not for the first time) in Ithaca from the bureau drawer. The broken phrases retrieved from that retrieval serve as the dead man's own funeral inscription, his attempt to write the post-humous message of importance ("it is of no use" *or* "with your dead mother" *or* "all for me is out"), but most graphically in the italicized final fragments:

das Herz...Gott...dein. (*U* 723)

(The great hotel proprietor called him home.) Carefully preserved, and handled only by the intended recipient, the suicide note withstands the onslaughts of time better than the "inked characters fast fading on the frayed breaking paper"—a paper, incidentally, that Bloom was intent on throwing away.

Far more substantial and permanent are words carved in stone (Shakespeare's "unswept stone, besmeared with sluttish time"), and none is as monumental as the Commandments, celebrated by Professor McHugh conjuring up the voice of John F. Taylor (and available to us in a gramophone recording made by greatgrandfather Joyce). Taylor is quoted as intoning: "*He would never have spoken with the Eternal amid lightnings on Sinai's mountaintop nor ever have come down with the light of inspiration shining in his countenance and bearing in his arms the tables of the law, graven in the language of the outlaw*" (*U* 143). The Mosaic tablature marks not a death and interment, but the birth of a religion, a people, a race, a civilization. The gravity of that engraving allows for no measure of levity, yet the Joycean perspective is often tempered by tables of a different color, particularly the *Smaragdine Tablet* of Hermes Trismesgistus, where Joyce found that "that which is below is like that which is above" (or, in Finneganese, "The tasks above are as the flasks below, saith the emerald canticle of Hermes"—*FW* 263.21–22). Bloom's tendency to trivialize, or perhaps merely to domesticate, reflects the temptation to reduce exalted properties to the mundane, and the Tables of the Law return in *Ulysses* to just a reduction. In Aeolus the subject had been the subjected Gaelic and Hebrew races, but in Ithaca it is the Gold Cup, and Bloom's awareness that he had inadvertently tipped Throwaway as the winner:

> when Frederick M. (Bantam) Lyons had rapidly and successively requested, perused and restituted the copy of the current issue of the *Freeman's Journal* and *National Press* which he had been about to thrown away (subsequently thrown away), he had proceeded towards the oriental edifice of the Turkish and Warm Baths, 11 Leinster street, with the light of inspiration shining in his countenance and bearing in his arms the secret of the race, graven in the language of prediction. (*U* 676)

The Ascot race replaces the Hebrew race, the newspaper the tablets; Bloom replaces Moses, the language of prediction the language of the outlaw.

The Tables of the Law come replete with an implied author, whose name remains ineffable and whose signature a constant in the landscape. Bloom's sense of caution prevents him from uttering the name of Jesus Christ, and that of Blazes Boylan (things above and things below), a moral censoring that may have less to do with his discomfort with the Christian religion, which had been so ineptly

assigned to him, than a carryover from the older faith that prohibited
the use of the Ineffable Name. Moses had requested a signatory
name for the tables and received instead the epigraphic ''I am that
I am.'' On the level of things below, Bloom attempted the signature
of self-identification on a tablature even less permanent than paper
or stone, the sandy beach at Sandymount, printing in virtual darkness
with a wooden stick ''I...AM. A. ''—the message remaining incomplete, the signature absent. Even as he begins, he realizes the futility
of the writing, simultaneously recognizing that a more permanent
script already exists around him: ''All these rocks with lines and
scars and letters.'' His final verdict on the transitory nature of his
effort is that ''All fades,'' an echo of his verdict on ''Inked characters
fast fading'' (*U* 381). His intended inscription might have been
more identifying, individuating, confessing, conjecturing, complaining than merely ''I travelled for cork lino'' or ''paid five shillings
in the pound.''

On the same strand Stephen had mused, ''Signatures of all
things I am here to read, seaspawn and seawrack, the nearing tide,
that rusty boot'' (*U* 37). Were he to repeat his stroll on Sandymount
Strand the next day, his might be the ''flatfoot'' that Bloom assumes
would ''tramp'' on his writing ''in the morning,'' which he prevents
by tramping on it himself, effacing ''the letters with a slow boot''
(*U* 381). If it was God's signature Stephen was intent on reading,
he had already proven himself master of that reading when the
writing was on material even more transitory than sand: he had
identified the combination of ''whirring whistle'' and preceding
cheers from the hockey field as ''God....A shout in the street''
(*U* 34). The shout and the whistle are then transcribed on the
printed page, in imitation of auditory effects, as ''Hooray! Ay!
Whrrwhee!''—on close inspection these prove to be the Tetragam-
maton, containing Y.H.W.H. in abundance, Yahweh written on the
wind. Stephen later attempts to codify *his own* identity, a historical
continuity of shifting selves from past into future:

> But I, entelechy, form of forms, am I by memory because under
> everchanging forms....
> I, I and I. I.
> A.E. I. O. U.
> (*U* 190)

In each case the self-signature represents a transitional stage of
selfhood, potentially seeking realization, nonetheless under the final

rubric of the accomplished self. Thereafter, Stephen codifies the interrelationship of that Self with an Other, in this mundane instance that of theosophist George Russell, his creditor. Russell had determined that most minimal of signatures in the digraph Æ—in itself reflected in that small word of vastness, *æon*—but to both Stephen and Bloom the linked letters are separated into commonplace initials, so that Bloom can conjecture on "Albert Edward, Arthur Edmund, Alphonsus Eb Ed El Esquire" (*U* 165), a further exercise in trivialization, a means of reducing the augmented and auspicious to human and mundane commodities—common names. Stephen has done precisely the same in "signing" an I.O.U. to Æ—"haggling over money."

In *A Portrait* Stephen learned early on that proper names were boxes into which people were put—or put themselves. "Victoria and Stephen and Simon, Simon and Stephen and Victoria. Names" (*P* 92). Boxed in between his father and the name of the hotel where they are staying, he is boxed in between the Name of the Father and the Name of the Queen, "a servant of two masters." To *re*-name himself posits a way of escaping from a preordained box, so when invited to consider a vocation as a Jesuit, "His new name in that new life leaped into characters before his eyes": "The Reverend Stephen Dedalus S. J." (*P* 161). The face he imagines as accompanying the name is not his own, however, but "a mental spectre of the face of one of the jesuits whom some of the boys called Lantern Jaws and others Foxy Campbell." Even the augmented and reverend name is externally determined, preordained and determining by ordination, so that in *Ulysses* he realizes that names are "impostures...Cicero, Podmore, Napoleon, Mr Goodbody, Jesus, Mr Doyle" *U* 622). Names are externally *imposed*, and the act of naming a part of the process of literary creation. Having slipped past the trap of a clerical calling, Stephen passes a "squad of christian brothers," and hears one of them addressed as "Brother Hickey" (*P* 165), and having decided that "Their piety would be like their names, like their faces," he goes on to impose names on the others:

Brother Quaid.
Brother MacArdle.
Brother Keogh.

(*P* 166)

"Low" Irish names box them in, diminish them, despite the elevation of their calling. In effect, Stephen is engraving their tombstones—irrevocably—as he does for all those who have betrayed him.

Of the three "friends" who span *A Portrait* and *Ulysses*, Cranly, Lynch, and Mulligan, each is disposed of with a unique method of entablature. Stephen effectively decapitates the unfaithful Cranly in the diary pages, "a stern severed head or deathmask" (*P* 248), and writes his epitaph at two stages in *Ulysses*: "Cranly's arm"; "Cranly's smile" (*U* 7, 184), relics of the dead friend (the embracing arm and the disarming smile designate the betrayer). Lynch is renamed as Judas and condemned to hanging ("*Exit Judas. Et laqueo se suspendit*"—*U* 600). But for Mulligan *three* affixing nails are chosen: looking at his golden teeth, he pronounces "Chrystostomos" (*U* 3); turning his back on the renter of the tower, he assigns "Usurper" (*U* 23); and mistrusting the intentions of Mulligan's embracing arm, he decides "Catamite" (*U* 204). In contrast to such serious and stately applications of summary accusations, we can turn to that of the Alf Bergan (or possibly Richie Goulding) deathnote for the pathetic Denis Breen, the devastatingly dismissive "U.P.: up" (*U* 158) and read that as Breen's epitaph.

The postcard sent to Denis Breen serves as a paper tombstone, equivalent in size and shape, one supposes, to those library slips that Stephen keeps forgetting to appropriate for the writing of his verse. Stephen had, on at least one previous occasion, found himself without the necessary sheet of writing paper, foolscap, sheepskin, parchment, papyrus, without which no writer since Homer could long survive: in *A Portrait* he awoke with nocturnal inspiration and no bedside tablet:

> Fearing to lose all, he raised himself suddenly on his elbow to look for paper and pencil.... He stretched his arm wearily towards the foot of the bed, groping with his hand in the pockets of the coat that hung there. His fingers found a pencil and then a cigarette packet, placed the last cigarette on the window ledge and began to write out the stanzas of the villanelle in small neat letters on the rough cardboard surface. (*P* 218–19)

In *Ulysses* an alternative expediency presents itself: on Sandymount Strand, reading the signature of all things, he is inspired to write his "pale vampire" quatrain, and like Hamlet calls for "My tablets." Again he searches his pockets:

> Paper. The banknotes, blast them. Old Deasy's letter. Here. Thanking you for hospitality tear the blank end off. Turning

his back to the sun he bent over far to a table of rock and scribbled words. That's twice I forgot to take slips from the library counter. (*U* 48)

When the poem resurfaces in Aeolus, Miles Crawford makes the obvious assumption and nastily asks, "Who tore it? Was he short taken?" (*U* 132).

The cloacal inference, assuming that the missing piece was used as emergency toilet paper, establishes the relationship between poetic inspiration and the excremental, just as the villanelle had fixed the relationship betwen poetic inspiration and nocturnal emissions, leading directly to the making of ink out of feces in *Finnegans Wake*. The formula for making "indelible ink" by producing "nichthemerically from his unheavenly body a no uncertain quantity of obscene matter not protected by copriright in the United Stars of Ourania" (*FW* 185.26–31) almost all Joyceans have now accomplished in their own laboratories, but what Shem uses in lieu of library slips is also significant in the inscribing of the Joycean tombstone: "every square inch of the only foolscap available, his own body" (*FW* 185.35–36). Writing on the body not only transcends such prosaic materials as cigarette packets and the bottoms of letters, or even Baudelairean bottoms, but places the Joycean inscription within a taboo area, violating the proscription in the Old Testament. Whereas Exodus 32.16 proclaims what God wrote and on what surface ("the tables were the work of God, and the writing was the writing of God, graven upon the tables"), Leviticus 21.5 specifies a surface that may *not* be engraved: "They shall not make baldness upon their head, neither shall they shave off the corner of their beard, nor make any cuttings in their flesh." Those who have been fortunate to have heard Jane Marcus's paper, "Laughing at Leviticus," will be familiar with the text that she explicates in the light of a violation of this prohibition, Djuna Barnes's *Nightwood*, in various ways a companion text to *Ulysses*, or perhaps a work that negotiates the space between *Ulysses* and the *Wake*.

In *Nightwood* Dr. O'Connor recalls a circus bear-fighter, tattooed over every square inch of his own unheavenly body:

There he was, crouching all over the arena without a stitch on, except an ill-concealed loin-cloth all abulge as if with a deep-sea catch, tattooed from head to heel with all the *ameublement* of depravity! Garlanded with rosebuds and hackwork of the devil—was he a sight to see! Though he couldn't have done a

thing (and I know what I am talking about in spite of all that
has been said about the black boys) if you stood him in a gig-
mill for a week, though (it's said) at a stretch it spelled
Desdemona.

O'Connor spares us none of his descriptive powers, reading ad
infinitum that writing on Nikka's body, ending with the inscription
on the bottom:

And just above what you mustn't mention, a bird flew carrying
a streamer on which was incised, *"Garde tout!"*

O'Connor's concern with Nikka's genitalia—in both tumescence
and detumenscence—is hardly casual, as he himself exposes his own
in the Church of St. Merri, bewailing its very existence and giving
it an appellation that serves as its death knell: Tiny O'Toole. At a
stretch Nikka's tool spells Desdemona (he therefore signs himself as
Othello the Moor), but at its far more usual repose, one can only
speculate that a variant of the hoary joke makes it a mere Mona.
Tumescence and detumescence bother the mind of Bloom-the-Scribe
on Sandymount Strand: his own masturbation he aligns with the
pyrotechnics: "My fireworks! Up like a rocket, down like a stick,"
(*U* 371). His attempted message in the sand, written with a "Bit of
stick," proves impossible, after which "He flung his wooden pen
away. The stick fell in silted sand, stuck" (*U* 381). He observes the
phenomenon with awe, and comments: "Now if you were trying to
do that for a week on end you couldn't." The wooden pen, the
Roman candle, the erect penis: Bloom, whose own body is undoubtedly innocent of any carvings proscribed by Leviticus, has in effect
written with his wooden pen on the naked flesh of Gerty MacDowell,
just as Nikka, himself a parchment for any and every tattoo artist,
is maligned as phallically unable to write on the body of Desdemona.

What literature offers regarding the esoteric art of tattooing
may be minimal—and marginal at best—but several instances are
worth noting, keeping in mind the able-bodied Murphy who shows
off the nautical and numerical carvings on his chest, also admitting
that his body is constantly in the process of being written upon by
lice and other vermin. In Garcia Márquez's *One Hundred Years of
Solitude* José Arcadio emerges from the jungle covered with tattoos:
"there was not a square inch of his body that was not tattooed,
front and back, and from his neck to his toes." (Compared to Nikka
and Shem and José Arcadio, the Marine who has "Mother" inscribed
on his bicep is a minimalist.) José Arcadio has been written upon

by his exile, his wanderings, his experiences in the jungle. In Kafka's "In the Penal Colony" the method of punishment employs a machine that carves its message into the flesh of the convicted felon, a sadistic analogue to God's brand on the forehead of Cain. The seafaring tradition accounts for the incredibly memorable Queequeg in Melville's *Moby Dick*, whose "dark, purplish, yellow skin" is covered with tattoos of "large, blackish looking squares"; and of the protagonist of John Hawkes' *Second Skin*, whose daughter Cassandra forces him to have a name tattooed on his chest in green, but not the name he expected. And in Shakespeare's *King John*, the dying monarch makes no secret that it is Death that is writing on his entire body:

> I am a scribbled form, drawn with a pen
> Upon a parchment, and against this fire
> Do I shrink up.

Almost in the same breath that God prohibits carving on the body, He also insists on circumcision, His own carving on every male body, of which Bloom is also innocent. Under that guise God is referred to by Mulligan as "the collector of prepuces" (*U* 13), and he underwrites the Nietzschean death notice by asserting that "Jehovah, the collector of prepuces, is no more" (*U* 201). Circumcision serves as God's signature on all things, and the Dedalian/Shemian insistence on writing on any available surface, even the human flesh, pronounces the open defiance of God's exclusive privilege. The artistic creator rivals God the creator, despite the awful threats from a Deity described in the *Wake* as "Him Which Thundereth From On High" (nonetheless capable of "abundant mercy"—*FW* 62.13–14). Shem, consequently, is characterized as "Tumult, Son of Thunder, self exiled in upon his ego, a nightlong a shaking betwixteen white or reddr hawrors, noondayterrorised to skin and bone by an ineluctable phantom (may the Shaper have mercery on him!) writing the mystery of himsel in furniture" (*FW* 185.36–186.2). Carving one's initials or name in furniture ("I, I and I. I"—or the word "Foetus") is minimal immortality compared to the message on the tombstone, and the transportation of the letter "F," missing from "himself," changes the tablature from furniture to funereal urn.

Shem insists that he has been denied "romeruled stationery," and must resort to making "synthetic ink and sensitive paper for his own end out of his wit's waste" (*FW* 185.5–8), yet in *A Portrait*, where such deprivations originate, the surfaces for inscriptions are as

numerous as they are ubiquitous; the desks in schoolrooms, the
bulletin boards on school walls, the flyleaves of books, the walls of
toilets, the signs on street walls, the slates in a school yard. From
his first days at Clongowes, Stephen claims his territory as the world,
inscribing himself as a resident of that world in his geography book,
yet Fleming usurps that privilege and rewrites Stephen's inscription—
"for a cod" (*P* 16). Also for a cod, the "thick slabs of slate" in
the Clongowes square[2] are anonymously inscribed, and

> Behind the door of one of the closets there was a drawing in
> red pencil of a bearded man in Roman dress with a brick in
> each hand and underneath was the name of the drawing:
> *Balbus was building a wall.*
> Some fellows had drawn it there for a cod. It had a funny face
> but it was very like a man with a beard. (*P* 43)

The bearded face is the obvious parody of the feminine genitalia,
the male "writing-over" of the woman's body, and Stephen comes
very close to reading the palimpsest. And a subsequent piece of
graffiti declares itself in palimpsestic punning, that *'Julius Caesar
wrote the Calico Belly''* (*P* 43). To achieve his own immortality,
Lynch admits to having written his name "on the backside of the
Venus of Praxiteles in the Museum" (*P* 205).

The maniacal insistence on transcribing oneself persists throughout the Penman chapter of the *Wake*, Shem having intoned the
Vulgate Psalm 44 while manufacturing his fecal encaustic: *"Lingua
mea calamus scribae veliciter scribentis''*—my tongue is the reed of
a scribe swiftly writing. Tongue/reed/wooden pen/moving finger
(that have writ moves on)/penis: the implement with which he
"scrabbled and scratched and scriobbled and skrevened nameless
shamelessness about everybody ever he met" (*FW* 182.13–14) and
to "stipple endlessly inartistic portraits of himself" (*FW* 182.18–19).
Pariah Shem represents the extreme outpost of the lonely artist, and
the act of writing on his own body displays itself as masturbatory.
In *A Portrait* Stephen had awakened from an erotic dream, a dream
he had already recorded on his own body, before he sets out to
record its "literary" translation on a cigarette packet, and when his
inspiration flagged, and mundane thoughts intruded, Stephen res-
timulated that inspiration through masturbation in order to complete
the villanelle, to write its *envoi*. In *Ulysses* Bloom follows his
masturbatory act with the added gesture of writing in the sand, a
replication of the futility of lonely self-expression. And in his own

life James Joyce wrote a series of letters to Nora, letters he saved and later worried about, letters of "nameless shamelessness," but letters that clearly delineated its Sender and its Receiver. Not on his own body, but on the body of the beloved, the writer writes the mystery of himself, using the penis as his pen, and, as he indicated in those letters, his tongue as well.

The erotic letters to Nora would not have fared well if they had been exposed in 1909 to the bourgeois Edwardian world, a world nicely depicted in *Ulysses,* its genteel pretentions apparent throughout *Stephen Hero* as well, as witnessed in the Irish language class Stephen attends:

> It was a beginners' class and its progress was retarded by the stupidity of two of the young men. The others in the class learned quickly and worked hard....The class was very serious and patriotic. The only time Stephen found it inclined to levity was at the lesson which introduced the word "gradh." The three young women laughed, finding something very funny in the Irish word for "love" or perhaps in the notion itself. But Mr Hughes and the other three young men and Stephen were all very grave. When the excitement of the word had passed Stephen's attention was attracted to the younger of the stupid young men who was still blushing violently. (*SH* 60)

Writing on the delicate fabric of genteel Irish society in late Victorian and Edwardian times required careful circumventions around the Irish word for love, a delicacy that Joyce displayed again in *Exiles,* where Robert Hand pens a clandestine note to Bertha that reads: *"There is one word that I have never dared to say to you."* When Bertha asks to hear the word (written communication had obscured, rather than revealed it), Robert merely reports "that I have a deep liking for you" (*E* 34). The word, which had remained unwritten, also remains unspoken, and Robert is offered a second opportunity to speak the word, this time by Richard: "Explain to me what is the word you longed and never dared to say to her. If you can and will" (*E* 75). Robert's second venture is no better than the first: "I admire very much the personality of your...of...your wife. That is the word. I can say it. It is no secret." Neither "liking" nor "admiring" is quite the same word as "love," and the potent word itself was destined to lie dormant for quite a while.

Reticence over the word love may have remained a Joycean concession to a verisimilitudinistic representation of his age had it not surfaced recently, many decades after the world had given up

on it. The new "Critical and Synoptic" edition of *Ulysses* has restored
some missing lines from that text, including the privileged positioning
of the banned word: "Love, yes. Word known to all men" (*U-G* I,
419). Love, then, in all senses, voices, connotations, declensions: over
which stupid young men blush and for which seducers seek euphe-
mistic substitutes. Those of us who might have despaired of anything
other than elliptical and indeterminate statements from James Joyce
(except perhaps for "Love that dare not speak its name"—*U* 202)
now hailed the advent of the word LOVE, if not exactly carved in
stone, at least lofted on high. The answer is especially welcome since
we have always known that there was a question, and it was asked
by Stephen of the ghost of his dead mother: "Tell me the word,
mother, if you know now. The word known to all men" (*U* 581).
Mrs. Dedalus, however, rattles on about her care and concern for
her wayward son, repeating her belief in the efficacy of prayer, and
insisting that Stephen repent. (If it were left to Mrs. Dedalus, the
Word would either have been *Prayer* or *Repentance*.)

Stephen's question derives from his mother's recollection of the
song he used to sing to her, "*Love's bitter mystery*," so Love
engenders the question and perhaps anticipates the answer. The
associations in Circe derive from the earlier appearance of Mrs.
Dedalus in Telemachus: Mulligan's admonition to "Give up the
moody brooding" brings Stephen's thoughts to the Yeats lyric—
"*And no more turn aside and brood/Upon love's bitter mystery*"—
which in turn invites thoughts of singing the song for his dying
mother, and her reaction then: "For those words, Stephen: love's
bitter mystery" (*U* 9). The confrontations between Stephen and his
mother in the morning and midnight scenes are mirror images of
each other, and whereas Mrs. Dedalus concerns herself with the *words*
("love" and "bitter" and "mystery"), Stephen strives for the single,
all-inclusive *word,* without bitterness and no longer a mystery. The
restored passage, occurring as it does between these two confrontations, demonstrates that Stephen *knows* the word in the afternoon—
why then is he asking to know the word late at night? Within the
context of Shakespeare's *Pericles* "love" functions as the word, but
only temporarily and within a given context that soon changes. The
one word that has *no* prevailing significance as the word known-to-
all-men may well be that overworked and slippery word, LOVE.

As the incomplete last sentence of *Finnegans Wake* may indicate,
Joyce could be exceedingly reticent to put the last word on anything.

His attitude toward epitaphs generally may be gleaned from the status of Robert Emmet's epitaph as the final words of Sirens, Emmet himself a reluctant epitaphist. His last words from the dock after his sentence of death are historically read as an epitaph for a dead Ireland, as well as a harbinger of a resurrected Ireland. Bloom sees a printed version of Emmet's words in a shop window:

> *When my country takes her place among....*
> *Nations of the earth....*
> *Then and not till then...*
> *Let my epitaph be...*
> *Written. I have...*
> *Done.*
>
> (*U* 291)

Bloom experiences gastric upset leading to flatulence as he reads these potent words, and he waits for the sounds of a passing tram to cover his farting, so that the Emmet epitaph vies with both the gurgling flatulence and the clanging tram for auditory privilege, causing the insignificant word "the" (destined to be the last word of *Finnegans Wake*) to be lost from the Emmet statement, a victim of contending nonverbal sounds, the noise of the tram and of broken wind.

Several Joyceans, notably Clive Hart, have commented on a tendency toward sentimentality that Joyce obscured with irony and irreverence, and the concept of LOVE conquering all, sweeping the country, making the world go round, might even be embarrassing to Leopold Bloom, who, compelled to deal with the word, defines it as "the opposite of hatred," and quickly adds, "I must go now." The enraged Citizen reacts with: "Love, Moya! He's a nice pattern of a Romeo and Juliet"—while the parodic narratives that evolve from the discourse in Barney Kiernan's provide a mocking commentary, beginning, "Love loves to love love," and concluding with: "and this person loves that other person because everybody loves somebody but God loves everybody" (*U* 333).

Not to be put off by irony and irreverence, as readers we search for the Joycean signature of all things, aware of the search that is in operation within the Joyce texts. At the dawn of protohistory, in the opening chapter of the *Wake,* the unswept stones of earliest civilization are being read by humans not quite erect on two feet: "He who runes may rede it on all fours" (*FW* 18.5–6). And we are invited to read along:

(Stoop) if you are abcedminded, to this claybook, what curios
of signs (please stoop), in this allaphbed! Can you rede (since
We and Thou had it out already) its world? It is the same told
of all. Many. (*FW* 18.17–20)

Rather than the words, the concentration is on the individual
letters of the alphabet, the "root language," from which all words
and names evolve in myriad patterns. Reading the runes, we uncover
in the *Wake* a footnote to the Doodles family, a series of seven
signs, sigla that represent members of the family and contiguous
outsiders, and even the book itself, the outline of a square that
Joyce used for his untitled mamafesta, his claybook, *Finnegans Wake*.
The quest for the signature of the individual author, or the individual
character, leads to the hieroglyphics of ancient inscription, the signs
of the human family.

The Doodles family, ⨅, △, ⊣, X, □, ∧, ⊏. Hoodle
doodle, fam.?

NOTES

1. On the building next to the Pakhus where the Symposium took place a
brass plaque high up announced that it had been erected in 1882.

2. An epitaph to Stephen Dedalus's terminated youth is the sign *Lotts* near
the morgue (*P* 86). Breathing in the "good odour" of "horse piss and rotted
straw" calms his heart—but that is the subject of a companion essay, "James Joyce:
The Olfactory Factor."

5

Joyce and Modernist Ideology

ROBERT SCHOLES

*I wish I could go to Denmark. Ferrero says that Abo, Stockholm
and Copenhagen are the finest cities in Europe.*

(*Letters II, 201*)

Following Joyce's wish, we have at last rearrived in Denmark, but I
have chosen to begin a discussion of the ideology of modernism with
these words from Joyce's Roman period not to direct attention to this
fine city but to notice the authority Joyce gives for his desire. The
mediator of this desire is Guglielmo Ferrero, whose book, *L'Europa
giovane (Young Europe)* Joyce was reading in 1906 (he lists it as next
to Mercredy's Map of Ireland on Shelf J, back, among his books in
Trieste). Joyce was much taken at this time with Ferrero, whose study
of European culture, published in 1897, is subtitled "studies and
voyages in the countries of the north." In September of 1906, Joyce
found a picture postcard of Ferrero in Rome, and wrote to his brother
about it:

> By the way, talking of faces I will send you a picture postcard
> of Guglielmo Ferraro and you will admit there is some hope for
> me. You would think he was a terrified Y.M.C.A. man with an
> inaudible voice. He wears spectacles, is delicate-looking and,
> altogether, is the type you would expect to find in some quiet
> nook in the Coffee-Palace nibbling a bun hastily and apologet-
> ically between the hours of half-past twelve and one. (*Letters II*
> 159)

Among other things, these remarks suggest that Joyce saw some
parallels between Ferrero and himself.

One day in November of 1906 Joyce wrote to Stanislaus that he
was thinking of beginning his story *Ulysses* but felt too oppressed
with cares. In the next sentence he turned to a discussion of Ferrero's
views of Jews and anti-Semitism, noting that "The most arrogant
statement made by Israel so far, he says, not excluding the gospel of
Jesus, is Marx's proclamation that socialism is the fulfillment of a
natural law" (*Letters II* 190). In the reference to this letter in the

91

index to Richard Ellmann's edition of the letters, what should be
"Ferrero on Marx" unaccountably appears as "Ferrero on Mary." This
tiny change, the Freudian slip of a pious compositor, no doubt, is
effected by simply cutting off a bit of Marx's X (a bit off the bottom,
so to speak), turning Marx into Mary with a minimum of fuss. How
Joyce would have loved this error! Roland Barthes would also no
doubt have found this emblematic castration of Marx both amusing
and significant.

   For me it also symbolizes the tension between Christianity and
socialism that constitutes one of the structuring polarities of modernist
ideology. The movement of W. H. Auden, for instance, from one
end of this polarity to the other over the decade 1929–1939 is
emblematic of this dimension of modernism. One can also find the
two opposites dangerously conflated in a typical thirties poem like C.
Day Lewis's *Magnetic Mountain*, as in the following lines from the
well-known section that begins, "You that love England...."

> You who go out alone, on tandem or on pillion,
> Down arterial roads riding in April,
> Or sad beside lakes where hill-slopes are reflected
> Making fires of leaves, your high hopes fallen:
> Cyclists and hikers in company, day excursionists,
> Refugees from cursed towns and devastated areas:
> Know you seek a new world, a saviour to establish
> Long-lost kinship and restore the blood's fulfilment.
> ...We can tell you a secret, offer a tonic; only
> Submit to the visiting angel, the strange new healer.
>
> ...You shall be leaders when zero hour is signalled,
> Wielders of power and welders of a new world.
>   (*Magnetic Mountain*, Poem 32)

This poem, which first appeared in the tendentious collection, *New
Country*, in 1933, is a communist manifesto, written by a committed
party member, but the rhetoric of saviour and angel is thoroughly
imbued with Christian connotations, as if Day Lewis could express
his hopes convincingly only through discursive features that he should
have repudiated. The poem is also full of a deeply felt sense of place
that is just a step from nationalism: "You that love England, who
have an ear for her music..." Similarly, "the visiting angel, the
strange new healer" may refer to your local CP recruiter, but it exudes
disturbing connotations of the *Führer Prinzip*. One of the other
structuring polarities of modernism is defined by the opposition

between equality and hierarchy or, in more purely political terms, between democratic and authoritarian notions of government. This is a polarity that existed *within* the socialist movement, for instance, and not simply as a difference between socialism and conservative or reactionary parties.

Let *x/y,* then, symbolize the whole set of polarities that shape the ideology of modernism as it emerged in the late nineteenth and early twentieth centuries. To describe these polarities fully is both theoretically and practically impossible, since each description would itself enter the play of ideological discourse. On an occasion such as this, one can only begin to sketch certain dimensions of this field. I propose, then, to examine some interactions between literature and politics, as we can trace them in the lives of a few young men of Joyce's generation, including of course, Joyce himself. We can begin with a brief summary of a paradigmatic life story of such a young man.

He was born in the early 1880s into a family with little money which managed nonetheless to send him away to religious boarding schools. A biographer describes his father as one who "like his son after him nurtured a mixture of contradictory ideals" (Mack Smith 2). The father's carelessness about money made life a struggle for the family. At school the young man was troubled by illness and was punished by the authorities. He preferred reading to playing with the other children. At one point he led a revolt against the quality of the food. He refused to go to mass and once had to be dragged to church by force. In his second school his interest in music flourished and he was asked to give a speech at a local theatre in honor of Giuseppe Verdi. At the age of 17 he was known as a hermit and misanthrope, but he made regular visits to a local brothel. He received his diploma shortly after the turn of the century, at which time his biographer describes him in this way: "there was already much of the intellectual bohemian about him. He was writing poems and trying, if unsuccessfully, to get them published. He knew long passages of Dante by heart and was a voracious reader of novels and political tracts" (Mack Smith 5).

After a brief job as a substitute teacher, borrowing money from a number of people, he went into self-imposed exile, leaving behind debts and unpaid rent. In his adopted country he drifted from one job to another. He was a socialist but he had (his biographer tells us) "little patience with sentimental reformist socialism or with democratic and parliamentary methods; instead he preached revolution to expropriate a ruling class that would never voluntarily renounce power and possessions'' (Mack Smith 7). He spent some time in Paris in 1904 but did not settle there. He worked on foreign languages and practiced translating books from both French and German. He taught school briefly but had trouble keeping order. His biographer tells us that ''his mother's death at the age of forty-six caused him great grief and perhaps some feelings of guilt for having been so inattentive a son'' (Mack Smith 9). He spent hours in a university library ''on a somewhat rambling and random course of reading that later stood him in good stead'' (Mack Smith 8). He set up housekeeping and started a family in a one-room apartment in the Italian part of Austria with a woman he later married, who is described as taking no interest in his writing or in politics and having ''no intellectual pursuits of her own'' (Mack Smith 16). A knowledgeable observer has described his political views while in his early self-imposed exile as follows:

> ...more the reflection of his early environment than the product of understanding and conviction; his hatred of oppression was not that impersonal hatred of a system shared by all revolutionaries; it sprang rather from his own sense of indignity and frustration, from a passion to assert his own ego....(Angelica Balabanoff, in Mack Smith 11)

He tried his hand at both journalism and fiction but had trouble finding a publisher for his fiction.

Whose early life is described in this brief sketch? It is much like that of James Augustine Aloysius Joyce, is it not, this early life of the man christened Benito Andrea Amilcare Mussolini? Joyce, of course, was named after three saints and Mussolini after three left-wing revolutionaries, but the patterns of their early lives are strikingly similar. In describing Mussolini's youth I have carefully followed Denis Mack Smith's biography, only I have suppressed the repeated incidents of physical violence and brutality that distinguished the personality of the young Mussolini from that of the young Joyce. Mussolini was quick to rape a reluctant female or stab an antagonistic male, actions that situate him at an enormous distance from the essentially gentle and monogamous Joyce. This violence led to a number of imprisonments that also distinguish the youth of Mussolini from that of Joyce. There are other differences as well, in class background for instance, but these very differences emphasize the strikingly similar patterns in the lives of these two young men who were born a year apart in two troubled countries.

Joyce seems to have abandoned socialism—and all political commitment—some time before war broke out in 1914, though I believe his socialistic views were entirely serious in the days when he was reading *Avanti!* and describing himself as a socialistic artist. Mussolini, of course, was fervent enough as a socialist to become the editor of *Avanti!* in 1912, at which time he also tried to establish another journal named *Utopia* in honor of St. Thomas More, whom he admired as the first socialist. For two years at *Avanti!* Mussolini upheld the international socialist line, but as the war approached he became more nationalistic, to the point where he was expelled from his editorship in November of 1914 and by December had founded the first *fascio d'azione rivoluzionaria*. In November 1906, at the height of his interest in socialism, Joyce had expressed his admiration for Arthur Griffith and said in a letter to his brother, "If the Irish programme did not insist on the Irish language I suppose I could call myself a nationalist" (*Letters II* 187). Both Joyce and Mussolini were responding to similar nationalistic feelings. One of the polarities that shape the modernist dialectic for several decades is this tension between nationalism and internationalism, which in extreme forms turns into a struggle between socialism and fascism. The Stalinist move to "socialism in one country," preserving the Russian revolution by sacrificing a number of others, is a response to the same nationalistic surge in the ideology of modern Europe felt by Joyce and Mussolini a decade or so earlier. For Mussolini, fascism was the answer to his disillusionment with international socialism. As his fascist party developed after the war, gaining more and more power, he gradually discarded the socialist elements of his program, abandoning both his anticlericalism and his sympathy for the proletariat. What he kept was his attitude toward parliamentary forms of government, an attitude highly visible in the *Avanti!* of 1906, for instance, which Joyce read and discussed regularly.

The view of parliamentary government that Joyce found most appropriate in the latter part of 1906 was that expressed by the syndicalist Arturo Labriola. Joyce explained this in a letter to Stanislaus which is worth quoting at some length:

> I am following with interest the struggle between the various socialist parties here at the Congress. Labriola spoke yesterday, the paper says, with extraordinarily rapid eloquence for two hours and a half. He reminds me somewhat of Griffith. He attacked

the intellectuals and the parliamentary socialists. He belongs or
is leader of the sindicalists. . . . They assert that they are the true
socialists because they wish the future social order to proceed
equally from the overthrow of the entire present social organi-
zation and from the automatic emergence of the proletariat in
trades-unions and guilds and the like. Their objection to parliamentarianism seems to me well-founded. . . . Of course the sindicalists are anti-militarists but I don't see how that saves them
from the conclusion of revolution in a conscriptive country like
this. (*Letters II* 173–74)

We should notice a number of things in Joyce's analysis, including
his lack of faith in parliamentary government (which we Americans
usually refer to as democracy), a position which he also takes in other
letters of this period. The evidence suggests that he accepted the
socialist critique of parliaments as tools of the bourgeois oligarchy for
maintaining their own power and wealth. Certainly his hatred for
what he called "the stupid, dishonest, tyrannical, and cowardly
burgher class (*Letters II* 158) and "these insolent whores of the
bureaucracy" (*Letters II* 164) is well documented.

Joyce's connection of Arturo Labriola to Arthur Griffith is also
interesting, but the truly devastating point of his commentary on
the syndicalists is his dismissal of any possibility of obtaining power
for the proletariat other than revolution. He is quick to reject (in
another part of the passage from which I have already quoted at
length) the syndicalist dream of a general strike. The most damning
thing he says against the syndicalists is that they have come to
resemble the English socialists. They repress the necessity for revolution because they ignore the fact that "the Italian army is not
directed against the Austrian army so much as against the Italian
people." In the years when Joyce gave his serious attention to politics,
he favored a revolution that would suppress parliamentary government, expropriate the vast wealth of the Catholic Church (*Letters II*
165–66), punish the bourgeoisie, and emancipate the proletariat
(*Letters II* 198). This became, in fact, the program of Mussolini's
fascists, until he abandoned the genuinely socialist elements of it in
1921, retaining only its antiparliamentarity.

I do not wish to suggest that Joyce was a proto-fascist in 1906,
but to point out that he had attended carefully enough to the
dialogue of the Italian socialists for several years to see the overwhelming problems facing the socialist enterprise in Italy, which
boiled down to the question, How do pacifist internationalists make

a national revolution in a country with a standing army? It took a world war to answer that question, and even in Russia after 1917 it finally took the authoritarian nationalism of Stalin to sustain that revolution. Joyce's turn away from politics, which took place around the time we have been examining, was no doubt determined by many things, among them the impossible contradictions he could see in the political position he found most congenial. But there is more to the story of Joyce's socialism than this, and we must examine certain features of it more thoroughly to discover some of what he learned during his political years.

For the space of about a year, in 1906 and 1907, when he was finishing *Dubliners* and planning *A Portrait* and his "story" *Ulysses*, Joyce thought of himself—frequently and earnestly—as a socialist. After that period he certainly took less interest in politics, but he neither repudiated his earlier views nor adopted any of the alternatives that were so visible and insistent around him. We are generally less aware than we should be of Joyce's socialism, mainly because Ellmann, who has been in most respects an exemplary steward of the Joycean oeuvre, adopted a view of Joyce that did not admit of a serious commitment of this sort, at one point in the biography observing, "At least Joyce can scarcely have been a Nietzschean any more than he was a socialist" (*JJI* 147), and at another arguing that any interest Joyce took in socialism was motivated by a petty hope for personal gain, believing that "the triumph of socialism might make for some sort of state subsidy of artists like himself" (204).

It is a wise biographer who knows the heart of his subject, but Ellmann is not seeing into a heart, of course; he is constructing a portrait of a writer as a young man. His young man frequently returned to the theme of socialism in letters to his brother. Ellmann's way of acknowledging this is to say that Joyce "labored to make socialism an integral part of his personality," the implication clearly being that such labor was in vain; but producing an integrated personality is more the biographer's problem than his subject's. Consider, for a moment the passage Ellmann introduced in the biography as an example of Joyce's vain labor:

> It is a mistake for you to imagine that my political opinions are those of a universal lover: but they are those of a socialistic artist. I cannot tell you how strange I feel sometimes in my attempt to lead a more civilized life than my contemporaries. But why should I have brought Nora to a priest or a lawyer to

make her swear away her life to me? And why should I
superimpose on my child the very troublesome burden of belief
which my father and mother superimposed on me. Some people
would answer that while professing to be a socialist I am trying
to make money: but this is not quite true at least as they mean
it. (205)

The passage goes on for some distance. What it reveals, among other
things, is that for Joyce his rejections of church and state in his own
life—as represented by rejection of formal marriage and baptism or
religious instruction for children—are aspects of what he calls his
socialism. Ellmann's comment on all this is a laconic put-down:
"socialism has rarely been defended so tortuously" (205). Unfortunately, however, socialism has been rarely defended in any way other
than tortuously, as a little reading in Marx, Adorno, or Lukács would
quickly demonstrate—and there are overwhelming reasons why this
must be so. One cannot argue for a new way of thinking from
within an old way of thinking except with the kind of self-conscious
complexity that is all too easily dismissed as "tortuous." My purpose
here, however, is not to defend socialistic discourse but to explore
the ways in which socialism and other ideological currents merge and
diverge during the period we call modernist. In particular I am
interested in the ways in which European culture shaped the minds
of those individuals who later helped to change the literary and
political map of Europe.

    In the case of Joyce, we have never, for instance, properly
appreciated the contribution of Guglielmo Ferrero to his thinking.
The only serious attempt I know of to accomplish this is Dominic
Manganiello's, in his useful book, *Joyce's Politics,* but the book has
not received the attention it deserves, and even Manganiello, who
treats Joyce's debt to Ferrero at some length, ignores some small but
extremely interesting matters.

    One of these is the fact that the immediate source of Joyce's
often repeated characterization of the style in which he had written
the stories of *Dubliners* is certainly to be found in Ferrero's *L'Europe
giovane.* Joyce alluded to Ferrero in a letter to Grant Richards
defending his stories "Counterparts" and "Two Gallants," in which
he went on to say that he had written *Dubliners* "for the most part
in a style of scrupulous meanness" (*Letters II* 133–34). This expression
is Joyce's translation of a phrase Ferrero applies to the treatment of
sensual love in French novels: "Che cosa si trova in Balzac, in Zola,

in Flaubert, in De Goncourt? Descrizione dell'amore sensuale, fatte bene o fatte male, fatte con scrupulosa esatezza di analista...." (175). Ferrero goes on to condemn the lack of attention to the mental and moral dimensions of sexual psychology in the French novelists. These are commonplaces of the period. One can find them, for instance, in Henry James's criticisms of Flaubert; but for our purposes that striking phrase, "scrupulosa esatezza di analista," is more important. In Italian, as in English, the idea of exaction has connotations of the sort of meanness one associates with the exaction of taxes, for the cognate of *esatezza, esatore*, means tax collector.

Stanislaus Joyce, in *My Brother's Keeper* (204) has claimed that "scrupulous meanness" is simply a revision of the phrase "studiously mean" which Joyce used in a 1902 review of William Rooney's *Poems and Ballads* that appeared in Dublin's *Daily Express* (and has been reprinted in Joyce's *Critical Writings*, 84–86). We should pause and examine this claim. Joyce wrote of Rooney's verses that little is achieved in them "because the writing is so careless and yet is so *studiously mean*. For, if carelessness is carried very far, it is like to become a positive virtue, but an ordinary carelessness is nothing but a false and *mean* expression of a false and *mean* idea" (85, emphasis added). Stanislaus argues that his brother should have said (and must have meant) that Rooney's poems "are the false and mean expression of a false and mean idea, but that studious (that is, careful) meanness can become a positive virtue" (204). He adds that he raised this objection in a letter to his brother at this time, thus laying the groundwork for Joyce's use of "scrupulous meanness" four years later. This may indeed be the case, but usage is often overdetermined, and I would argue that Ferrero's phrase was a more immediate stimulus, providing the key word, "scrupulous," that had previously been lacking. After all, Ferrero was so much on Joyce's mind that he was mentioned in the very same letter, and Joyce's phrase is in exactly the same vein as Ferrero's, connecting Joyce to the French naturalists Ferrero was discussing: "I have written it for the most part in a style of scrupulous meanness and with the conviction that he is a very bold man who dares to alter in the presentment, still more to deform, whatever he has seen and heard."

Ellmann's note on Ferrero in his edition of the letters describes him as an "Italian historian and antifascist social critic," which is true enough but doesn't really locate him politically; moreover, Ellmann's description of what Joyce learned from Ferrero is bizarre:

"Ferrero finds a secret alliance between Puritanism, sexual aberration, and military destructiveness, using Bismarck as his example" (133). In the passage Ellmann cites, Ferrero speaks of Bismarck's hatred of France and his desire to destroy Paris by cannon fire as the action of a puritan, not an ascetic, describing Bismarck as "un rude monogamo" who detested the city of "aesthetic vice." If Ellmann is right, we must add "rude monogamy" to the list of sexual aberrations, but I doubt if Ferrero would approve.

Ferrero was in fact a classic liberal humanist, a true child of the Enlightenment. It is also the case that he was infected by nineteenth-century racialism to some extent. His explanations according to racial characteristics appear ludicrous now, but there is much in *L'Europa giovane* that is still interesting. Joyce's "tortuous" defense of his socialism no doubt owes something to passages like this one:

> A man can become a socialist through class interest; that is, because he sees in the socialist party the best defense of his own interest. But a man can also become a socialist against the interest of his class, for moral reasons, because the numerous defects and the many vices of modern society have disgusted him; and that is the case of many bourgeois socialists, independent professionals, scientists, rich people, who in many countries of Europe, and especially in Italy, participate in one way or another in the socialist movement. (361, my translation)

That is not so bad for 1897. Ferrero was friendly to socialism, and accepted much of Marx's criticism of bourgeois society as justified, but he thought that when it came to the crucial matter of the future, Marx had substituted Semitic religiosity for the science he claimed to profess. Joyce told Stanislaus in a letter of November 1906 that he had just finished reading Ferrero's *Young Europe*:

> He has a fine chapter on Antisemitism. By the way Brandes is a Jew. He [Ferrero] says that Karl Marx has the apocalyptic imagination and makes Armageddon a war between capital and labour. The most arrogant statement made by Israel so far, he says, not excluding the gospel of Jesus is Marx's proclamation that socialism is the fulfilment of a natural law. In considering Jews he slips in Jesus between Lassalle and Lombroso: the latter too (Ferrero's father in law) is a Jew. (*Letters II* 190)

This passage is Joyce's own conflation of many pages in Ferrero's book. (Ellmann's note on the passage cites many sections, but they are simply taken from the "Indice" and are not accurate.) Joyce learned about Brandes's Jewishness, for instance, from Ferrero's report on an interview with Brandes in this city of Copenhagen. In Ferrero's book Joyce's interest in Jews and this interest in socialism were both fed. Here are excerpts from a crucial passage:

> The great men of the Hebrews have almost all had a transcendent consciousness of their own missions. . . ; they have all felt themselves, more or less lucidly, to be Messiahs. The old popular legend has become a living sentiment, a reality, in the consciousness of the great representatives of the race. Every great Hebraic man is persuaded, even if he does not say so, of having a mandate to inaugurate a new era for the world; to make, in the abyss of darkness in which humanity lives, the opening through which will enter for the first time, and forever, the light of truth. Of course this consciousness may be more or less clear, take one form or another, have a greater or lesser amplitude according to the times and the individuals, but it is there in all of them; it is in the ancient prophets who were precursors of the Messiah, it is in Jesus come to announce the heavenly kingdom; it is in Marx come to announce the proletarian revolution; it is in Lombroso, come to deliver the true scales of justice, after so many ages in which men through ignorance and malice have adopted the false. (366, my translation)

This passage obviously made an impact on Joyce, providing much of what he reported to his brother in the letter already cited, but it also provided something else: a verbal formula that came in handy when he sought a ringing phrase for the conclusion of his first novel. Listen to it again, this time in the Italian: "La vecchia leggenda del popolo é diventata sentimento vivo e realtà nella coscienza dei grandi rappresentanti della razza." For years we have wondered where that curious phrase "conscience of my race" came from. Now we know: "nella coscienza. . .della razza." Ferrero contributed something to the creation of both Stephen Dedalus and Leopold Bloom (as Dominic Manganiello noted in *Joyce's Politics*). It is supremely ironic, then, that when Joyce and Ferrero met it was at a PEN meeting at Paris in 1937, where a virtually blind Joyce listened to the exiled Ferrero lecture passionately on the burning of Joyce's books by the fascists, thinking all the time only of the infringement of his copyrights and afterwards complaining bitterly that politics had spoiled the meeting (see W. Potts, *Portraits of the Artist in Exile*, 155–56). Ferrero died the year after Joyce, also in Switzerland, where he was teaching at the University of Geneva.

We do not know exactly when the apolitical Joyce whom Ferrero encountered in 1937 displaced the political Joyce of 1906, with his syndicalism and revolutionary fervor, but it may be that Ferrero, by directing Joyce's attention to a religious element in Marxism, helped to disillusion him. We can no longer ignore the fact, however, that certainly in *Dubliners* and probably in much of his other work, Joyce felt himself to be engaged in a bringing to consciousness the social problems that beset his nation, or in his own language, in a style of scrupulous meanness creating a conscience for his race. We know enough about his thinking in those years to attempt a summary of his literary and political attitudes.

He was antibourgeois, anticlerical, antiparliamentary, antimilitaristic, antibureaucratic, an Irish nationalist, and definitely not an anti-Semite, though extremely interested in Jews. In literature he admired Ibsen, Hauptmann, Tolstoy, Maupassant. In particular he liked the "scrupolosa esatezza di analista" that he found in these writers. What he did not like is well expressed in his comments on George Gissing in a letter of November 1906:

> I have read Gissing's *Demos: A Story of English Socialism*. Why are English novels so terribly boring? I think G has little merit. The socialist in this is first a worker and then inherits a fortune, jilts his first girl, marries a lydy, becomes a big employer and takes to drink. You know the kind of story. There is a clergyman in it with searching eyes and a deep voice who makes all the socialists wince under his firm gaze. (*Letters II* 186)

In this critique Joyce's socialism and anticlericalism are inextricably bound up with his sense of realities and his aesthetic judgment. He is judging by a standard in which realism and aestheticism are allied rather than antagonistic.

Certainly one of the polarities that structure modernist ideology is that between naturalism and aestheticism. That particular division of what had been in the nineteenth century a unified realism is one of the decisive breaks that constitutes modernism as a cultural hegemony. Joyce in 1906 was poised right on that break, seeking a way of extending realism without its fragmenting into aesthetic and naturalistic poles. Certainly, the stories of *Dubliners* can be usefully seen in exactly that light. It will be helpful in appreciating his position to look carefully at his thoughts on a writer whom most critics would see as tending toward the naturalistic pole to a greater extent than Tolstoy, Maupassant, or Ibsen may be said to do. I refer to Gerhard Hauptmann, whose *Rosa Bernd* Joyce acquired, though he could scarcely afford it, at a time in the autumn of 1906, when he was also taking Danish lessons to read Ibsen more easily in the original. Joyce had admired Hauptmann for some years but his appraisal of Hauptmann's drama was this side idolatry:

> I finished Hauptmann's *Rosa Bernd* on Sunday. I wonder if he acts well. His plays, when read, leave an unsatisfying impression on the reader. Yet he must have the sense of the stage well developed in him by now. He never, in his later plays at least, tries for a curtain so that the ends of his acts seem ruptures of a scene. His characters appear to be more highly vivified by their creator than Ibsen's but also they are less under control. He has a difficulty in subordinating them to the action of his drama. He deals with life quite differently, more frankly in certain points...but also so broadly that my personal conscience is seldom touched. His way of treating such types as Arnold Kramer and Rosa Bernd is, however, altogether to my taste. His temperament has a little of Rimbaud in it. Like him, too, I suppose somebody else will be his future. But, after all, he has written two or three masterpieces—"a little immortal thing" like *The Weavers*, for example. I have found nothing of the charlatan in him yet. (*Letters II* 173)

Joyce's praise of Hauptmann's vividness of characterization, his frankness, and his freedom from charlatanry is balanced by a dissatisfaction that is partly aesthetic (a disparity between characters and actions) and partly ethical: he deals with life "so broadly that my personal conscience is not touched." The immediate contrast, only partly explicit here, is with Ibsen, whose control and balance brings him near the top of Joyce's aesthetic scale. The young Joyce's reactions to Gissing and Hauptmann can help us to locate his own position with respect to naturalism. He rejects the sentimentalized naturalism of Gissing and prefers the harsher, franker naturalism of Hauptmann. But he is troubled by two features of Hauptmann's work, a certain lack of aesthetic "control" (which Ibsen so obviously had) and a crudity or broadness that left his "personal conscience" untouched— a criticism similar to Ferrero's critique of the French novelists. The need to reconcile the naturalistic presentation of life with an aesthetic control that would affect the personal conscience merges from these critiques as the central problem for Joyce as a writer. It is the paradigmatic problem for the modernist writer of plays or stories, a problem that other modernists, such as Hemingway and Lawrence, would also have to solve.

This problem became central in the work of another young man of Joyce's generation, whose experience will serve to close this little

excursion into modernist ideology. He was born in the 1880s in a
city on the edge of Europe. Though raised in a bourgeois family he
rebelled against bourgeois manners and values. He was a bright
student in school: outwardly conforming but inwardly rebellious.
One of the earliest literary works to impress him was Lamb's *Tales
from Shakespeare*. At a later age he discovered "Baudelaire, Verlaine,
Swinburne, Zola, Ibsen, and Tolstoy as leaders and guides" (*Record
of a Life* 147). As he matured, he continued to admire the radicalism
of Scandinavian and Russian literature. Years later he recalled his
relationship with his family in this way:

> I was completely estranged from my family, or at least from a
> part of it. I did not have any relationship with the family at
> all.... My mother was a shrewd woman who soon saw what
> was happening. She fell seriously ill and died of cancer of the
> breast. Under pressure from other members of the family, I
> wrote her a letter. When she received it she said, "I must be
> very ill for [my son] to write me a letter." (35)

Rejecting marriage as a bourgeois convention, he went into self-
imposed exile. Looking back on his twenty-third year, he wrote, "In
my case...absolute independence in order to produce, and for that
reason silent rejection" (151). This was his version of the Joycean
"silence, exile, and cunning." He came to admire the work of a
poet who expressed his own values, seeing in this poet in 1906, as
he later recalled, "a revolutionary who regarded the revolution as
indispensable for his own self-realization" (39). He had ambitions
to write a treatise on aesthetics and to be a dramatist. "I started to
write plays in the manner of Hauptmann and Ibsen" (31), he later
recalled, and he translated *The Wild Duck* into his native language
(34). Writing about Hauptmann some time after his youthful en-
thusiasm, he praised in particular the dramatists "great and beautiful
honesty." Living in Italy in his twenty-sixth year he began a major
work on aesthetic theory but set it aside the following year. When
he was about twenty-five he discovered French syndicalism, which,
he says, "at the time I regarded as the only oppositional socialist
movement that could be taken seriously" (41). He condemned
conditions in his own country, which he seriously hoped to change
through his own work, but, as he has said, "this did not mean that
I was prepared to accept English Parliamentarianism as an alternative
ideal."

The young man I have been describing, as you have no doubt realized was Georg Lukács, the Hungarian Jew who became Europe's leading Marxist literary critic and theoretician. Considering the fact that he came to be a major opponent of the kind of modernism he felt to be manifested in Joyce's work, it is useful to see how much the two writers shared in the cultural matrix from which modernism emerged. But at the point where Joyce turned from politics to art, Lukács turned in the opposite direction. At the end of his life an interviewer asked him about shift of interest:

> *Int:* You said you gave up aesthetics because you had begun
>   to be interested in ethical problems. What works
>   resulted from this interest?
> *G.L.:* At that time it did not result in any written works.
>   My interest in ethics led me to the revolution. (53)

Both of these young men reached a similar point of decision and made their choices, living the lives that followed from them. They had also made other choices, Joyce abandoning criticism as Lukács abandoned drama, but these were more personal, matters of talent primarily. Perhaps the ideological choices stem as much from personality as anything else, but there is a lot we do not know about these things. In the case of Joyce, for instance, what may have been a crucial year of intellectual decision, 1908, is simply a blank on the biographical record. For the first eleven months of that year we have five lines of correspondence and precious little else. We know a lot about what Joyce was in 1906 and what he later became. About the transition itself, we are ignorant.

We know, however, that Georg Lukács became the most articulate critical opponent of modernism in literature (with the possible exception of Wyndham Lewis). Lukács's critique of modernism has a philosophical basis that allows him to set modernism against realism, in fact to see modernism as a perverse negation of realism. For Lukács realism is based on the view of man as a *zoon politikon*, a political animal. Modernism, on the other hand, is based on a view of human existence as, in Heidegger's expression, a *Geworfenheit ins Dasein*, a "thrownness into being." Realism, says Lukács, depends upon perspective and norms of human behavior, whereas modernism destroys perspective and glorifies the abnormal. Realism assumes the objectivity of time and modernism assumes time's subjectivity. For Lukács, Joyce acquired the proportions of the arch-modernist, whose works displayed an exaggerated concern with form, style, and technique in general, along with an excessive attention to sense-data, combined with a comparative neglect of ideas and emotions.

Lukács's unfavorable comparison of Joyce to Thomas Mann, however, has affinities with Joyce's comparison of Hauptmann to Ibsen. It should also be noted that Lukács does not trivialize Joyce's enterprise. He is perfectly ready to call *Ulysses* a masterpiece, as he does in the following passage:

> A gifted writer, however extreme his theoretical modernism, will in practice have to compromise with the demands of historicity and of social environment. Joyce uses Dublin, Kafka, and Musil the Hapsburg Monarchy, as the locus of their masterpieces. But the locus they lovingly depict is little more than a backcloth; it is not basic to their artistic intention. (*Realism in Our Time* 21)

Lukács particularly criticized Joyce's use of the stream of consciousness, in which, as he argued, "the perpetually oscillating patterns of sense and memory-data, their powerfully charged—but aimless and directionless—fields of force, give rise to an epic structure which is static, reflecting a belief in the basically static character of events" (18). This is by no means a trivial or inaccurate description of Joyce's major enterprise, though I think the Joycean stream of consciousness is more directed and purposeful than Lukács gives it credit for being. Lukács is surely right, however, when he borrows Walter Benjamin's description of Romantic and Baroque art to characterize the allegorical tendencies of modernism: "Every person, every object, every relationship can stand for something else." (42). It is surely this, and the Joycean sense that history is an endless repetition of such transformations that make Joyce a fearful object to Lukács, whose faith in progressive possibilities could only abhor what he called the "religious atheism" that animated Joyce's modernism.

For all their differences, however, they were products of very similar cultural interests and pressures. To emphasize that, I shall close by presenting to you some excerpts from one of the last things Lukács wrote, his *Gelebtes Denken* or preliminary notes for an autobiography that he did not live to finish. To my ears they connect him across time, across politics, across experiences, across Europe, with the writer who most symbolized for him the mistaken ways of modernist prose. Listen:

> Objectivity: the correct historicity. Memory: tendency to relocate in time. Check against the facts. Youth. . . .

No poet. Only a philosopher. Abstractions. Memory, too, organized to that end. Danger: premature generalization of spontaneous experience. But poets: able to recall concrete feelings.... That already means at the right place at the right time. Especially: childhood....

Live here: over 80—subjective interest in reality maintained—at a time when the contact with early youth often lost. Long and even now, an undeniably industrious life—my right to attempt to justify this posture....

Thus an old Hungarian Jew, back from exile, planning to justify his life, lapses into a prose somewhere between an outline and a stream of consciousness. He wants to fight the tendency of memory to relocate in subjective time, seeks the objective, the facts, but also says "No poet, Only a philosopher. Abstractions." He fought to the end the tendency of his own discourse toward modernism and the power of his own subjectivity, which had been formed in the same European crucible as that of those he criticized. Sometimes, at some levels, $x = y$.

WORKS CITED

Hauptmann, Gerhard. *Rosa Bernd.* In *The Dramatic Works of Gerhard Hauptmann,* Vol. II, edited and translated by Ludwig Lewisohn. New York: Huebsch Press, 1913.

Joyce, Stanislaus. *My Brother's Keeper: James Joyce's Early Years,* edited by Richard Ellmann. New York: Viking Press, 1958.

Lewis, C. Day. *Magnetic Mountain.* In *Collected Poems, 1929-33.* London: Hogarth Press, 1945.

Lukács, György. *Realism in Our Time: Literature and the Class Struggle,* translated by John and Necke Mander. New York: Harper & Row, 1964.

——— . *Record of a Life: An Autobiographical Sketch,* edited by István Eörsi; translated by Rodney Livingstone. London: Verso Press, 1983.

Mack Smith, Denis. *Mussolini.* London: Weidenfeld and Nicolson, 1981.

Manganiello, Dominic. *Joyce's Politics.* London: Routledge & Kegan Paul, 1980.

Potts, Willard, ed. *Portraits of the Artist in Exile: Recollections of James Joyce by Europeans.* Seattle: University of Washington Press, 1979.

CRITICAL
STUDIES

6

Farrington the Scrivener:
A Story of Dame Street

MORRIS BEJA

I might as well be talking to the wall as talking to you.
—Mr. Alleyne, in James Joyce, "Counterparts"

At the start of Herman Melville's short story "Bartleby the Scrivener: A Story of Wall Street," originally published in 1853, the narrator, an elderly lawyer, speaks of a "singular set of men" of whom, as far as he knows, "nothing" has "ever been written—. . .the law-copyists, or scriveners" (92). Since then, at least one other major writer—James Joyce—has written a story centering on such a scrivener: "Counterparts." Melville's lawyer says of his scrivener that he was "the strangest I ever saw, or heard of" (92). Nothing that we shall discover in this essay about Joyce's scrivener, Farrington, will match Bartleby for strangeness. Nor, I should stress at the outset, is my bringing the two scriveners together meant to discuss or even suggest any sort of possible "influence." I am confident that Joyce would not have known what was at that time an obscure tale by a largely neglected writer when he wrote his own story in 1905. I am not in any case interested in the question of influence; for my purposes, the fact that there was surely no awareness on Joyce's part of Melville's story makes it all the more intriguing to compare and contrast the two works, and above all the two men: Joyce's brutal bully and Melville's passive victim.

So different are the two characters, actually, that at first it would seem that only the contrasts between them and their tales are worth mentioning, and that their one genuine point of convergence is their mode of employment. On the evidence of both stories, the job of the scrivener—that is, of copying legal documents in those pre-Xerox days when typewriters were also either nonexistent (as in Bartleby's time) or not yet widely accepted for legal purposes (as in Farrington's)—would seem to have been tedious, mechanical, and alienating: a daily grind demanding no thought and yielding little self-respect.

111

Such characteristics seem especially emphasized in Melville's story. It is narrated by Bartleby's employer, a New York lawyer who tells about his office and its two scriveners, Turkey and Nippers, and the errand-boy, Ginger-Nut; the lawyer had determined that there was too much work for his current staff and so advertised for another scrivener. In response, one day "a motionless young man" (99) stands upon his threshold: Bartleby. The lawyer hires him, and for a time the young scrivener's work is exemplary, and Bartleby does "an extraordinary quantity of writing" (100). So it is all the more surprising when the lawyer, having asked him to help examine some previously copied work, hears from Bartleby the reply, "I would prefer not to" (101). The lawyer feels at that moment too busy to pursue his anger, but he does so a few days later upon again hearing the scrivener use that enigmatic phrase: "I would prefer not to." The other members of his staff agree with him that Bartleby's behavior is reprehensible and even outrageous, but in view of the young man's excellent work otherwise, and his quiet demeanor, the lawyer does not turn him out, even when, as the days go by, the same response is forthcoming when any request is made of Bartleby—and indeed when he eventually stops copying altogether. At around that time, as well, the lawyer discovers that Bartleby apparently never leaves the office premises, before or after work hours, subsisting on "nothing but ginger-nuts" (104). Attempting to be sympathetic, the lawyer pleads with the young man to provide information about his background, but Bartleby replies only that he would prefer not to reply. The lawyer at last fires him, but to no avail: Bartleby simply remains in his little corner, behind his screen and facing a wall opposite the office window.

The lawyer comes to feel that he is no longer in control of his own offices, and in a kind of panic he resolves that if Bartleby will not leave, he will; so he changes his premises. Even after the move takes place, Bartleby continues to haunt the old offices—and then, when turned out by the new tenant, the building. Returning there on the plea of the landlord, the lawyer is so touched by Bartleby's plight that he offers to take him with him—not to the new offices but to the lawyer's own home; but Bartleby replies that he would prefer not to. Days later, the lawyer hears that the police have removed Bartleby and taken him to the Tombs, the prison in the Halls of Justice. The lawyer visits him there, where Bartleby says, "I know you...and I want nothing to say to you" (128). The lawyer arranges for the young man to be treated and fed well, but when he returns a few days later he finds Bartleby huddled at the base of the wall, dead. In a postscript of sorts, the lawyer informs us that some months later he heard a rumor that Bartleby had once worked at the Dead Letter Office. "Ah, Bartleby!" he ends his narrative, "Ah, humanity!" (131).

"Bartleby the Scrivener" is a complex, packed work, perhaps overdone in parts and not always in full control of its ambition; but for all that it is a genuine masterpiece, an obsessively haunting tale. Joyce's "Counterparts" is finally less ambitious, but on its own it is also masterful, perhaps even flawless. It succinctly recounts the events of a single day in the life of a man who would seem to be not so much a Bartleby as an anti-Bartleby.

Farrington, already regarded by his employer—the lawyer Mr. Alleyne—as a shirker, has failed to complete some copies when they are needed, and when asked to provide them he tries to pretend he knows nothing about them. In front of the entire staff, his furious employer asks him, "do you take me for a fool? Do you think me an utter fool?" Before he realizes it, Farrington replies, "I don't think, sir...that that's a fair question to put to me" (91).

Threatened with the loss of his position, Farrington must apologize abjectly for his witticism. At the end of the day, he is still thirsty—despite his having sneaked off to a pub during working hours—and in need of a night out with his friends, so he pawns his watch. His story of the incident at the office is a success with his chums, but as the pub crawl continues the evening is disappointing. He spends too much money, is frustrated when he feels unable to respond to an apparently flirtatious woman in one pub, and then loses an arm-wrestling contest to Weathers, a younger man. On his way home, he feels "humiliated and discontented; he did not even feel drunk; and he had only twopence in his pocket. He cursed everything. He had done for himself in the office, pawned his watch, spent all his money; and he had not even got drunk" (96–97). His wife not at home, he asks his son Tom about his dinner. The young boy says he is going to cook it; but Farrington sees that the fire has been allowed to go out and, furious, viciously beats him with a walking-stick. Terrified, the boy squeals, "Don't beat me, pa! And I'll...I'll say a *Hail Mary* for you...I'll say a *Hail Mary* for you, pa, if you don't beat me.... I'll say a *Hail Mary*..." (98).

Obviously, there is a marked difference in the reader's degree of sympathy or, certainly, identification with the protagonist of each story.[1] Joyce forces us to understand a brute like Farrington, and—I shall attempt to show—to realize our own kinship with him, but most of us are readier to identify with his son, or even with Bartleby. Many readers who seem to have no qualms about identifying themselves with a catatonic and schizophrenic like Bartleby—as the existential victim—would recoil with repugnance at any attempt to associate them with Farrington, or indeed with either of the employers in the stories. Such readers are ready enough to sentimentalize Bartleby's plight by turning him into a prophet, wiser in his "irrational" existence than the rest of humanity in its desperate "sanity." Yet it does not take so romanticized a view of Bartleby to feel that there is an integrity in his self-destructive and futile mode of behavior that is lacking in Farrington's self-deceptive and futile modes of rebellion.

Not to put too fine a point on it, Farrington is after all a "ruffian." The term is Mr. Alleyne's—hardly a totally sympathetic or unbiased judge of Farrington's character—but the narrative voice of the story uses not dissimilar terms, as we hear that Farrington feels "savage and thirsty and revengeful" (92), or that he is "full of smoldering anger and revengefulness" (96). Bartleby, in contrast, is said to be a "poor, pale, passive mortal...a helpless creature" (123). Each character is given the sort of physique that would be expected, given their roles: Bartleby the victim is described as "lean," and as "thin and pale" (109, 111), while Farrington the bully is "tall and of great bulk," and he walks "with a heavy step" (86).

They contrast with one another in additional physical ways as well. Bartleby is constantly in stasis. He seems never to move: "I like to be stationary," he remarks in his exasperating mode of understatement (126). Farrington is constantly hyperkinetic: "his body ached to do something, to rush out and revel in violence" (90). He leaves the office whenever he gets the chance (Mr. Alleyne accuses him of taking extra-long lunches, and of never being there when he is wanted; and we see him pretend to go to the men's room when he is actually going out to a pub)—in contrast to Bartleby, who is at first praised by the lawyer for the fact that he is always *there*: "I observed that he never went to dinner; indeed, that he never went anywhere. As yet I had never, of my personal knowledge, known him to be outside of my office" (104). In time the lawyer becomes less sanguine about this clinging, static quality in his scrivener, who finally refuses to quit the lawyer's office altogether.

As all that suggests, the relationships between employee and employer in the two stories are also studies in antithesis, as are the employers themselves. Mr. Alleyne is impatient and short-tempered. While there has been some critical disagreement about the efficacy of the lawyer's good intentions in "Bartleby the Scrivener," and some critics have attacked, for example, his "exploitative" role as a representative of "Wall Street," few of us mere mortals (as distinct I gather from literary critics) could claim to be as patient, as generous, or as long-suffering as Melville's lawyer, who tries—truly sincerely, it seems quite clear, however ineffectively or hopelessly—to deal with and confront Bartleby's painful case. It is true that he is the one to tell us, but there seems little reason to disbelieve the lawyer's assertions that, for example, "I seldom lose my temper; much more seldom indulge in dangerous indignation at wrongs and outrages" (93); and it is clearly accurate for him to claim, as he does, that (unlike Mr. Alleyne, certainly) he resorts to "no vulgar bullying, no bravado of any sort, no choleric hectoring" (117). In contrast, we see no reason to doubt Farrington's fear that from now on "Mr. Alleyne would never give him an hour's rest; his life would be a hell to him" (92). To give Mr. Alleyne his due, he does not have a model employee in Farrington, who surely would be an exasperating person to have in one's office.

So would Bartleby, no doubt. Yet in the end it is the psychological and spiritual differences between the two scriveners that seem, at least at first, to control our views when we look at them together. Both men are self-defeating; but Farrington's mode of self-destruction follows what is, unfortunately, probably the more usual pattern. For he strikes out, bitterly and openly, at other people as well, even resorting to—seeking out, and ready to "revel in"—violence: "he longed to execrate aloud, to bring his fist down on something violently" (90). In some ways, he seems closer to the other scriveners in the office of Melville's lawyer than to Bartleby himself: to Nippers, for one, who, "if he wanted anything, it was to be rid of a scrivener's table altogether" (96). Nippers, however, is "at least, a temperate man" (98), so Farrington—with his determination "that he must have a good night's drinking" (87)—seems even more like Turkey, as they both practice a profession that Joyce's scrivener would agree is, in Melville's lawyer's words, "a dry, husky sort of business" (98). Turkey is notorious in the office for becoming less agreeable and more irascible and cantankerous after his lunch, when he has had some beer, which leads him to be (like Farrington, after his glass of porter) "rash with his tongue—in fact, insolent" (95). The alcohol also makes both men prone to violence: in the morning, Turkey seems the soul of patience with respect to Bartleby's odd conduct; after experiencing the "effects of beer," however, he displays "combativeness," throwing "his arms into a pugilistic position" and offering to "go and black his eyes" (105, 106). In contrast, Bartleby, whose "pale face clearly indicated that he never drank beer like Turkey" (111)—or Farrington—displays "freedom from all dissipation," and "great stillness" and "unalterableness of demeanor under all circumstances" (107). He is a completely nonviolent person, whose stance takes the form of totally passive resistance—a "poor, pale, passive mortal" (123). Fascinatingly, his rebellion is ultimately no less real than Farrington's, and much more effective in many essential ways: "nothing," as Melville's lawyer points out, "so aggravates an earnest person as a passive resistance" (104). Yet, after all, Bartleby's rebellion is also self-defeating, and hardly a model for others to emulate.

In that and in other key ways as well, despite all these contrasts between the protagonists of the two stories, the similarities between the two men, and between their plights, are much more revealing and suggestive, if subtle and surprising. The comparison may suggest that similar forces are present in their lives—however ultimately difficult it may be to pin down those forces—which make them both not merely unwilling but unable to get down to work, to copy their papers: to get along in their worlds. Bartleby's inability (or unwillingness) to copy is all too obvious as his story proceeds. Farrington's inability is less extreme, but it seems acute from the start, as he has for some reason been unable to finish his copy of an important contract for Mr. Alleyne, who accuses him right off of having "always some excuse or another for shirking work" (87). Farrington too would prefer not to; and he doesn't, sort of. He may not have the absolute courage of his convictions we see all too present in Bartleby, but in this pivotal matter he is his counterpart.

And indeed they are genuine "counterparts." Above all they are so to each other, but they are also counterparts to secondary figures in their respective stories. If we had any doubts about that in Joyce's story, the title makes it clear enough, with a near explicitness in which Joyce rarely indulges, except—as here—in some of his titles

(A Portrait of the Artist as a Young Man, Exiles, Ulysses, Finnegans Wake). Farrington is played off against Mr. Alleyne; against Weathers, the young man who beats him at arm wrestling (and who has apparently slipped out from work in order to join them at the pub); and most compellingly against his young son, Tom. The counter-pointing is so close and so effective that even in the short space of this brief tale we come to understand that, at least in respect to Mr. Alleyne and Tom, it is not a question of their merely being "foils" for Farrington: they are in fact his *counterparts*, his doubles or "doppelgangers."

As a number of critics have shown, "Bartleby the Scrivener" is also a tale of doubles,[2] with its major and minor characters serving as "counterparts" to one another: above all, the lawyer and Bartleby; but also the other two scriveners, Nippers and Turkey (mirroring one another like the morning and afternoon personalities of a single character—the nip and tuck, as it were); and the lawyer and each of those two characters (especially the elder, Turkey); as well as those scriveners (and, perhaps, Ginger Nut) and Bartleby. It is one thing to recognize that all these characters are doubles, however, and quite another to perceive the full significance of their doubling in this mysterious tale. An especially crucial area of exploration is the relationship each scrivener has with his employer/double.

Joyce's Mr. Alleyne, as we have seen, is petulant and in general apparently a hard, irritable man to work for. In the first sentence of the story he rings the bell "furiously," and speaks through the tube in "a furious voice" and in "a piercing" accent (86). In contrast, Melville's lawyer is apparently justified in claiming at the start that "I seldom lose my temper" (93). Yet he finds Bartleby's behavior so provoking that he responds at times in ways that, by his standards in any case, come quite close to the mode of response of Mr. Alleyne: at first he merely reports his "rising in high excitement," but he soon enough finds himself speaking "in a louder tone"—indeed " 'Bartleby,' I roared"; and "sometimes, to be sure, I could not, for the very soul of me, avoid falling into sudden spasmodic passions with him" (101, 106, 107).

The two employees, however, are portrayed as powerless—impotent—in their respective spheres. Bartleby manifests impotence through passivity (although through passive resistance), Farrington through impotent rage. But in each their sense of powerlessness and alienation seems exacerbated by the contrasts between themselves and their employers—and their employers' positions in the world. Bartleby shares the traits his employer ascribes to himself: he too wants a "snug retreat" and acts—with a vengeance—as though he has a "profound conviction that the easiest way of life is best" (92–93). But within the social world of the story—given, that is the socio-political and economic forces at work—the lawyer can convert these traits into success, authority, and power, while for Bartleby they are self-destructive.

Both Bartleby and Farrington live and work in a system in which they cannot succeed. Bartleby's "passive resistance" occurs in a society far removed from Thoreau's; or, more accurately, given his class, his social status, and the economic realities of his situation— all of them more comparable to Farrington's than Thoreau's—there is no possibility of Bartleby attaining some genuine mode of triumph or success through such passive resistance.

Farrington clearly envies his employer's potent, active rage and energy, manifested in an ability to fire Farrington or to see that "his life would be a hell to him" (92). Mr. Alleyne's forcefulness has an outlet that society sanctions; Farrington's only outlets—or so it would seem to him—are through drink and abusing his son. But, as with Bartleby, his mode of behavior is self-destructive.

In Melville's story, all that does not make us lose sight of how the lawyer takes on a positively fatherly role in regard to his young employee—just as, perhaps, it is a similar recognition of their paternal relationship that leads Bartleby in his turn to choose the lawyer for his own needs. Those needs, as much of what I have said would suggest, seem at least twofold: for one thing, to involve a young man's need for a father, but for another to include a son's presumably inevitable need to rebel against that father. Moreover, the lawyer seems more or less to recognize his role in such a pattern, and the necessity for it. At one point, he even suggests that his own needs are thereby being met, when he says in regard to Bartleby's actions that "I burned to be rebelled against again" (106). In the end, he goes so far as to offer to bring Bartleby into his own home—to adopt him, in effect. But Bartleby would prefer not to.

Paternal benevolence is not enough, nor is mere kindness. Bartleby's employer is much more humane than Farrington's (or, as I have argued, than most employers would ever be), but that does not save Bartleby, and it would not save Farrington either.

The paternity theme in "Counterparts" is illuminated if complicated by the fact that in portraying and naming Mr. Alleyne,
Joyce is—as a loyal son—paying off one of "his father's scores," as
Richard Ellmann puts it (16); for a Henry Alleyn was a dishonest
businessman and supervisor of a firm with which the older Joyce had
worked, and he had run off with the firm's funds. But Farrington
himself, unlike Bartleby (we can only assume), is also a father, not
merely a son: in that context, the biographical associations are
complicated by the fact that Farrington seems at least partially based
on Joyce's father, John Joyce, as well as on Joyce's uncle, William
Murray. According to Stanislaus Joyce in an entry in his diary during
1904, "the manner in which Uncle Willie tyrannizes his children is
to me an intolerable and stupid cowardice," and Stanislaus goes on
to report that "on one occasion Bertie, then an infant of six or
seven, begged Uncle William not to beat him and promised to say
a 'Hail Mary' for him if he didn't" (37). Stanislaus' attitude toward
such brutality is commendable, but it is one of my arguments that
James Joyce's presentation, while no less damning, also brings us
closer to a genuine understanding, even a degree of compassion, for
Uncle William's counterpart. As Joyce once wrote in a letter to
Stanislaus, "if many husbands are brutal the atmosphere in which
they live (vide Counterparts) is brutal..." (*Letters II* 192).

Intriguingly, the authors of both stories use similar imagery in
evoking the anguish and situations of their scriveners. Bartleby's story
is a "Story of Wall Street," and he is constantly associated with
walls, particularly "the dead brick wall" upon which his office
window looks (111); at the Tombs he at last dies "strangely huddled
at the base of the wall" (130). Farrington is "tall and of great
bulk," and Mr. Alleyne claims that "I might as well be talking to
the wall as talking to you" (86, 87). And Farrington (we are told
several times) has "heavy dirty eyes" (94; cf. 86), while Bartleby,
at death, has "dim eyes" (130).

In a well-known letter of 1904 to Constantine P. Curran, Joyce
said that he was calling his book "*Dubliners* to betray the soul of
that hemiplegia or paralysis which many consider a city" (*Letters I*
55); two years later he reiterated, to Grant Richards, that "I chose
Dublin for the scene because that city seemed to me the centre of
paralysis" (*Letters II* 134). If anything, the sense of paralysis is even
greater in Bartleby's tale than in Farrington's, for Bartleby is for all

practical purposes quite literally paralyzed and static—even to the
degree of seeming at last catatonic. He displays "great stillness,"
and "long-continued motionlessness" (107, 111); the mildness and
stasis with which he utters his "I would prefer not to" portray not
action but inaction, and a preference for it; he goes nowhere—"I
like to be stationary"—and finally the lawyer is the one who is
forced to move, since Bartleby does not and will not.

Farrington would seem to be constantly active, yet the effect is
often curiously similar. Confronted with Mr. Alleyne's anger at his
not yet having done his copying at the start of the story, Farrington
remains in front of his employer's desk, immobile, until at last Mr.
Alleyne bursts out, "Are you going to stand there all day?" Returning
to his desk, and despite the urgency of his need to get down to
work, or because of it, Farrington is paralyzed with an inability to
copy even a single word: "he continued to stare stupidly at the last
words he had written" (88). At the end of his evening's pub crawl,
this clerk who has longed to leave his office "loathed returning to
his home" (97), so that Bernard Benstock's phrasing is right on the
mark when he observes that Farrington "moves from pub to pub
until time and money run out and he is fixed in a catatonic moment
of entrapment" (35).

The social context of each story brings out the stasis and paralysis
on the communal level; both men are paralyzed by the worlds in
which they live. Their resulting immobility and inertia are personally
ruinous and seemingly irrational, as are, in context, the comments
each makes to his employer which bring on the respective crises.
Bartleby's "I would prefer not to" makes no ordinary "sense" at
all. And for his part Farrington's reply to Mr. Alleyne's demand
that he answer the question about whether he takes him for a fool—
that, in effect, he would prefer not to ("I don't think, sir, he said,
that that's a fair question to put to me" [91])—is similarly disastrous.
It is precisely equivalent to Bartleby's answer at one point in *his*
story: "'At present I prefer to give no answer,' he said..." (113).

It is essential to understand the significance of the closeness of
their responses, which are in substance interchangeable. For in each
case the behavior of the given scrivener is to himself not as outrageous,
as incomprehensible or as irrational, as it will necessarily seem to the
rest of the world. *It is a mode of coping.* Even perhaps a strategy,
a tactic. Their action and inaction seem to them the only means
they have to handle what they regard as an unlivable situation.

Bartleby's behavior is clearly ludicrous, absurd, even sick, if you are not Bartleby; Farrington's behavior is clearly crude, brutal, even cruel, certainly indefensible, if you are anyone else in the world except Farrington. "At present I would prefer not to be a little reasonable," says Bartleby for both of them (113).

The ultimate point of the comparisons I have discussed, after all, is to attempt to illuminate what happens in both stories, and why—or out of what forces. I feel especially that the comparisons help us to comprehend "Counterparts" more fully. Bartleby certainly remains a mysterious figure, and any attempt to explain completely—or to explain away—his motivation, or the sources in his psyche for what he does, is doomed to failure. There are ambiguities enough in Joyce's story, but for once another writer seems even more indeterminate than he. Yet however uncertain we remain about the true sources of Bartleby's behavior and his plight, we must—given the comparisons I have pointed out—feel that at least some may well be shared with Farrington: and among those their frustration and alienation and social plight are surely central. And for my present purposes, it is Farrington's character which is particularly illuminated in this light, for the comparison enables us to see him from a perspective that grants us a greater receptivity to compassion for this fierce and ill-natured man with a wasted life. We become his as well as Bartleby's counterparts.

Ah, Farrington! Ah, humanity!

NOTES

1. I have argued elsewhere against the frequent assertion that it is the lawyer, rather than Bartleby, who is for most readers the central interest in Melville's story. In that same essay, I pursue the relevance of "schizophrenia" as a clinical term in attempting to comprehend Bartleby, his state, and his behavior. See "Bartleby and Schizophrenia."

2. See for example the works cited for Marcus, Widmer, Rogers, Keppler, and Beja.

WORKS CITED

Beja, Morris. "Bartleby and Schizophrenia." *Massachusetts Review* 19 (Autumn 1978): 558–68.

Benstock, Bernard. *James Joyce.* New York: Ungar, 1985.

Joyce, James. "Counterparts." In *Dubliners,* 86–98, edited by Robert Scholes. New York: Viking Press, 1967.

Joyce, Stanislaus. *The Complete Dublin Diary,* edited by George H. Healey. Ithaca: Cornell University Press, 1971.

Keppler, C.F. *The Literature of the Second Self.* Tucson: University of Arizona Press, 1972.

Marcus, Mordecai. "Melville's Bartleby as a Psychological Double." *College English* 23 (February 1962): 365–68.

Melville, Herman. "Bartleby the Scrivener: A Story of Wall Street." In *Selected Tales and Poems,* 92–131, edited by Richard Chase. New York: Holt, Rinehart & Winston, 1950.

Rogers, Robert. *A Psychoanalytic Study of the Double in Literature.* Detroit: Wayne State University Press, 1970.

Widmer, Kingsley. *The Ways of Nihilism: A Study of Herman Melville's Short Novels.* Los Angeles: California State Colleges, 1970.

7

The Language of *Exiles*

CLIVE HART

*I am simply using the language of people whose opinions
I don't share*

—Robert

Robert, the journalist, the glib professional, bases his hopes of an affair with Bertha on the utterance of a "word": "There is one word which I have never dared to say to you" (34.7).[1] Superficial, conventional, false, the language which he manipulates is nevertheless the vehicle by which he hopes to achieve gratification of the flesh: "Your eyes...I want to speak to you. Will you listen to me? May I speak?" (35.10–11). Incapable of saying the true, simple word "love," he has recourse to lame paraphrase: "I have a deep liking for you" (34.10). However clumsy, the avowal brings the reward of the first kisses. There follows a curious passage:

> BERTHA
> *(closes her eyes and kisses him quickly)* There. *(puts her hands on his shoulder)* Why don't you say: Thanks?
> ROBERT
> *(sighs)* My life is finished—over.
> BERTHA
> O don't speak like that now, Robert. (40.27–41.2)

I begin with this because the language is double-edged. Rather than wince at the exchange, trying to imagine it as the potential speech of real people living in Dublin in 1912, we might feel more comfortable responding to the dramatic artifice. The "thanks" which Bertha proposes he offer would be at once an expression of Robert's linguistic conventionality and of the essentially self-seeking emotional bargaining in which he indulges. He responds, instead, with a still more conventional piece of emotional melodrama, which attracts Bertha's mild protest: "O don't speak like that now." Hear! Hear!: one is inclined to voice warm agreement. This passage is as much about possible modes of speech, desirable and undesirable ways of relating words to emotions and situations, as it is about the experience of two dramatic characters.

Critics have often been troubled by *Exiles*, the trouble arising in many cases, I believe, because the dialogue has been understood as an attempt at pure realism. There are at least three good reasons why that should have been so: first, the play is in the "well-made" tradition, in direct line of descent from the realism of Ibsen's middle period; second, most readers and theatre-goers are influenced by the undeniable realism of the dialogue in nearly all of Joyce's prose before *Finnegans Wake*; third, the play is tricked out with realist settings and props, and bears many stage directions having a flatly documentary tone. We would nevertheless do better, I believe, to look beyond these comparisons and assumptions and to recall, on one hand, that Joyce had early shown an immediate sympathy with the double vision of Ibsen's last plays, and, on the other, that he had only recently finished work on *A Portrait of the Artist*, one of the most salient stylistic characteristics of which is the "Uncle Charles Principle": "the narrative idiom need not be the narrator's" (Kenner 18). That principle is at work in the play also: the dramatic tone need not be the dramatist's. Nor, of course, entirely that of the characters: the idiom of *Exiles* is curiously poised between the two, leaving the characters and their actions half real, half reinterpreted with a critical, ironic voice. Clearly aware that our responses are baffled if we try to locate the play within any of the familiar dramatic categories, Mr. Kenner writes:

> Unhappily *Exiles* refuses to be farce; it wants to be a strenuous drama of ideals. Drama is more ritualistic than Joyce appears to have supposed. If it is not to enact straightforwardly the ritual of farce or the ritual of pathos, then its recourse must be, as Shakespeare knew, to the ritual of a formal language which can hold the farcical and the tragic in suspension. (25–6)

He goes on to say: "But Joyce wanted his actors to exchange sentences of plain decent prose" (26). Here I begin to differ. *Exiles* is conceived, it seems to me, in a thoroughly mixed genre of a new kind, both farce and strenuous drama simultaneously, the two not held in suspension but welded together by subtle manipulations of language. If we take full note of its manifold uses of reflexive techniques we begin to see that the prose is neither so plain nor so straightforwardly decent as we first thought. Although unusual in the theatre, the mixture is familiar enough to readers of *Ulysses*, who experience a similar double vision in some of the later chapters.

Mr. Kenner says of Joyce's apparent intentions: "He needed to write something with no point of view, no narrator, whatever: something wholly 'objective': something in which the only point of view would be that of the spectator" (24). It may well be that Joyce set out to do something of the kind; in the event, his rapidly developing sense of multiple vision led him to a somewhat different execution. Unable, except in the stage directions, to deploy his own wide range of third-person voices, Joyce resorted to a texture of reflexions and inversions which radically qualify the play's apparent objectivity. Speaking of the characters, Ruth Bauerle rightly says that they "often echo one another in speech, and appear to have been conceived by Joyce as complex double images of one another" (x). Similar statements could be made about most other elements of the play.

I shall examine the language of *Exiles* in relation to the play's governing polarities: speech and silence, bondage and freedom, certainty and doubt. Returning to the passage with which I began, I take up the matter of self-reference by comparison with another, earlier passage. According to the stage direction, Richard speaks *"fiercely"* about his dead mother, using highly colored, emotional, and histrionic phraseology. As in the later exchange, the female interlocutor, in this case Beatrice, asks him not to do so. He nevertheless persists, growing ever more clichéd:

> RICHARD
> *(fiercely)* How can my words hurt her poor body that rots in the grave? Do you think I do not pity her cold blighted love for me? I fought against her spirit while she lived to the bitter end. *(he presses his hand to his forehead)* It fights against me still—in here.
>
> BEATRICE
> *(as before)* O, do not speak like that!
>
> RICHARD
> She drove me away. On account of her I lived years in exile and poverty too or near it. I never accepted the doles she sent me through the bank. I waited too. Not for her death but for some understanding of me, her own son, her own flesh and blood. That never came. (24.7–19)

The motif "Do not speak like that" closely associates these two passages of false male speech, both about love and death. Here, as on many other occasions, both men say too much and with too little effect. The theme is further developed through another motif, the opening stage direction "*fiercely.*" Of no great weight when considered here in isolation, the word gains powerful connotations through its later association with Swift, in whose *saeva indignatio* Robert sees a model for Richard's character: "You have that fierce indignation which lacerated the heart of Swift" (51.34–52.1). Both in Richard's unavailing speech about his mother, and in the vision of him as an escapist which lies at the core of Robert's newspaper article (128.28–129.12), it is nevertheless an impotent verbal ferocity capable of achieving only pain for others and wholly lacking Swift's creative energy.

Less directly associated with Swift, the phrase "*almost fiercely,*" which occurs twice in stage directions, forms an independent motif with a life of its own. Both occurrences are embedded in the intense dialogues of Act II, and both are used in association with the idea of freedom in love. First Richard speaks "*almost fiecely*" about the need to allow Bertha the possibility of personal development:

RICHARD
(turns towards him, almost fiercely) Not that fear. But that I will reproach myself then for having taken all for myself because I would not suffer her to give to another what was hers and not mine to give, because I accepted from her her loyalty and made her life poorer in love. That is my fear. That I stand between her and any moments of life that should be hers, between her and you, between her and anyone, between her and anything. I will not do it. I cannot and I will not. I dare not. (87.5–13)

Towards the end of the act, Robert adopts the same tone to pursue the subject to his own advantage:

ROBERT
(still more warmly) I am sure that no law made by man is sacred before the impulse of passion. *(almost fiercely)* Who made us for one only? It is a crime against our own being if we are so. There is no law before impulse. Laws are for slaves. Bertha, say my name! Let me hear your voice say it. Softly! (112.30–34)

While Robert's ferocity is applied as a melodramatic dramatization of his sensuality, Richard is trying to hold himself in check, to maintain control. Acutely aware of the danger and difficulty of words, he is oppressed by his heavy responsibility to use their power correctly or not at all. At times he seeks to be silent rather than to involve himself in unsatisfactory exchanges. When Bertha herself takes up his talk about emotional freedom, she challenges him "*hotly*" with "You love her." He *"throws out his hands with a sigh"* and responds: "Love! [...] I cannot argue with you" (67.5–9). When Richard is at his most human, is most like the others—when emotion gets the better of him and he relaxes his grip—he is able to use language most freely. At such times, however, he capitulates to the words which lie outside him, is unable to escape from the accents of the market place. When, by contrast, he is most aware of words, he is paradoxically reduced to silence, can generate nothing from within. We learn that he has written a book, but in his present phase he appears paralyzed, sterile, his control over language having been reduced to little more than the power to throttle it.

For the others, silence is a threat, a trap. As soon as Richard confronts Robert, in Act II, with his awareness of betrayal, Robert says: "Listen to me, Richard [...] Let me speak frankly, will you? Let me tell you everything" (74.21–2). When assured that Richard already knows everything, he takes up the motif of his approach to Bertha, saying that "a word," which had the power to start the train of events, could also have stopped it: "And you never spoke! You had only to speak a word—to save me from myself" (75.30–31). Now, at last, the word has been uttered: "I cannot tell you what a relief it is to me that you have spoken—that the danger is past [...] Because...there was some danger for you too [...] if you had not spoken" (77.15–22). Later in the act he makes a similar point to Bertha: "Why did you not stop me? You could have—with a word" (97.29–30). The motif appears for the last time in Act III when Richard contemplates the bitter possibility that freedom may entail separation. After Bertha has cursed the day that she met him, he says "I am in the way, is it? You would like to be free now. You have only to say the word" (134.28–29). In the next exchanges of this low-leveled quasi-marital dispute, there is irony at Richard's expense as Bertha repeats his taunt about her "lover," using the word in ways which he fails to recognize.

In a wry moment in Act II, Robert comments to Bertha: "We all confess to one another here. Turn about" (106.2–3). But it is rare for confession to flow freely. Early in the play, when interrogated by Richard about her awareness of her inspirational role, Beatrice says that she can respond only to direct inquiry: "I cannot say it. You yourself must ask me, Mr Rowan" (19.9–10). Invited thus to pursue his questioning, Richard attributes to Beatrice the same fear of uttering a word which has inhibited her cousin Robert: "Could not because

you dared not. Is that why?'' (19.18–19). Much later, discussing the
same subject with Bertha, he invites her to act as her own interrogator:
''You know why, Bertha. Ask yourself'' (95.8). Even when handing
the words over to others, Richard always assumes that he remains in
charge of them.

The repeated acts of confession, ''turn about,'' form one of the
ways in which the play exploits symmetry and inversion. Readily
apparent in the relationships of the principal characters and in the
a–b–a structure of the three acts, this architectural harmony is a
fundamental feature of the play's design. A cyclic pattern, establishing
an inverse relationship of beginning and end, was Joyce's norm. A
major shaping force in *Dubliners, A Portrait,* and *Ulysses,* it is also
dominant in *Exiles,* the last act of which may be seen as a shortened
mirror-image of Act I. Acts I and III both explore a daytime world
of social order, in contrast to the potential misrule of the night of
Act II. Although all three acts take place indoors, Act II, with its
garden, its rain, and its relatively remote location, offers a somewhat
sardonic parallel to the green-world experience at the center of much
Elizabethan comedy and romance. Like Act IV of *The Winter's Tale,*
Act II of *Exiles* is in a sense a dream: ''You dreamt that I was yours
last night'' (138.2–3). As we enter Act III, the sense of return to
reality is immediate, the contrast with the previous night being
unwittingly underlined by Brigid's question to the now exhausted
Bertha: ''Had you a bad dream that woke you?'' (115.23). The
pattern of return is developed not only through thematic parallels in
the dialogue, but also by recurrences of stage business, such as Bertha's
offering and being offered tea, and by incremental repetition of image
and motif. Recurrences in Act III of the language used in Act I are
often quite detailed. In the third speech of Act I, Brigid solicitously
asks Beatrice ''[. . .] Were you long in the train?'' (14.5), a question
echoed at the equivalent point in Act III, when she asks Bertha: ''Are
you long up?'' (115.19). In Act I she comments to Beatrice: ''You're
tired out, I'm sure'' (14.10), while in Act III she says to Bertha
''[. . .] you must be dead tired [. . .]'' (115.28). In her first speech
about Richard in Act I, Brigid says of him ''Up half the night he
does be'' (14.27), which, as soon as he is mentioned in Act III, she
echoes with ''[. . .] he does be in there [. . .] half the night at his
books'' (116.16–17). Most poignant of all is a growth in resonance
of the thematically important word ''back.'' First heard in the play's
opening speech—''Did you send word you were back, Miss Justice?''

(13.31–32)—it is soon repeated by Beatrice, whose life is little more than a long and hopeless waiting; "I can wait here till they come back if they are not long" (14.30–31). The tensions surrounding absence and return are hinted at a few moments later by Richard when he speaks of the two women in succession: "Bertha will be back any moment [. . .] I had begun to think you would never come back" (16.2–6). In Act III, however, Richard is the one who is emotionally absent, in voluntary exile, Sensing this, Brigid tries in vain to comfort Bertha: "Leave him alone. He'll come back to you again" (116.17–18). Although Richard professes to be unaware of his emotional distance, Bertha puts the matter plainly before him: "You left me: and I wanted for you to come back to me" (145.8). As we hear in the highly charged last lines of the play, she must nevertheless continue her vigil: "O, my strange wild lover come back to me again!" (147.18–19).

Important echoes bear on the theme of truth and falsehood. The Italian newspapers of which Brigid is faintly dismissive and which at first seem to be introduced merely to fill out Richard's adopted foreignness, serve as a valuable preparatory gloss on Robert's journalistic betrayal in Act III. Both are implicated in the language of disguise, a theme emphasized by the secretiveness inherent in Richard's keeping the domestic letterbox locked. The half-disguised quality of the attack in the leading article is entirely appropriate to Richard's personality. Although wishing to establish himself as the proponent of total openness and truthfulness, in contrast to the "liar, thief and [. . .] fool" (63.29) which he deems his friend to be, he is himself tortuous, evasive, and capable of outright lying. Although Bertha would not mean to be understood literally when making her anguished statement "Every word you say is false" (133.28–29), there is more truth in her criticism than Richard is willing to recognize. His fallibility as the custodian of language and honesty is clearly demonstrated when Act I closes, a few minutes after his outburst to Bertha, with the very painful little scene in which he lies to his son. Bertha leaves, reminding Richard that she "did not deceive" him (70.30) immediately after which Richard unashamedly deceives Archie:

ARCHIE
(quickly) Well, did you ask her?
RICHARD
(starting) What?

ARCHIE

Can I go?

RICHARD

Yes.

ARCHIE

In the morning? She said yes?

RICHARD

Yes. In the morning.
[*He puts his arm round his son's shoulders and looks down at him fondly*] (71.5–17)

Richard did not ask her.

Richard's evasiveness contaminates others. Unwilling to confront Robert in Act I, he invites Beatrice to lie on his behalf: "I cannot see him now. Say I have gone to the post" (26.9–10). In another context, this formal social excuse might well pass for relatively innocent; in the context of such intense care for nuances of meaning and honesty as permeates the world of *Exiles*, it can only be seen as culpable evasion, a denial by Richard of his primary role as truth-teller. Although Beatrice, who lives on the fringes of that world, is willing to cooperate with Richard's excuse (29.31–32), she is not seriously tainted by it. Bertha, on the other hand, suffers a nightmarish period during which she succumbs to it wholly. Parallel to Richard's lie in Act I is her panic-stricken response to the arrival of Beatrice in Act III: "Say I'm not up, that I'm not well [. . .] No, say I'm in [. . .] Say I've just got up" (120.7–19).

More important than straightforward lying is the pervasive uncertainty as to the relationship of appearance and reality, statement and intent. The tension is most clearly felt in the case of Robert, the conscious deceiver. The gap between the surface of his words and the thoughts that lie beneath is developed in a little motif coupling the words "saying" and "thinking." It first occurs in Act I, after his avowal of affection for Bertha, who wonders "if that is what you say—to the others" (35.29–30). Robert reassures her, after which she adds, rather cautiously, it seems: "Thank you for saying it—and thinking it" (36.17). Already made a little doubtful of Robert's sincerity (though his physical desire is real enough) we are given an open expression of the distinction between words and thoughts during the subsequent confrontation between Robert and Richard. Adopting a wholly theatrical style at a moment of great stress, Robert pauses, "*strikes his forehead with his hand*," and continues: "What am I saying? Or what am I thinking? I wish you would upbraid me, curse me, hate me as I deserve. You love this woman [...]" (78.26–28).

For Robert, the gap between saying and thinking appears briefly to close at the moment when he believes he has won Bertha. The moment is neatly signaled by his use of an endearment which is both caressive and possessive: Bertha says, with downcast eyes, "I too want to speak to you," to which he responds *"tenderly,"* with the phrase "Yes, dear, I know" (41.21–23). That he does not in fact "know," is almost immediately indicated by a painful and ludicrous blunder:

> ROBERT
>
> *(tenderly)* Yes, dear, I know. *(he kisses her again)* I will speak to you, tell you all then. I will kiss you then, long long kisses—when you come to me—long long sweet kisses.
>
> BERTHA
>
> Where?
>
> ROBERT
>
> *(in the tone of passion)* Your eyes. Your lips. All your divine body.
>
> BERTHA
>
> *(repelling his embrace, confused)* I meant where do you wish me to come. (41.22–33)

The irony attaching here to the inadequacy of Robert's knowledge of human responses casts an interesting and cautionary light on the scene between Richard and Bertha which follows soon afterwards. Richard is guilty of a similarly ludicrous if less painful misunderstanding:

> BERTHA
>
> He asked me to give him my hand.
>
> RICHARD
>
> *(smiling)* In marriage?
>
> BERTHA
>
> *(smiling)* No, only to hold. (58.20–25)

In the middle of his inquisition about Robert's physical behavior, Richard reveals himself more seriously when he twice asserts his control of the whole situation in a tone of emotional arrogance:

> BERTHA
>
> [...]   *(she breaks off suddenly)*
> Tell me, Dick, does all this disturb you? Because I told you I don't want that. I think you are only pretending you don't mind. I don't mind.

RICHARD

(quietly) I know, dear. But I want to find out what he means
or feels just as you do.

BERTHA

(points at him) Remember you allowed me to go on. I told you
the whole thing from the beginning.

RICHARD

(as before) I know, dear...And then? (59.15–27)

There is little to choose, it seems, between Robert's and Richard's
knowledge of Bertha.

Among the most resonant motifs in the play is the reason
offered by Beatrice for her visit to Richard's house: "Otherwise I
could not see you" (18.8). At first an apparently straightforward
statement of fact, it acquires a mysterious quality through repetition
and modulation.[2] Immediately after she has first uttered it, Richard
repeats the phrase, "*uncertainly.*" Thrown into confusion by Richard's
attention to her words, Beatrice threatens to leave but is persuaded
to stay and to listen to Richard's comments on his literary relationship
with her. At the approximately equivalent point in Act III, Richard
again repeats the phrase, this time attributing it to malevolent
demons:

RICHARD

(stands in the doorway, observing her for some moments) There
are demons *(he points out toward the strand)* out there. I heard
them jabbering since dawn.

BEATRICE

(starts to her feet) Mr Rowan!

RICHARD

I assure you. The isle is full of noises. Yours also. *Otherwise I
could not see you,* it said. And her voice. And his voice. But,
I assure you they are all demons. I made the sign of the cross
upside down and that silenced them. (127.27–128.5)

Inability to see is an important theme. "I cannot see him
now," says Richard of Robert (26.9–10); "I cannot see her now,"
says Robert of Bertha (91.6); "I can't see anyone," says Bertha,
tired and in distress (120.8). Physically unable to see Robert in Act
II, Bertha experiences a moment of undefined panic—"I feared
something. I am not sure what" (102.26–27)—from which she feels
secure only when Robert reappears: "O, now you are here. I can
see you. Now it has passed" (102.31). But it is Richard's raising of
the motif to an almost metaphysical level by his parable of the
demons which most firmly establishes the failure of people to see

each other clearly. The demons on the strand, impersonating "the voices of those who say they love me" (142.12–13), tell Richard to despair. Although he refuses to do so, silencing the demons by the use of their own symbolic weapons, he himself has chosen to avoid what the inhabitants of the everyday world consider immediacy and clarity of focus. Out of touch with Bertha, he gazes at her *"as if to an absent person"* (147.4). In the final words of the play, Bertha, unseen, unable to penetrate Richard's mask, *"closes her eyes" (147.20).*

Reflecting the self-conscious role-playing of many of the characters, an appropriate degree of theatricality pervades the stage directions. Indeed, the actors are guided by so many stagy adverbs—*"darkly," "moodily," "earnestly," "desperately," "bitterly"*—that readers have sometimes wondered whether *Exiles* should not after all be played as burlesque. While many of the directions have to do with physical action—*"half closing her eyes"* (21.24)—or are directly expressive of manner—*"intensely"*—others exhibit an interesting interplay of language, personality, and implicit authorial comment. A simple example is found in the description of Brigid's first action in Act III: *"she halts suddenly and blesses herself instinctively"* (115.11). Fresh from writing *A Portrait,* Joyce well knew the meaning of "instinctively." Indeed, still with a trace of the Uncle Charles Principle but this time applied more correctly, the word is used again later in the act, in relation to Beatrice: "[. . .] *instinctively*) It is true then!" (127.20). Prone to appeal for sympathy because of his "fight," his "struggle," Richard is twice described as *"struggling with himself"* (87.34, 95.27). Apparently nurtured, like others of Joyce's women, on the naive style of magazine stories, Bertha *"tosses"* her head, *"flings"* a slip of paper on to the couch, gestures *"impulsively."* Robert, who fears the "torture" of an emotional trap, and who sentimentally describes Richard as "torturing" himself, adopts a *"tortured expression."*

Interesting distinctions may also be seen in the longer, more descriptive stage directions. Beatrice is introduced on the first page with grace of language and clarity of focus: "BEATRICE JUSTICE is a slender dark young woman of twentyseven years" (13.25–26). This contrasts both in rhythmic quality and precision of statement with the clumsy description of Robert: "ROBERT HAND is a middlesized rather stout man between thirty and forty" (26.24). We learn still less about Richard's age, but once again the prose, assured and

fluent, is expressive of character: "He is a tall athletic young man
of a rather lazy carriage" (15.4–5). Of Bertha also, introduced in
simple, pleasing rhythms, we learn that she is "young," but her
age is left imprecise: "BERTHA *is a young woman of graceful build.*
She has dark grey eyes, patient in expression, and soft features"
(30.10–11).[3] Although relatively unassertive, the language of the stage
directions is by no means featureless. As in the case of the dialogue,
much of the meaning arises from echo and antithesis.

Only once, at the beginning of Act II, is there any significant
period of dumb show. Joyce takes the opportunity to tune his prose
to the curious blend of lumpiness and high color which characterizes
Robert:

> [ROBERT HAND, *in evening dress, is seated at the piano. The*
> *candles are not lit but the lamp on the table is lit. He plays*
> *softly in the bass the first bars of Wolfram's song in the last*
> *act of* Tannhäuser. *Then he breaks off and, resting an elbow*
> *on the ledge of the keyboard, meditates. Then he rises and,*
> *pulling out a pump from behind the piano, walks here and*
> *there in the room ejecting from it into the air sprays of perfume.*
> *He inhales the air slowly and then puts the pump back behind*
> *the piano. He sits down on a chair near the table and, smoothing*
> *his hair carefully, sighs once or twice. Then, thrusting his hands*
> *into his trousers pockets, he leans back, stretches out his legs*
> *and waits.*
> *A knock is heard at the street door.. He rises quickly]* (72.16–27)

It is entirely appropriate if at this stage the audience is, as Mr Kenner
suggests, "helpless with laughter" (25). But the farce coexists with
seriousness and pain. Deaf to rhythmic and other subtleties, Robert
assuredly does not realize how much irony he addresses to himself
by evoking the strenuous clash of sacred and profane loves in
Tannhäuser.[4] Nor is it for nothing that in the verbal model of
Robert's movements on stage the word "then" should appear so
often. Marking off the successive phases of his preparations with a
heavy, unsubtle narrative hand, the word is an echo of Richard's
insistent questioning of Bertha toward the end of Act I: four times
Richard asks "And then?" urging her to continue her anatomy of
the wooing. Even in performance, Robert's step by step arrangement
of the scene in his love nest may remind us of the tone of the
previous analysis. The pattern of repeated "then," expressive of
Robert's manipulative approach to life, turns up again, and for the

last time, in the "story [...] not very nice" (141.9), which he tells of his night out with "the divorced wife of a barrister." Joyce's sensitivity to the word is further shown by his having deleted it from the last stage direction of Act I, which originally read "[He puts his arm round his son's shoulders, and then looks down at him fondly]" (MacNicholas 1979:66, 91). Rendering Richard's movements less consecutive, less mechanical, the change softens the tone, increases the sentiment, and further distinguishes the relationship of father and son from that of father and mistress.

Do people really go on in that embarrassingly flamboyant way? Considering each scene in isolation and without reference to the distancing effect of the artistic context, many might be prepared to agree that the personal encounters dramatize something not far from everyday truth. But the interest of *Exiles* lies neither in the realism of the action nor in the psychology of the characters, expressed in language which is by turns stiff, overlush, trite, or muted to extinction. It lies, rather, in the curious blending of a serious plot about freedom and bondage, creativity and sterility, with a gamut of language which explores, without, as it were, sparing the characters' feelings, how to talk about it all, how not to talk about it, how to engage with each other, how to make a mess of personal relationships. Selecting, juxtaposing, counterpointing the registers, an "arranger" makes the play as much an artifact as a slice of other people's lives. The distancing created by that comparative linguistic exercise allows the work, however painful it may sometimes seem, to be perceived as essentially comic. As in *Ulysses*, the comedy collaborates with rather than attenuates the seriousness of the thematic content.

Living inside this subtle verbal framework, the characters of the play are isolated as much by words and silence as by their personal circumstances. For much of the time Beatrice is almost unable to speak; Bertha's prelapsarian simplicity of language fails to connect with the complex world into which she has been drawn; Robert's ready-made narrative glibness gives him only the illusion of communication. Richard's many-sided difficulty is in a sense a superfluity of communication. Only partly aware of his own tendency to degrade language by histrionics and cliché, he acts as though he were the sole custodian of words, often using them in attempts to mold others to his liking. He admonishes Bertha: "do not say things you will be sorry for" (65.5–6), and his first reaction to the news of Robert's latest sexual advances is to "Tell him [...] A few words will do"

(64.4–5). In cringing support of Richard's self-assessment, Robert twice alludes to Bertha as if she were one of Richard's verbal creations: "She is yours, your work" (78.29); "You have made her all that she is" (84.21–22). In similar vein, Richard speaks of himself as a godlike artist, pre-existent, unchanging: "I did not make myself. I am what I am" (133.24). Asserting his authority over the power of words, he poses as if he may utter when he pleases, be silent when he pleases. Others suffer accordingly. But while enjoying his position of power, Richard also suffers. Sensing, with half-justified arrogance, that everyone else looks to him for guidance and strength, he seeks a means of escape from the unwelcome role of a fallible god whose creatures appear to lack free will. By urging on Robert and Bertha the freedom to act, he arranges for himself the gap between words and truth which troubles all the others but which he sees as a necessary condition of liberation for the artist. In place of the physical wound in which Thomas found assurance, Richard seeks an intangible wound of doubt in the soul, a wound which, unlike that of Amfortas, will never be healed: "You will tell me. But I will never know" (133.8); "Yes, yes. The truth! But I will never know, I tell you" (133.13–14). Richard's last self-imposed exile is from the certainty of language.

NOTES

1. Page/line references in parentheses are to the edition of *Exiles* published by Penguin Books, Harmondsworth and New York, 1977, corrected in accordance with the information supplied by MacNicholas (1979). Suspension points within brackets are my own; others are authorial. I do not deal with Joyce's notes to the play, nor with the fragments reproduced in MacNicholas. I am grateful to Simon Evans for many useful comments on an early draft of this essay.

2. Cf. its appearance in *GJ*:
"Why?"
"Because otherwise I could not see you."
Sliding—space—ages—foliage of stars—and waning heaven—stillness—and stillness deeper—stillness of annihilation—and her voice (16).

3. In Joyce's notes to the play her age is given as 28 (148.13).

4. For further discussion of the relevance of Wagner, see MacNicholas (1975).

WORKS CITED

Bauerle, Ruth. *A Word List to Joyce's* Exiles. New York: Garland, 1981.
Kenner, Hugh. *Joyce's Voices.* London: Faber & Faber, 1978.
MacNicholas, John. "Joyce contra Wagner." *Comparative Drama* 9 (1975): 29–43.
———. *A Textual Companion to James Joyce's* Exiles. New York: Garland, 1979.

8

And the Music Goes Round and Round: A Couple of New Approaches to Joyce's Uses of Music in *Ulysses*

ZACK BOWEN

Musical scholars continue to seek out additional song references, operatic motifs, and musical parallels to the structure of individual episodes and scenes from Joyce's great Bloomusalem in song. Just when we think we've located them all, more come along, with new methods of interpretation, new applications of fugal structure, new references to popular songs long forgotten. But while the identification of songs and motifs is important, it does not tell the whole story of Joyce's genius in interweaving music into the text of his fabulous voyage.

I would like to consider in this paper two examples of ways Joyce used music differently from any other writer before or since, ways which, unless the reader were a professional singer familiar with the history of music theory, would normally escape comment or seem to be of little special significance.

I deliberately chose the first example from the "Sirens" episode, and the second from "Circe." "Sirens" is transitional from the earlier, realistic section of the novel to the book's latter half, with its concentration on language and linguistic variation. "Circe," while squarely in the second category, is largely recapitulatory, seeking new ways to represent motifs already established in the novel. It draws much of its material from earlier episodes, but transforms and transmutes earlier situations and language, combining seemingly disparate characters and events into interchangeable, if amorphous, new entities.

For the first example, try to put yourself into the position of aging singers, whose professional performances have largely evolved into amusements for drinking buddies—singers who no longer practice continually in preparation for concerts, operas, or oratorios, but who maintain a repertoire of old favorites, accompanying themselves on the piano when there is no professional accompanist handy, and in the process generally seeking to entertain rather than impress their friends. On occasion they may be capable of the glories their voices could once command, but they don't want to take too many risks to prove that they can still do it. Mix into your scenario an old musical purist like Father Cowley, who knows how the music should be performed and what the singers were once capable of vocally accomplishing. The result is so realistic it hurts.

Simon Dedalus, Ben Dollard, and Father Cowley are performing on a stage in the back of the Ormond bar while Bloom sits eating liver and bacon in an adjoining room.

> Over their voices Dollard bassooneed attack, booming over bombarding chords:
> —*When love absorbs my ardent soul...*
> Roll of Bensoulbenjamin rolled to the quivery loveshivery roof-panes.
> —War! War! cried Father Cowley. You're the warrier.
> —So I am, Ben Warrior laughed....
> —Sure, you'd burst the tympanum of her ear, man, Mr Dedalus said through the smoke aroma, with an organ like yours.
> In bearded abundant laughter Dollard shook upon the keyboard. He would.
> —Not to mention another membrane, Father Cowley added. Half time, Ben. *Amoroso ma non troppo.* Let me there. (*U* 270)

In reading the passage one might think that Dollard merely belts out every song that he sings, but we are to learn later that is certainly not the case in his rendition of the "Croppy Boy," when his tender and modulated tones nearly provoke his audience to tears. What Joyce does not say is that the song Ben is singing is a duet for tenor and bass. The tenor line, "When love absorbs my ardent soul," is a fourth higher than its counterpart melody, "When War absorbs my ardent soul," sung by the bass. Father Cowley, correcting Ben, cries "War! War! You're the Warrior." But that still doesn't explain why Dollard was singing so loudly. Joyce, an experienced singer, knew that when basses are called upon to sing in their top register, in this case up to a high G, they often are able to sing the higher notes only by increasing their volume. Cowley, who has been dying to play, takes Ben's seat at the piano, either to transpose the key downward so that Ben can sing the lover-tenor part in a normal voice, or to continue the accompaniment as Dollard starts to sing the bass part. But a transposition of key, if Dollard were singing the bass solo line, would take him down to a low E. We don't know whether Dollard in fact switched to the bass line, because the words "when (love or war) absorbs" are replaced by an ellipsis in the text. But the supposition is that he was singing the warrior's (bass) part because the music stopped so abruptly, presumably at the place where the bass and the tenor join and the bass is forced to sing harmony to the tenor melody line. Had Ben been singing the tenor line he could have finished the song.

Bloom, who is sitting in the next room, can tell by the touch on the keys that Cowley is playing and is surprised by the abrupt cessation of the music. Ben, corrected by Cowley, is forced to give up both piano stool and musical choice to his ungrateful but accurate accompanist, as Cowley resumes playing another unnamed song, and presumably asks Simon Dedalus, a tenor, for a rendition of *"M'appari."* It is only natural that Ben Dollard, the bass, whose belongings in tight trousers underscore his manliness, should be a little chagrined at having to yield the stage to his tenor counterpart, Simon. While Joyce doesn't explicitly say this, Dollard's growl, "Go on blast you. Get it out in bits," assumes what Joyce as a singer and performer well knew, the perennial sensitivity and even occasional jealousy among singers who on the surface seem the closest of friends. Simon, however, is not the professional musician that Dollard is, despite a tenor voice which we will learn is capable of genuine brilliance. Cowley, the musician, wants to hear *"M'appari"* in Italian, but Simon will sing it in English. Cowley momentarily abandons the piano stool to sing a brief version of *"M'appari"* to a girl painted on a seascape which hangs behind the stage. Then Simon, a bit reluctantly and apologetically, looks to Dollard, who has been offended and slightly miffed, for approbation, and when Dollard's mood changes Simon sits down at the piano.

> —Go on, Simon.
> —Ah, sure my dancing days are done, Ben... Well...
> Mr. Dedalus laid his pipe to rest beside the tuningfork and, sitting, touched the obedient keys. (*U* 271)

It is a Joycean irony that while Dedalus earlier sounded the tuningfork to check the piano's pitch, he now sits down to play the song, not in F major, the original key, but transposed, probably down to D. In other words, he does not have the requisite confidence that he will be able to hit the high B flat called for at the end of the song, and so wants to transpose the song downward a minor third. He has evidently been taking it easy on himself for a number of

years, because he seems to remember how to play the song only in
the lower key, and when Cowley, who has already ruined Dollard's
performance, insists that Simon put the song back in the original,
Simon has forgotten how to play it.

> No, Simon, Father Cowley turned. Play it in the original.
> One flat.
> The keys, obedient, rose higher, told, faltered, confessed,
> confused. (*U* 271–72)

The confession of the errant keys is that Simon would have been
happy to settle for less than a brilliant performance in the habitually
lower key of recent past performances, but that the old musical pedant
and perfectionist, Father Cowley, will not let him get away with it.
"Here, Simon. I'll accompany you, he said. Get up" (*U* 272). And
so, a magnificent performance of "*M'appari*," an aria that relates
Lionel's plight over his lost love to Bloom's four o'clock cuckoldry
predicament, is rendered by Simon. It is "Heard from a person
wouldn't expect it in the least" (*U* 274), who at the end of the song
becomes *Siopold*, a combination of Simon, Lionel and Leopold. Thus
does Joyce take trivial realistic musical details and weave them into a
delicate but exceptionally realistic drama of musical performance and
musical sensibilities.

The second example, like "Circe" itself, is both transformative
and recapitulatory, as well as considerably more complicated. Instead
of simple song references, Joyce uses harmonics, Greek modes, and
musicology as well as direct references to several musical works to
develop what is perhaps the primary motif of the entire novel: the
transformation process, with its attendant variations on language,
characters, and themes.

When Bloom, still in front of Bella Cohen's, hears Stephen
playing Benedetto Marcello's psalms on the piano inside, he makes
the same shrewd sort of guess he did when he identified Father
Cowley by his touch earlier in the Ormand. "A man's touch. Sad
music. Church music. Perhaps here" (475). Zoe, who greets him on
the street, is identified as Jewish by singing "I am black yet comely,
O ye daughters of Jerusalem" from "The Song of Songs." Her suspect
Semitic origins are not so much at issue here as the ancient Jewish
chant. Marcello (1686–1739) set the psalms to melodies patterned
after ancient Hebrew musical settings for the poetry, acting on the
assumption that these compositions were closest to the tonal patterns
of the Greeks.

This brings us around to harmonics and Greek modes based on the mathematical relations of string vibrations, or nodes. It is pointless to recapitulate here Edmund Epstein's brilliant explication of Stephen's speech about the hyperphrygian and mixolydian modes (*JJQ* 6, 1968, 83–86) except to say that Marcello transformed the Greeks' musical worship of Demeter and Ceres, through an emulation of Jewish religious music, into Roman Catholic ecclesiasticism. This is what Stephen means when he refers to ''texts so divergent as priests haihooping round David's that is Circe's or what am I saying Ceres' altar and David's tip from the stable to his chief bassoonist about his almightiness'' (504).

As Tindall has pointed out so many years ago (*James Joyce*, pp. 31–32), we are led to the observation that all religions, characters, and situations converge. ''Jewgreek is greekjew. Extremes meet'' (504). As Epstein points out, Stephen's subsequent observations on musical intervals and the relation of dominant to tonic in terms of their reconciliation in the octave form a harmonic analogy to the diverse religious music sources of Marcello's composition, and set the stage for the commonality between Stephen and Bloom. When Stephen turns and sees Bloom, whom we have earlier in Cyclops seen as a Christ figure, Bloom's entrance is associated with the Antichrist; and his fundamental unity with Stephen, whose Christlike and Satanic credentials have already been verified, is established. Epstein and I have long shared Tindall's theory of the commonality of characters in *Ulysses*.

There is still another melody to be played at the transformative concert, however. It concerns the idea of the messianic-prophetic figure who will lead the Irish people out of their bondage. Stephen has seen himself in that light ever since the concluding passages of *Portrait*, and Bloom has been cast into the role of prophet-messiah repeatedly in earlier episodes. In Circe, however, hints become concrete images, as Bloom's messianic turn comes. The conversation between Bloom and Zoe on Bella's doorstep, in which Semitism has played a considerable role, gives way to Bloom's utopian visions of himself as politician-soldier-statesman-savior of Ireland, who promises ''the new Bloomusalem in the Nova Hibernia of the future'' (484). Just as Stephen later tries to apply musical composition to the problem of interchangeable identities, an appropriate musical accompaniment is heard blending harmonics with a song about transformation. The speeches about harmonics which follow act as a unifying

agent for both Marcello's blend of religions and the interchangeability
of Bloom and Stephen as messiah figures:

> STEPHEN
>   Here's another for you. *(He frowns.)* The reason is because
> the fundamental and the dominant are separated by the greatest
> possible interval which. . .
> THE CAP
> Which? Finish. You can't.
> STEPHEN
>   *(With an effort)* Interval which. Is the greatest possible
> ellipse. Consistent with. The ultimate return. The octave. Which.
> THE CAP
> Which?
>   *(Outside the gramophone begins to blare* The Holy City.)
> (504)

Thus to harmonic transformations Joyce adds the transformational message of the song popularly known as ''Jerusalem'' because
of the name reiterated so often in the chorus. Bloom's ''new
Bloomusalem'' is a Joycean distortion of the refrain of the song,
which only now appears. We have not heard the last strains of this
particular melody, and neither has Stephen, who, caught up in
delineating the very thesis of interchangeability or consubstantiality
or transformation, calls the musical theme which embodies his concept
a ''noise in the street'':

> STEPHEN
>   *(Abruptly.)* What went forth to the ends of the world to
> traverse not itself. God, the sun, Shakespeare, a commercial
> traveller, having itself traversed in reality itself, becomes that
> self. Wait a moment. Wait a second. Damn that fellow's noise
> in the street. Self which it itself was ineluctably preconditioned
> to become. *Ecco!*

Bloom enters to the triumphal strains of the refrain of ''The Holy
City.''

> THE GRAMOPHONE
> Jerusalem!
> Open your gates and sing
> Hosanna. . . (507)

The meaning of the song's text was long since discussed in my
musical allusions book. For our purposes here, however, it should
be noted that the song is about a twofold transformation of the city
as it transpires in the dream of the singer. In the first dream vision

the city is alive with the voices of children and antiphonal angels singing "Jerusalem," etc. The scene shifts and the voices are quieted in the darkened city under the shadow of a cross. The third stanza envisions a regenerated egalitarian Jerusalem where all might enter, the prototype of Bloom's new Bloomusalem.

If Stephen fails to grasp the significance of the music with its transformational utopia, Joyce is not about to let the reader do the same thing. The next voice we hear is that of (Ben Bloom) Elijah, identified at the conclusion of the "Cyclops" episode, and transformed during the course of his "Circe" speech into A. J. Christ Dowie, whose ringing message concluded the "Oxen of the Sun" chapter. Ben Bloom Elijah A. J. Christ Dowie's inspirational message is that the entire company are consubstantial or interchangeable with the Son of God himself:

ELIJAH

...Just one word more. Are you a god or a doggone clod? If the second advent came to Coney Island are we ready? Florry Christ, Stephen Christ, Zoe Christ, Bloom Christ, Kitty Christ, Lynch Christ, it's up to you to sense that cosmic force. Have we cold feet about the cosmos? No. Be on the side of the angels. Be a prism. You have that something within, the higher self. You can rub shoulders with a Jesus, a Gautama, an Ingersol. Are you all in this vibration? (508)

Dowie does not let us forget that the entire metamorphosis is essentially musical in nature:

It vibrates. I know and I am some vibrator. Joking apart and getting down to bedrock, A. J. Christ Dowie and the harmonial philosophy, have you got that? ...Now then our glory song. All join heartily in the singing. Encore! *(He sings.)* Jeru...

THE GRAMOPHONE

(Drowning his voice.) Whorusalaminyourhighhohhh...
(508)

If the characters are interchangeable with God, they also inhabit the bodies and abodes of whores. The first last and the last first, according to the classless society of the new Jerusalem.

One final word. If Dowie's pronouncement is definitive here, it is no wonder that Joyce uses him to conclude the coda to Oxen. The narrative parodies are fairly chronological throughout the episode, but when we come to the concluding pages, most often described by critics as a modern polyglot, it is Dowie who restores understand-

ability to the conclusion in the verbiage of an evangelical cough mixture salesman. Now we know that the elixir is the harmonial philosophy; and it's got a punch in it for you, my friend. Just you try it on!

WORKS CITED

Bowen, Zack. *Musical Allusions in the Works of James Joyce: Early Poetry through* Ulysses. Albany: State University of New York Press, 1974.

Epstein, Edmund. "King David and Benedetto Marcello in the Works of James Joyce." *James Joyce Quarterly* 6 (1968): 83–86.

Tindall, William York. *James Joyce: His Way of Interpreting the Modern World.* New York: Charles Scribner's Sons, 1950.

9

"Roll Away the Reel World, the Reel World": "Circe" and Cinema

AUSTIN BRIGGS

Although casual references to cinematic qualities in Joyce's work are commonplace and although extended discussions of Joyce and the cinema have appeared, significant affinities between "Circe" and film have remained largely unnoted.[1] I will discuss those affinities and along the way will describe a moving picture show that Bloom once saw.

Even in his teens Joyce demonstrated an interest in projections upon screens. Among his earliest efforts at fiction that we know of are the "Silhouettes" he composed at Belvedere College. In the one recalled by Stanislaus, the narrator stands in a dark street before "a lowered window blind illuminated from within" (*JJII* 50). He watches the action projected on this blind (the artist who will follow Homer is already playing with sight and sightlessness) as a burly male figure staggers and then strikes the figure of a woman.

In the "Ithaca" episode of *Ulysses,* Stephen and Bloom stand in the dark looking at a different window, at a "visible, splendid sign" cast by a "paraffin oil lamp...projected on a screen of roller blind supplied by Frank O'Hara, window blind, curtain pole and revolving shutter manufacturer" (*U-G* 1547.1173–76). A lamp, a screen, and a revolving shutter, of course, put us well on the way to cinema.

As has long been recognized, we find references to cinema throughout the *Wake*—including the inevitable *real/reel* pun in my title (*FW* 64.25–26)—and more than once we encounter what Andrew Sarris would call "the primal screen." In the cinematic dumbshow of Book III, for example, "the man on the street can foresee the coming event" of the Earwickers in their bedroom, "casting such shadows to Persia's blind" that their intimacy is "photoflashing... far too wide" (*FW* 583.14–16).

145

There is no historical impediment to Leopold Bloom's viewing a film in *Ulysses*. Although Ireland's first movie theater, Joyce's Cinematograph Volta, did not open until shortly before Christmas, 1909, films were shown from time to time after April 1896 in such Dublin locations as the Erin Variety Theater and the Rotunda (Werner 135, n. 6). Among the films that Bloom could have seen on or around Bloomsday was the most famous production of 1903, Edwin S. Porter's *The Great Train Robbery*; more to his tastes, however, would have been another work by Porter of the same year, *Gay Shoe Clerk,* a film remembered for its close-up of a woman's ankle and foot (Fell 36).

In ''Nausicaa,'' we are told of one and possibly two or even three moving pictures that Bloom actually has seen. Soon after Gerty MacDowell limps away, Bloom muses as follows:

> A dream of wellfilled hose. Where was that? Ah, yes. Mutoscope pictures in Capel street: for men only. Peeping Tom. Willie's hat and what the girls did with it. Do they snapshot those girls or is it all a fake? (*U-G* 793.793-96)

Was there a movie titled ''A Dream of Wellfilled Hose,'' or is Bloom remembering something like *Gay Shoe Clerk*? (''Love's young dream'' for Bloom, we recall, was to be a shoefitter and ''lace up... the dressy kid footwear satinlined, so incredibly impossibly small of Clyde Road ladies'' [*U-G* 1149.2815-17].) Or is Bloom recalling a more direct experience, like the stylish woman he gazed at in ''Lotus Eaters''? A tram deprived him of his glimpse of ''silk flash rich stockings white'' and left him with ''flicker, flicker: the laceflare of her hat in the sun: flicker flick'' (*U-G* 149.130, 139-40).

''Flickers'' or ''flicks'' are names for moving pictures, of course, reflecting the uneven shutter speed of early projection apparatus. When he visited the Capel Street parlor sometime after the Mutoscopes were introduced in 1895, though the machines required no shutter, Bloom would have seen flicker aplenty, for the illusion of movement was produced by the ''flickerbook principle.'' ''The peephole machine,'' we read in Gerald Mast's *Short History of the Movies*, used

> large photographs mounted on individual cards. The viewer flipped a series of cards with a hand crank....The hand crank added to the viewer's pleasure by allowing the motion to go either forward or back, to go slower, faster, or stop altogether. (25-26)[2]

Given Bloom's masturbation in "Nausicaa," one sees the appropriateness here. Hand crank indeed! And in Bloomian—or Wakean—Latin, "mutoscope" gives us "dumbshow," the silent language we have just seen eloquently demonstrated between Gerty and Bloom. In "Circe," Stephen declares his quest for a "universal language" of gesture (*U-G* 933.105–06); as Eisenstein recognized when he quoted Stephen's remark for the epigraph to his 1932 essay "A Course in Treatment" (84), that quest was realized in the cinema as never before.

Impatient, Bloom could have cranked the Mutoscope faster; or to extend the experience, he could have turned more slowly, a procedure that would have increased the flicker produced by the dark intervals between the photographic images. Had Bloom viewed a film on a screen in some rented hall, he might also have seen the pace and even the direction of time altered, for Cecil Hepworth recalled how as an itinerant showman he amused audiences by turning his hand-cranked projector faster, slower, and in reverse, and by stopping films entirely to freeze actors in particularly awkward positions (37).

Even without playful showmen, early projection machinery was likely to produce tricks of its own; the English "scenics" he projected with his primitive apparatus, Hepworth said, were often so unsteady that "thus the Scriptures were fulfilled, and the mountains skipped about like young rams" (38). It is worth noting that the novelty of the medium, the whimsy of the showman, and mechanical problems in filming and projecting all conspired to make early cinema inherently self-reflexive to its audience.

One looked at the Mutoscope peepshow through a little eyepiece, but the reference to "Peeping Tom" in "Nausicaa" may refer not only to Bloom's voyeurism on the beach and in the Capel Street parlor but also to a Mutoscope production, for there was a 1901 film *Peeping Tom* made by George W. Smith.[3] I do not know what this Peeping Tom saw, but Smith, who has been described as a "pioneer in the matter of sex," was also the creator of the 1899 *The Kiss in the Tunnel* and the 1900 *Things Seen Through a Telescope* (Shipman 23). The things seen through Smith's telescope include "a couple embracing and a woman undressing," reminding us, perhaps, that the twelve naked plaster sisters who make up the nine new muses of the New Bloomusalem include in their uncertain number "Astronomy for the People" (*U-G* 1063.1710).

Less conjectural than "Peeping Tom" and "a dream of wellfilled hose" is "Willie's hat and what the girls did with it." As George C. Pratt notes in his invaluable *Spellbound in Darkness,* the *Willie's Hat* that Bloom recalls was an 1897 release of the American Mutoscope-Biograph Company (18).[4] Apparently considering the film too spicy for their regular catalogue, AM&B carried it only on their special "Club List." The film must have been in demand, for five years later, the company applied for a U.S. copyright in the only way possible at the time, by registering a so-called paper print, a series of still photographs of the entire film.

The entry on *Willie's Hat* in the catalogue of the paper print collection in the Library of Congress describes what Bloom saw:

> In a drawing room, four young women are frolicking about. There is a silk hat on the table and one of the young women picks it up and holds it above her head, while the remaining three girls attempt to reach the hat by kicking high over their heads. One of them apparently overextends herself for she falls over, landing flat on her back as the film ends. (Niver 367)

The film plays off nicely against Gerty's reflections on Cissy Caffrey's running: "It would have served her right if she had tripped over something accidentally on purpose...and got a fine tumble. *Tableau!* That would have been a very charming exposé for a gentleman to witness" (*U-G* 773.484–88). The action of *Willie's Hat,* moreover, provides added appropriateness to Gerty's identification with women in "pictures cut out of papers of those skirtdancers and highkickers" (*U-G* 787.703–04), and to her "wondrous revealment half offered like those skirtdancers behaving so immodest before gentlemen looking" (*U-G* 789.731–33).

When Bloom recalls *Willie's Hat,* our text has him asking himself, "Do they snapshot those girls or is it all a fake?" (*U-G* 793.795–96)[5] Earlier, Joyce wrote, "Do they snapshot those girls or is it imagination of some fellow?" (*U-G* 792.9). This is essentially the question readers ask themselves as they try to understand "Circe." What "really happens" and what is "the imagination of some fellow"?

The answer, of course, is that everything in "Circe" must be granted equal authenticity. So, too, cinema claims the same reality for everything it shows. As René Clair says, it "tends to present an action exactly as it would have been had it really taken place and had been photographed" (quoted in Barsacq 7). The effect is quite that of the archetypal sequence of the wall being demolished in the Lumière First Program as it was run forward and backward. First we see workmen tug and strike at the wall until it comes down; then the wall rises up and reconstructs itself out of rubble. The law of gravity is demonstrated in the first sequence and repealed in the second, yet the ontological authority of each occurrence is unimpeachable.

As has long been recognized, the pantomime is a prime source for *Ulysses* and *Finnegans Wake* (on the very first page of *Ulysses*, Buck's "whistle of call" to transubstantiate lather into Christine body may echo a cue for a panto transformation).[6] Especially in the theatrical "*Circe*"—with all of its costume changes and sound effects, and its sets and characters that appear and disappear and metamorphose—the pantomime is near at hand (Herr 158–61). Like many other popular arts, however, pantomime went directly into the cinema; and cinema—child of the Phantasmagoria and the Magick Lantern (and the Daedaleum, later patented as the Zoetrope [Fell 9])—is even more suggestive than is pantomime of the technic of "*Circe*," Hallucination, and the art of "*Circe*," Magic.

For all its ingenuity, the stage machinery of traps and flaps and pulleys cannot begin to duplicate the instantaneous appearances, disappearances, and transformations of cinema. Nor, Edward La Valley points out, can the panto stage engage us in the way the screen does by confirming our sense of a realistic spatial and temporal continuity in the very act of producing the impossible (147–48). From the day of Méliès to the present, we almost reflexively speak of film "magic," whether in the somber existentialism of Bergman or the witty fantasy of Fellini or the dreary effects cranked out for Steven Spielberg by Industrial Light and Magic.

Vachel Lindsay's pioneering 1915 *The Art of the Moving Picture* conveys what movies must have looked like to first-generation film-goers like Joyce. In terms that repeatedly evoke "*Circe*," Lindsay discusses the "Hallowe'en witch-power" of cinema. He argues that our natural "yearning for personality in furniture" is wonderfully gratified in cinema (61). We recall the buttons that bip and the gas jets that speak in "*Circe*," and we recall as well the description of Shem as the man "writing the mystery of himsel [*sic*] in furniture" (*FW* 184.9–10).

"It is a quality...of all photoplays," Lindsay says, "that human beings tend to become dolls and mechanisms, and dolls and mechanisms tend to become human" (53). Note how quickly, he continues, "the borderline between All Saints' Day and Hallowe'en can be crossed. Note how easily memories are called up and appear in the midst of the room. In any [photo]play whatever, you will find these apparitions and recollections" (65).

In "Circe," the Art designated by Joyce in the Linati schema as *Visione animata fino allo scoppio*—which Ellmann translates "Vision animated to the bursting point" (Appendix)—jumps and jerks and flickers through its astonishing transformations and wonders with time in a fashion analogous to the cinema. It is as magical as film first seemed to the audiences who turned cranks to see women undress or who gathered in cafés and store fronts to look at Fred Ott sneeze.

According to the well-known story, Méliès discovered the trick of stop-action substitution after his camera jammed while he was filming an omnibus on the street. Only in the darkroom did he discover what he had done by restarting the stalled mechanism: the omnibus turned before his eyes into a hearse, exactly the sort of transformation that is one of the striking features of "Circe" (and, incidentally, a Viconian transformation that Joyce would have relished).

Though the anecdote is probably apocryphal, it does explain the principle behind much of the trick photography that made Méliès's magic possible. Combining sex, horror, and sentimentality, elements of popular art Joyce was by no means above, Méliès used his discovery to produce marvels that repeatedly suggest Joyce's transformations (the films should be seen, of course, but they are lovingly described in John Frazer's *Artificially Arranged Scenes*). In *The Wrestling Sextette,* female Turkish wrestlers become men; in *The Brahmin and the Butterfly,* a fakir turns a cocoon into a flying butterfly-woman who turns into an Oriental princess who thereupon turns *him* into a caterpillar when he prostrates himself to kiss her foot; in *The Famous Box Trick,* one boy turns into two boys who fight each other (shades of Shem and Shawn); in *One-Man Band,* Méliès becomes six of himself, playing six different instruments; in the *Temptation of St. Anthony,* a man whom Joyce (and Luis Buñuel) would have understood contemplates a skull only to see Jesus materialize and then metamorphose into a half-clad woman. (Terry Ramsaye, the so-called first film-historian, aptly dubbed cinema "the Prayer Wheel of Wish" [lxx].)

Old Virag unscrews his head in "Circe" and tucks it under his arm, a commonplace miracle in films by Méliès and other film pioneers (Ferdinand Zecca's Slippery Jim eludes capture by such stratagems as unscrewing his feet). And in film and "Circe" alike—to repeat—such wonders are perceived as "real" even while recognized as impossible.

In the tableaux of "Circe"—which Joyce called a "costume episode" (*Letters I* 148)—characters play elaborate roles, yet somewhere underneath, presumably, stands reality. A speech addressed to Bloom by the prostitute Zoe used to perplex me. "I hate a rotter that's insincere. Give a bleeding whore a chance" (*U-G* 1083.1977–78). One of Joyce's notes for "Ithaca" suggests what sort of sincerity Zoe may be asking for. "Fuck," the note reads, "only time people really sincere" (Herring 429).

Although Bella Cohen's is a place designed for such carnal sincerity, the closest we get to it is when Bloom and Shakespeare play Peeping Tom, looking through the keyhole at Molly and Blazes. "Show! Hide! Show!" (*U-G* 1237.3815), Bloom cries (giving the flicker effect, incidentally). "Circe" promises the truth in its foray into the red light district, a place where reality can be seen unveiled and without disguise—"the raw, naked truth," as film posters put such matters.

We discover disguises we had never dreamed of in "Circe," however. The camera, invisible, indifferent, paring its fingernails, was to reflect reality with a purity only a machine could boast, yet from the start, the movie camera projected dreams and illusion; like the whores of Nighttown, the cinema promises the real thing but turns tricks.

However radically costumes and roles change from film to film, we almost always see actors on the screen as themselves. The titles promise Max Linder Aviator, Boxer, Virtuoso, Toreador, King of the Circus—but whatever the role, Max is always Max. And so, too, whether Moses, Michelangelo, Gordon of Khartoum, or endorser of Ronald Reagan, Charlton Heston remains Charlton Heston. Similarly, Bloom appears in "Circe" in a myriad of costumes and roles, yet we have no trouble recognizing him even when he is sex-changed or transformed into a drooling Mongolian idiot. As in the cinema, the theater of "Circe" presents a place where individuality triumphs over all other roles.

Throughout the history of the cinema—but especially in its early days, as Panofsky points out—we confront instantly recognizable stereotypes (253–54). Playing Scotsman, Bloom must wear kilts;

playing schoolboy, he must wear Eton jacket. When Charles Laughton was proposed for the role of Bloom in a proposed film of *Ulysses,* Joyce suggested George Arliss instead (*JJII* 654). In at least one respect Arliss might have been perfect. Because he played not only Disraeli and Rothchild (two of Bloom's roles in "Circe") but a host of other historical figures including Richelieu, Wellington, and Alexander Hamilton, publicity releases proclaimed Arliss "the man of a thousand faces"; "a thousand faces," Hollywood quipped, "all the same." Thus with Bloom (not to mention HCE): the hero with a thousand faces, all the same.

The magic of "Circe" is reminiscent not merely of the trick photography that has been a stock in trade of film from Méliès's time to the present. Consider Maxim Gorki's description of the documentary films in the First Program of the Lumière Brothers which he saw at the Nizhni-Novgorod Fair in 1896. "Last night I was in the Kingdom of Shadows," Gorki begins.

> Carriages coming from somewhere in the perspective of the picture are moving straight at you...; somewhere from afar people appear and loom larger as they come closer to you; in the foreground children are playing with a dog, bicyclists tear along, and pedestrians cross the street.... All this moves, teems with life and, upon approaching the edge of the screen, vanishes somewhere beyond it. (407)

"You feel," Gorki continues, "as though Merlin's vicious trick is being enacted," compressing buildings and dwarfing people.

> Suddenly something clicks, everything vanishes, and a train appears on the screen. It speeds straight at you—watch out! It seems as though it will plunge into the darkness in which you sit....
> But this, too, is but a train of shadows. (408)

In his description, which seems almost a Circean hallucination, Gorki catches the marvel that even so-called *actualité* presented to early filmgoers. They experienced a reality so palpable that they flinched as the train seemed to plunge toward them from the screen, a reality so persuasive that in 1904 one viewer, Nora Joyce, cried aloud after an escaping villain on the bioscope screen, "O, policeman, catch him" (*Letters II* 75). Yet at the same time, audiences gazed at a silent world of shadows where figures are myseriously compressed or expanded and in which "suddenly something clicks" and images appear out of nowhere.

In "Circe," too, we see figures dramatically compressed and enlarged. And Joyce uses cuts abruptly to move not only from place to place but forward and back in a time continuum which is, as is necessarily the case in cinema, that "one continuous present tense" in which Shem writes (*FW* 185.36–186.1). "And time," Bloom muses, "well that's the time the movement takes" (*U-G* 805.988–89).

Even Joyceans who teach *Ulysses* year after year often cannot quite recall how terribly difficult the work is to first-time readers; harder still is it to imagine what movies must have first looked like to members of Joyce's generation. René Clair reminds us that "for a new eye, one image replacing another in a flash. . .[produces] the impression of a magical substitution or a lightning-like metamorphosis" (quoted in Frazer 60–61). Something of that speed must have hit Joyce when he wrote from Trieste to Stanislaus in 1909 of his flight from depression in "the sixty-miles-an-hour pathos of some cinematograph" (*Letters II* 217).

At the climax of "Circe," Joyce returned to the projection that had interested him as early as "Silhouettes." "Against the dark wall a figure appears slowly, a fairy boy of eleven." Eleven, Joyce's number of renewal and the number on the ad for Kino's which is always in motion, bobbing on the ever-moving river that is, Bloom muses, not only the Liffey but life itself (*U-G* 323.90–95). The fairy boy materializes slowly, a fade-in rather than the typical jump-cut, because we are leaving kinesis for the silence and arrest of timeless (albeit temporary) epiphany. Like some image from an early hand-tinted film, the figure has a "delicate, mauve face"; like an actor in a movie the figure "gazes, unseeing" out at the viewer (*U-G* 1335.4956–1337.4964); like a character in a silent film, the figure mimes his role, reading "inaudibly" (how often is that the stage direction in Joyce's epiphanies?). And like all images in cinema, the figure is present and substantial, yet he is at the same time a phantom of the past, strangely transparent and insubstantial.

Earlier in "Circe," J. J. O'Molloy projects on a courtroom wall a lantern picture of Bloom's extensive mortgaged property at Agendath Netaim. The Gabler *Ulysses* restores "image" for "mirage" in the description of O'Molloy's slide of "blurred cattle cropping in silver haze" (*U-G* 1005.985–6). A crude realism would prefer the "mirage" of the Random House edition in order to dismiss both Rudy and the Promised Land, would find both of them mere illusion in contrast to the time-bound reality of the drunken Stephen lying on the solid

on the solid pavement of a Dublin gutter. But in "Circe," as in
film, all images—even "fake" ones—command belief.

In this moment in "Circe," as in its dreamlike transformations
and transitions, in the Magic that is its Art, we see instructive
analogies between Joyce's art and cinema. The figures and objects
shrinking and swelling in the gray space on the screen at the Nizhni-
Novrogod Fair—the world of Gorki's Kingdom of Shadows—and
Joyce's Nighttown border on each other as projections of a modern
way of seeing.

NOTES

1. The best overall treatment of Joyce and Cinema is Spiegel 71–82, *et passim*.
Palmer is especially persuasive on Eisensteinian montage and *Ulysses*. Bazargan's
stimulating note on cinema and "Aeolus" is much in keeping with my own
thinking. See also: Murray 126–141, *et passim*; Cohen 147–56, 172–79, 187–204,
et passim; Barrow; and Pearce 38–47 (Pearce's excellent discussion of "Circe," 41–
43, focuses on the cinematic usurpation of the narrator by the medium).

2. I understand that original Mutoscope machines are still in operation at
Disneyland, presumably offering different titles than those C. W. Ceram reported
on the Hamburg Reeperbahn in the early sixties, titles such as *When Women
Become Hyenas, The Mouse at the Tea Party*, and the Joycean-sounding *Yes, Yes,
Love is Blind* (92). As Andrew Eskind notes, "the glory of the International
Mutoscope production must rest with its 'Girlies,' dance and strip-tease subjects."
On 218 and 220, Ceram offers stills from Robert W. Paul's 1896 Kinetoscope
Undressing Extraordinary (identified elsewhere as *Exhibition*), in which a gentlemen
ogles the classical statue of a naked woman; the man's sight line appears to be
somewhat higher than Bloom's at the National Library.

3. Niver describes a 1905 American Mutoscope and Bioscope *Peeping Tom
in the Dressing Room* (247); given peep-show devices like the Mutoscope and given
the nature of cinema, there must have been number of works featuring Peeping
Toms.

4. Pratt asks whether the Buck Mulligan in Josef von Sternberg's 1927
Underworld may be a tribute to Joyce (456).

5. Twenty-five words into his workbook entry "Circe" for the *Wake*, Joyce
wrote, "cinema fakes, drown, state of sea, tank: steeplejack, steeple on floor, camera
above: jumps 10 feet, 1 foot camera in 6 foot pit" (Connolly 119).

6. An early 19th-century letter believed to be by Charles Dibden, the younger,
one of the "arrangers" who worked with Grimaldi at Covent Gardens, is a rarity
for its details on well-guarded secrets of panto "trickworks"; the letter speaks of
"the whistle...for change" as the cue for a transformation (Meyer 147–48).

WORKS CITED

Barrow, Craig Wallace. *Montage in James Joyce's* Ulysses. Madrid: Studia
        Humanitatis, 1980.
Barsacq, Léon. *Caligari's Children and Other Grand Illusions: A History of Film
        Design*. Revised edition. Boston: New York Graphic Society, 1976.

Bazargan, Susan. "The Headings in "Aeolous': A Cinemagraphic View." *James Joyce Quarterly* 23 (Spring 1986): 343–50.

Ceram, C.W. *Archaeology of the Cinema*. New York: Harcourt, Brace & World, n.d.

Connolly, Thomas E., ed. *Scribbledehobble: The Ur-Workbook for* Finnegans Wake. Evanston, Illinois: Northwestern University Press, 1961.

Eisenstein, Sergei. "A Course in Treatment." In *Film Form: Essays in Film Theory,* edited by Jay Leyda, 84–107. New York: Harcourt, Brace & World, 1949.

Ellmann, Richard. *Ulysses on the Liffey*. New York: Oxford University Press, 1972.

Eskind, Andrew H. " 'She Banked in Her Stocking; or Robbed of her All': Mutoscopes Old and New." In *"Image" on the Evolution of Film,* edited by Marshall Deutelbaum, 26–31. New York: Dover Publications, 1979.

Fell, L. John. *A History of Films*. New York: Holt, Rinehart & Winston, 1979.

Frazer, John. *Artificially Arranged Scenes: The Films of Georges Méliès*. Boston: G. K. Hall, 1979.

Gorki, Maxim. Rev. of Lumière Program, 4 July 1896. Jay Leyda, *Kino: A History of the Russian and Soviet Film*. 3rd ed., 407–9. Princeton, N.J.: Princeton University Press, 1983.

Hepworth, Cecil. "Those Were the Days: Reminiscences by a Pioneer of the Earliest Days of Cinematography." In *The Penguin Film Review, 1946–49,* Vol. 2, 33–39. Totowa, N.J.: Rowman and Littlefield, 1977.

Herr, Cheryl. *Joyce's Anatomy of Culture*. Urbana: University of Illinois Press, 1986.

Herring, Phillip F., ed. *Joyce's* Ulysses *Notesheets in the British Museum*. Charlottesville: University Press of Virginia, 1972.

La Valley, Albert J. "Traditions of Trickery: The Role of Special Effects in the Science Fiction Film." In *Shadows of the Magic Lamp: Fantasy and Science Fiction in Film,* edited by George Slusser and Eric S. Rabkin, 141–58. Carbondale: Southern Illinois University Press, 1985.

Lindsay, Vachel. *The Art of the Moving Picture*. New York: Liveright, 1970.

Mast, Gerald. *A Short History of the Movies*. 2nd ed. Indianapolis, Ind.: Bobbs-Merrill Educational Publishing, 1981.

Mayer, David, III. *Harlequin in His Element: The English Pantomime, 1806–1836*. Cambridge: Harvard University Press, 1969.

Murray, Edward. *The Cinematic Imagination: Writers and the Motion Pictures*. New York: Ungar, 1972.

Niver, Kemp R. *Early Motion Pictures: The Paper Print Collection in the Library of Congress*. Washington, D.C.: Library of Congress, 1985.

Palmer, R. Barton. "Eisensteinian Montage and Joyce's *Ulysses*: The Analogy Reconsidered." *Mosaic* 18 (1985): 73–85.

Panofsky, Erwin. "Style and Medium in the Motion Pictures." In *Film Theory and Criticism,* 2nd ed., edited by Gerald Mast and Marshall Cohen, 243–67. New York: Oxford University Press, 1979.

Pearce, Richard. *The Novel in Motion: An Approach to Modern Fiction*. Columbus: Ohio State University Press, 1983.

Pratt, George C. *Spellbound in Darkness*. Revised edition. Greenwich, Conn.: New York Graphic Society, 1973.

Ramsaye, Terry. *A Million and One Nights: A History of the Motion Picture*. New York: Simon & Schuster, 1926.

Shipman, David. *The Story of Cinema*. New York: St. Martin's Press, 1982.

Spiegel, Alan. *Fiction and the Camera Eye: Visual Consciousness in Film and the Modern Novel.* Charlottesville: University Press of Virginia, 1976.

Werner, Gosta. "James Joyce, Manager of the First Cinema in Ireland." In *Nordic Rejoycings—1982,* 125–36. Norberg, Sweden: James Joyce Society of Sweden and Finland, n.d.

10

Images of the Lacanian Gaze in *Ulysses*

SHELDON BRIVIC

Stephen Dedalus and Leopold Bloom are both preoccupied in *Ulysses* with defining for themselves the operations of their own perceptions, and the workings of these perceptions for the two men parallel each other. Moreover, these perceptual patterns also parallel one of the best-known theories of Jacques Lacan, the theory of the split between the eye and the gaze, which appears in *The Four Fundamental Concepts of Psycho-Analysis*.[1] Lacan's concept of the gaze can help us to see how perception is arranged for Joyce's two protagonists, how they see the world and each other, and how they see the world through each other.

The key principle of Lacan's idea of the gaze is that one can only see something by imagining that it is looking back at one: "this is the essential point—the dependence of the visible on that which places us under the eye of the seer."[2] One's perception, even of landscapes and still lifes, must be motivated by being drawn toward its objects by desire, and desire is always based on an imagined response. This imagined response on the visual level is called the gaze and comes from a locus which is built into the structure of perception.

As perception depends on being perceived by a gaze in Lacan's system, so does existence. Being is being seen, and seen more completely than one can oneself see: "I see only from one point, but in my existence I am looked at from all sides."[3] The point from which I see is the eye and the surrounding watchfulness is the gaze that constitutes me as the subject of a larger human consciousness. This view is an extension of Lacan's theory of the mirror stage, which holds that an individual's personality is formed by the way others see him, that a child's image of himself is a reflection of the views of others.

The structure of visual perception for Lacan, however, is more complex than this. What the eye sees is a field in which the eye itself is an invisible center, and this field is seen by focusing on a particular point. At the same time, the subject maps himself in the picture, so that I project myself as a formal composition onto the field before me in the act of perception. At the center of the visual field or picture is a blind spot or hole, a reflection of my pupil, and behind this blind spot is situated the gaze. I can't see what is regarding me in all of my perceptions any more than I can see a person watching me by looking in his or her eyes. Lacan says, *"You never look at me from the place from which I see you."*[4] The gap in the center corresponds to what Lacan calls the *objet petit a*, with the lower case *a* standing for *autre*. This little point of otherness is the focal point of desire.

For Lacan, the point that is the object of desire always stands for an absent phallus. Moreover, in Lacan's system, the phallus itself is absent by nature, a symbolic organ defined by negation because we first become aware of it through the sense of castration.[5] The hole or lack which is the object of desire stands for the flaw through which the other shows its need for one. Desire, for Lacan, is always the desire of the Other, which is to say that it always comes from a source one can't locate; and the center of any pictorial composition is always the desire of the Other to show itself behind which is the power of the Other to create one's being.[6] This power is represented by the phallus, an organ which is invisible in its fully realized state, or as Joyce describes it, put "out of sight." The implication of Joe Hynes's question, "I wonder did he ever put it out of sight" (*U* 12.1655), is that if he hasn't put it out of sight, he doesn't have it.

What can actually be seen is neither the gaze nor the subject, neither the Other nor the self, but the image or screen that mediates between them as they create each other. Lacan diagrams the eye and the gaze as overlapping cones pointing in opposite directions, an image like Yeats's gyres. The screen appears at the point where the intersecting cones of perspective—the one widening out from the eye and the other narrowing down to the gaze at the other end—have equal diameters.[7] This screen corresponds to what Stephen calls the diaphane or veil of appearance. It manifests what is behind it at the same time that it conceals it.

Stephen has been studying perception and concerned with what is behind it ever since his theories of epiphany in *Stephen Hero*. On the first page of "Proteus" he conceives of the diaphane or field of vision as having an aperture, as something to be passed through:

"Diaphane, adiaphane. If you can put your five fingers through it it is a gate, if not a door" (*U* 3.7–9). Later, under the influence of Berkeley, the diaphane becomes a "veil of space with coloured emblems," and here again Stephen thinks of going "beyond the veil" (*U* 3.417, 425).

On the other side of this field of light lies the darkness which he calls "adiaphane," and when Stephen closes his eyes to escape the veil of appearances, he hopes and fears to pass beyond the diaphane into absolute darkness: "If I open and am for ever in the black adiaphane" (*U* 3.26). The darkness on the other side of light corresponds to outer space and the void on which the world is founded, but also to the darkness within that Stephen finds when he closes his eyes.

Stephen longs for the adiaphane because he feels trapped in his own mode of perception: the "ineluctable modality of the visible" is "thought through" his eyes (*U* 3.1). He derives from Berkeley the idea that the visual is a flat field and that distance is produced by forces in the mind: "Flat I see, then think distance..." (3.418). According to Lacan, distance results from a structure projected by desire.

Bloom also thinks of closing his eyes as an experiment in the course of his meditation on what perception would be like for the blind: "They say you can't taste with your eyes shut.... Want to try in the dark to see" (*U* 1123, 1142). One of his main experiments with perception occurs when he tries to see a clock on top of a bank in "Lestrygonians":

> Can't see it. If you imagine it's there you can almost see it. Can't see it.
>
> . . . . .
>
> The tip of his little finger blotted out the sun's disk. Must be the focus where the rays cross. (*U* 8.562–67)

Here he moves toward the conclusion that the perception of depth is subjective, shaped by the mind's patterns, and that vision is focused on a screen.

Stephen makes an extensive effort to understand where the thought of distance comes from. He recognizes that it involves the stereoscopic operation of two points of view. And as he has this recognition, he divides himself into two viewpoints, addressing himself in the second person and in the first person plural so as to recognize another within: "You find my words dark. Darkness is in our souls do you not think?'' (*U* 3.420). This darkness within is equated with the soul (*anima*) as a woman: ''Our souls, shamewounded by our sins, cling to us yet more, a woman to her lover clinging...'' (*U* 3.421–23). By recognizing the other within through the reality of a woman, Stephen could see the depth of things, the reality of the world and its beauty. But he will not be ready to do so until after he makes contact with Bloom.

Bloom's thoughts are arranged to complement Stephen's and his equivalent of the veil Stephen wants to penetrate appears when he daydreams about meeting a girl with a veil in church (*U* 5.376). A few pages after this, he visualizes Molly, her darkness, her mystery, and her gaze partially covered by a linen veil: ''Brings out the darkness of her eyes. Looking at me, the sheet up to her eyes, Spanish, smelling herself...'' (5.494–95).) Here he puts himself into her mind as she looks at him. When he projects Molly in her most authoritative form in ''Circe,'' emphasis is placed on her being heavily veiled with a ''yashmak'' (*U* 15.300), and Bloom is ''spellbound.'' The most immediately effective form of the veil is the semitransparent hose Bloom is watching on Gerty MacDowell when he has the strongest physical satisfaction of his day in ''Nausicaa'': ''O, those transparent!'' (*U* 13.1262).

On one level the veil stands for the surface of material reality, which transfixes Bloom so that he can scarcely imagine penetrating it. But Stephen is also preoccupied by such a veil, and it is debatable whether his attempts to penetrate it are any more successful. The veil, then, is a general, constitutive feature of human perception. It corresponds to the screen in Lacan that is all we can see of the interaction between what is within and what is beyond that screen. Lacan says that in order to constitute the illusion of visual reality, a screen is needed: ''if one wishes to deceive a man, what one presents to him is the painting of a veil, that is to say, something that incites him to ask what is behind it.''[8]

In traditional psychosexual terms, veils, like stockings, are fetishes, which is to say that they stand for the phallus. According to Lacan's theory, the object of focus conceals a phallic power, and the image of Molly that draws Bloom continually conceals a dark power that is manifested by Blazes Boylan. Molly certainly would not attract Bloom as she does if she did not have the will to seek satisfaction beyond what he can provide. Stephen's equivalent to Molly is his mother, and his preoccupation with her involves the dark powers of the father and God, to both of whom she has given herself. These powers emerge in "Circe," where she appears in a torn bridal veil and says, "Beware! God's hand!" (*U* 15.4219).

In the first episode Stephen strains to see the beauty of the world, but his vision is dimmed by the thought of his mother's violation (*U* 1.225). When he tries to see the "great sweet mother" Mulligan speaks of, he soon perceives his mother's wound. Behind that gap at the center of his perception is his mother's lost power, which appears in Lacanian terms as an occulted phallus through the memory of his mother that occurs to him:

> She heard old Royce sing in the pantomime of *Turko the Terrible* and laughed with others when he sang:
> *I am the boy*
> *That can enjoy*
> *Invisibility.*

(U 1.258–62)

This bright, attractive moment of her life has now passed beyond the veil: "Folded away in the memory of nature with her toys" (*U* 1.265).

As Stephen strives to comprehend the source of depth in "Proteus" and thinks of the darkness behind light (1.409), he apparently sees a pair of gypsies watching him and this leads to a series of feelings of being watched. He thinks, "If I were suddenly naked here as I sit?" (*U* 3.390), and wonders, "Who watches me here?" (3.414). He also refers to himself in different persons as an object of perception: "Me sits there with his augur's rod of ash... unbeheld" (3.410–11). His efforts to perceive the visual field, in accordance with Lacan's recognition, are accompanied by a sense of being perceived, and this pattern is acted out on a more physical level by Bloom.

In "Calypso," at the butcher shop, when Bloom's senses are first stirred to excitement, the text describes "his soft subject gaze" (*U* 4.163). Bloom's impotence is connected to a sense of constantly being watched by the authorities who are finally manifested in "Circe." Two of the main representatives of authority there are referred to as "the watch" (*U* 15.276). Bloom's sex life presents a parody of the theory of the gaze because as a voyeur he likes to have the women he watches watching him. Gerty knows what he is up to in "Nausicaa," and even when he imagines himself watching through a keyhole in "Circe," Blazes and Molly know that he is there. In fact, he needs to know that Molly knows that he knows about Blazes. Bloom's need to be seen watching something he shouldn't see is a need for shame, and shame may be a strong feature of all desire. It corresponds to what Lacan calls the invidious aspect of the gaze.[9]

The feeling of being watched that Stephen has in "Proteus" leads through meditation on the visual field as a veil to the image of the soul as a woman. Thoughts of woman evoke a longing for contact with universal humanity, the entire outside environment which the gaze that looks at one from all sides represents. The first objects through which this contact is to be made are his mother's eyes: "Touch me. Soft eyes. Soft soft soft hand. I am lonely here. O touch me soon, now. What is that word known to all men?" (*U* 3.434–36). Later, when Stephen asks his mother this question again, her eyes are gaping holes and she carries behind her the power of God. Stephen tries to overcome this hidden malignance, which has really been in his field all day, by shattering the perceptual field to cause the "ruin of all space" (*U* 15.4245).

The "word known to all men," which Stephen at one point thinks may be "love" (*U* 9.429), seems to designate a common knowledge that would bind Stephen to humanity. The only figure in the book who possesses love and could give Stephen such knowledge is Bloom. The coincidences between their thoughts that I have cited here—such as the experiments with the visual field and such images as closing the eyes, the veil, and perception returned—are part of a long series of signs that they are meant to meet. Each is designed to serve as the aim of his opposite, the ultimate limit of the other man's perception. The constant blind spot in the center of Stephen's vision may be associated with Bloom's compassion, while the blind spot in Bloom's vision is Stephen's independence. Bloom represents the Other for Stephen and Stephen represents the Other for Bloom, and so each tends to constitute the gaze for the other.

It may seem foolhardy to suggest that all of their perceptions lead to each other, but I won't be departing far from established perspectives if I point out that their main actions of the day prepare them to meet as they do. It is well known that Stephen's theory of Shakespeare as a cuckold predicts Bloom, and in "Proteus," as I have indicated, Stephen finds in himself a need for the world. If Stephen hadn't argued with his friends, if Molly hadn't committed adultery, or even if Bloom hadn't masturbated with Gerty, the two men might not have met, and one can go on finding a kind of preparation in virtually any perception either man has. After all, Stephen believes in ''Ithaca'' that his collapse in ''Circe'' was caused by a cloud he saw in the morning (*U* 17.36–42). If he hadn't collapsed, he wouldn't have come home with Bloom, and his reason for collapsing wouldn't exist if he hadn't seen this cloud. Everything they see and do prepares Bloom and Stephen to meet with exactly the kind of uncertainty that allows for the potential of their interaction.

Stephen and Bloom draw each other, each the center organizing the other's perception, to lead themselves to realization. Lacan says that the gaze guides us through what appear to be the accidents of life: ''The gaze is presented to us only in the form of a strange contingency, symbolic of what we find on the horizon, as the thrust of our experience, namely, the lack that constitutes castration anxiety.''[10] What draws us on is what we need, and whether it leads to fulfilment or failure—for the contact between Stephen and Bloom remains ambiguous—it leads us to actualize what is in us. As Stephen says in ''Scylla and Charybdis,'' we wander through the world ''always meeting ourselves'' (*U* 9.1046).

Of course, no one person should be identified with Lacan's gaze, but Stephen and Bloom, as the prime objects for each other, tend to dominate each other's destiny. As I pointed out earlier, Molly also tends to embody the gaze for Bloom, as May Dedalus does for Stephen. If the men have the potential to complete each other, they are capable of helping each other to relate to the women in their lives. Stephen, for example, stands for and brings out an adventurous element in Bloom that binds Molly to him, while Bloom shifts Stephen from the spirit of his mother toward the earth of Molly.

The optical reciprocity of Stephen and Bloom is presented in images that extend from their meeting to their parting, and begin even before their meeting. Harry Blamires believes that the ship Stephen sees at the end of ''Proteus,'' the Rosevean, prefigures Bloom. Blamires points out that the sense of someone behind him that the ship gives Stephen—''Behind. Perhaps there is someone?'' (*U* 3.502)—is parallel to the feeling he later has when Bloom passes by him at the end of ''Scylla and Charybdis'': ''About to pass through the doorway, feeling one behind, he stood aside'' (*U* 9.1197). Blamires says that the ''crosstrees'' of the ship foretell the crisis Stephen will encounter when he meets Bloom.[11]

If we accept this reading as one level of what is going on, and I do, then Bloom is first manifested to Stephen when Stephen feels something inanimate watching him, a vivid representation of the gaze. Moreover, the sense of looking back involved in Lacan's *le regard* appears here as Stephen is described in heraldic language as ''rere regardent'' (*U* 3.503). The English *regard*, while it is still commonly used for affection, is rarely used for visual fixation, which is why *gaze* is the best translation of Lacan's term. But our *regard* can still denote gazing in extreme and old-fashioned usages such as Stephen's fixation on the ship and Mulligan's ironic statement, ''Any object, intensely regarded, may be a gate of access to the incorruptible eon of the gods'' (*U* 14.1166–67).

Here is the sentence in which Bloom first sees Stephen in ''Hades'': ''Mr Bloom at gaze saw a lithe young man, clad in mourning, a wide hat'' (*U* 6.39). The primary meaning of ''at gaze'' seems to be that Bloom is simply staring, but the word *at* suggests that he is being watched. Such nondirected perception seems for Joyce to put one in touch with mental forces outside consciousness that manifest themselves as something looking back.

In ''Oxen of the Sun,'' the episode in which Bloom's mental contact with Stephen is established with hardly any conversation between them, Bloom stares for a long time at a bottle of Bass ale. As he does so, a heavenly bride appears, presumably looking at Bloom: ''It is she, Martha, thou lost one, Millicent, the young, the dear, the radiant. How serene does she now arise...'' (*U* 14.1101–2).

In ''Eumeus,'' Bloom tells how he defeated the citizen by his mildness: ''A soft answer turns away wrath.... Am I not right?'' After asking this question, Bloom is described as turning ''a long you are wrong gaze on Stephen of timorous dark pride'' (*U* 16.1085–89). Rather than accusing Stephen, I think ''you are wrong'' answers ''Am I not right?'' and characterizes Bloom's ''timorous'' self-defeating expression, ''a glance also of entreaty'' (*U* 16.1089). I believe that Bloom's insecurity about his own authority is an important component of his appeal to Stephen. At this point Stephen, with irony, sees Bloom as an embodiment of Christ and the protagonists are described as having ''their two or four eyes conversing'' (*U* 16.1091), a phrase that multiplies their visual interaction.

The imagery of the gaze in *Ulysses* reaches its climax with a description of Stephen and Bloom looking at each other on the last full page they spend together in "Ithaca": "Silent, each contemplating the other in both mirrors of the reciprocal flesh of theirhisnothis fellowfaces" (*U* 17.1183–84). This occurs immediately after Bloom has "attracted Stephen's gaze" to the "screen" in the window of his house that covers the lamp that denotes Molly. "Each contemplating the other in both mirrors" means that each is seeing his own face in the other's and is seeing the other's in his own. The infinite regress of this is accompanied by the effect of fusion in the world *theirhisnothis*. The effect of this mutual mapping of subjects in vision is to evoke the larger Otherness behind the individuals.

This is one of the chief moments at which the possibility is felt of passing beyond the visual field, as it may be argued (elsewhere) that *Ulysses* does in "Penelope." But to pass beyond the veil is to pass into the realm of dream, a realm in which, according to Lacan, the gaze shows itself.[13] This dream vision cannot be apprehended by the organized mind of waking except in distorted, fragmented, indirect form. As personalities, Stephen and Bloom are stuck in the world of separation, of the split between the eye and the gaze.

Though Stephen feels the enclosure of the structure of perception more acutely and consciously, Bloom is enclosed more firmly by it, for he has a concrete object to fix his desire on. He is focused on Molly's *objet petit a* all day, no matter what he looks at, and his story ends with it in the form of the black dot that concludes "Ithaca."

Stephen, at odds with everyone, does not have a concrete attachment. His connection with Bloom is the closest he comes to such an attachment all day, and it remains potential. The structure of the gaze for Stephen is highly internalized, a mental system he consciously controls, analyzes, and seeks to escape. He never can escape as Stephen the attachment to desire that encloses him in a shape that screens reality and leaves him subject to the gaze of others; but he shifts or jolts this structure into new possibilities, new margins of reality, by his centrifugal dynamic of defiance. This endeavor of his is parallel to his author's. Joyce's techniques of narrative and description throughout *Ulysses* work to realize the structure of the gaze not only in the sense of enacting it, but in that of understanding it in order to penetrate it, to carry out the inevitable and hopeless, but fruitful aim of passing beyond it.

NOTES

1. Though the theory of the gaze is not one of the four fundamental concepts, it does make up one of the four quarters of the book, filling a section called "Of the Gaze as *Objet Petit a,*" 67–119. I should point out that there are serious problems involved in translating Lacan's difficult style. For example, while Joyce's use of the word *gaze* often seems to have Lacanian overtones, it is only the best English translation of Lacan's term *le regard.*

2. *Four Concepts* 72. Lacan's *voyant* has some of the prophetic overtones of its English equivalent, *seer.* See the French text, *Les Quatre Concepts* 69.

3. The idea of being seen from all sides suggests God. Lacan says, "The spectacle of the world, in this sense, appears to us as all seeing. This is the phantasy to be found in the Platonic perspective of an absolute being to whom is transferred the quality of being all-seeing" (*Four Concepts* 75). I believe that in the largest sense Joyce assumes this aspect of the gaze by seeing his characters from all sides, but I will not develop this idea in the present essay.

4. *Four Concepts* 103. Lacan's italics.

5. This is well explained in Jacqueline Rose's "Introduction II" to *Feminine Sexuality* 40–44.

6. *Four Concepts* 102, 103, 108. Lacan makes a big distinction between the lowercase *autre* and the capital *Autre.* The little other is the object on which one focuses. The big Other is harder to define, and seems to stand for the whole idea of otherness, the total structure of language from which any signifier is distinguished. Rose comments, "Lacan calls this the Other—the site of language to which the speaking subject necessarily refers. The Other appears to hold the 'truth' of the subject and the power to make good its loss. But this is the ultimate fantasy" (*Feminine Sexuality* 32).

7. The diagrams appear on 92 and 106 of the *Four Concepts.*

8. *Four Concepts* 112. The passage is about how a painting can seem real (*trompe-l'oeil*), but coming after discussion of the screen, it seems to apply to all visual reality.

9. *Four Concepts* 115. Lacan here points out that *invidia,* "envy" comes from *videra,* "to look at."

10. *Four Concepts* 72–73. Lacan's word for "thrust," butée (*Quatre Concepts* 70) involves a play on "beauty."

11. *Bloomsday Book* 19. Frank Budgen, *Making of Ulysses* 56, points out that Joyce insisted on using the word *crosstrees* though it was nautically inaccurate.

12. *Four Concepts* 75. Lacan here emphasizes that coherence and self-consciousness are impossible in a dream.

WORKS CITED

Blamires, Harry. *The Bloomsday Book: A Guide through Joyce's* Ulysses. London: Methuen, 1966.

Budgen, Frank. *James Joyce and the Making of* Ulysses. Bloomington: Indiana University Press, 1960.

Lacan, Jacques. *The Four Fundamental Concepts of Psycho-Analysis,* edited by Jacques-Alain Miller; translated by Alan Sheridan. New York: W. W. Norton, 1978.

————— . *Le Séminaire de Jacques Lacan: Livre XI: Les Quatre Concepts Fondamentaux de la Psychanalyse,* edited by Jacques-Alain Miller. Paris: Seuil, 1973.

Lacan, Jacques, and the école freudienne. *Feminine Sexuality,* edited by Juliet Mitchell and Jacqueline Rose. New York: W. W. Norton, 1982.

11

Jellyfish and Treacle:
Lewis, Joyce, Gender and Modernism

BONNIE KIME SCOTT

Wyndham Lewis, who coined the phrase "the men of 1914" to privilege Joyce, Pound, Eliot, and himself as modern writers, will serve me in discussing the relatively new designation, "male modernism," and in considering whether James Joyce belongs in such a category. Lewis has entered the field of modernist definition previsiously. Before modernism had become a widely used designation, Hugh Kenner proposed that Lewis's term, "vorticism," might supply a name to the movement of which both Joyce and Lewis were a part, and for which Eliot's "still point of the turning world" from "Burnt Norton" provides a most memorable image (Faulkner ix). Vortex: "a shaped, controlled and heady circling, centripetal and three-dimensional, around a funnel of calm" (Kenner, *Gnomon* 6). With its calm, its control, and its geometric design, the vortex overcame the fear of the void, the unconscious, and the cosmic chaos suggested by the modern world and entered by other artists, ones Lewis would have labeled "feminine."

The theory that modernism can be divided on gender lines into "male modernism" and "female modernism" serves to remind us how little female modernists were once read and studied. Lewis named no women of 1914, though he knew some—Virginia Woolf, Rebecca West, Beatrice Hastings, and Harriet Shaw Weaver among others. Until about ten years ago, what we studied and taught as modernism was (with the occasional exception of Woolf or Stein) the product of male artists and in large part male critics. To cite Kenner once again, we might note that he assigns Joyce to an eighteenth-century tradition (*Dublin's Joyce*) rather than connecting him to the romantic era or to the company of such female modernists as Virginia Woolf, whom he denounces for middle-brow aesthetics and a "treacly" mind (*Pound Era* 553). Feminist critics Sandra Gilbert and Susan Gubar work with the term "male modernism" and suggest that Joyce deserves assignment to this limited category. In particular, they find in Joyce the practitioner of a "patrilinguistic ethic." Indeed, a logocentric, classicist vision of Joyce was encouraged by Joyce critics. But the current wave of Joycean feminist criticism suggests that Joyce was capable of feminine as well as masculine writing. I don't propose to take up the charges of Joycean phallogocentricity here. A more appropriate topic to a comparison of Wyndham Lewis and Joyce is male modernism, as deliberately defined and practiced by Lewis. I hope to demonstrate how Joyce coincides with some of Lewis's definitions early in his career, and how he and Lewis parted company in the 1920s, partially over the issue of the feminine. It is a debate that previously came to us under the masculine designation of Joyce as "the time man." As we play with new definitions involving gender and modernism, we discover that "the time man," one of "the men of 1914" was at least part woman, and that there was a great deal of "treacle" on and in his mind.

One way of comparing aspects of gender and modernism in Lewis and Joyce is to turn to their two early novels, *A Portrait of the Artist as a Young Man,* and *Tarr,* run in immediate sequence by Harriet Shaw Weaver's *The Egoist* in 1918. I think it is interesting that Miss Weaver could identify with Stephen Dedalus in Joyce's novel, but never took to *Tarr* in the same way. Lewis's work was "clever and interesting and unusual" and "a conglomeration of smart views." Weaver's relationship to Joyce's work was personal; Lewis's brought only an intellectual response. Dora Marsden, former editor of *The Egoist,* worried that Pound and the vorticists would use *Tarr* as a "bridgehead" to occupy their journal (Lidderdale 111–14). It seems typical of Lewis's incapacity for friendship, or his capacity for envy that he tipped off Miss Weaver to Joyce's considerable drinking. Joyce's letter in his own defense has been analyzed in various ways, but one interpretation is to see in it a critique of male camaraderie:

> There is a curious kind of honour code among men which obliges them to assist one another and not hinder the free action of one another and remain together for mutual protection with the result that very often they wake up the next morning sitting in the same ditch. (Lidderdale 186–87)

Molly Bloom implicates the same male pattern in the (presumably) alcohol-related death of Paddy Dignam in *Ulysses*: "they call that friendship killing and then burying one another" (*U-G* 18.1270–71).

Tarr and *A Portrait* are most comparable for their exploration of the aloof young male artist, for the aesthetic discussions they offer, and for their encounters of women in art and life. In the life cycle,

Lewis's novel might be said to take up where Joyce's leaves off. Lewis offers no sympathetic evocation of childhood; he had little sympathy for children. There is no mother figure in *Tarr*. Lewis was strongly attached to his own mother, and vice versa, but he refuses to grant the mother an important place in his writings. (It has been argued by Colin MacCabe [66] that Joyce did the same through much of *Dubliners*.) There are many more young women in Lewis's novel than in Joyce's, and Tarr has become involved in relationships, however imperfectly, while Stephen Dedalus merely blunders at initiating one with E.C., or avoids his sisters, or visits prostitutes. Tarr has left his native England to live in Paris, a city which already disappoints him; Stephen is only approaching such a move.

Tarr and Stephen have quite a few attitudes in common. They are egocentric, aloof to bourgeois middle-class culture, and distant from women. The misogyny of both young men has been noted, Suzette Henke, for example, writing on Stephen, and Michael Levenson on Tarr (241–42). Tarr and Stephen tend to be protective of their artistic energies. For Stephen, this means denying equal education, and even food to his siblings, and particularly to his sisters. To Tarr, this means a different deployment of sexuality:

> The artist is he in whom this emotionality normally absorbed by sex is so strong that it claims a newer and more exclusive field of deployment. Its first creation is *the Artist* himself, a new sort of person; the creative man....
>   The tendency of my work...is that of an invariable severity. Apart from its being good or bad, its character is ascetic rather than sensuous, and divorced from immediate life. There is no slop of sex in *that*. But there is no severity left over for the work of the cruder senses either. (12–13)

Tarr and Stephen are both ascetics and classicists in education, and they orient their intellectual lives toward other men. The above passage, for example, comes from a largely one-sided dialog of Tarr with Hobson. We might compare this performance to Stephen's aesthetic discussions with Temple and Cranly. Tarr and Stephen conceive of God and power as male, and like Aristotle and Nietzsche, place the female at the bottom of their conceptual hierarchies, with the mud, the vegetables, and the jellyfish. Tarr elaborates in a later dialog:

> Woman and the sexual sphere seemed to him to be an average from which everything came: from it everything rose, or attempted

to rise. There was no mysterious opposition extending up to Heaven, and dividing Heavenly beings into Gods and Goddesses. There was only one God, and he was a man. A woman was a lower form of life. Everything was female to begin with. A jellyfish diffuseness spread itself and gaped on the beds and in the bas-fonds of everything. Above a certain level of life sex disappeared, just as in highly organized sensualism sex vanishes. And, on the other hand, everything beneath that line was female.... He enumerated acquaintances evidently below the absolute line and who displayed a lack of energy, permanently mesmeric state, and almost purely emotional reactions. He knew that everything on the superior side of that line was not purged of jellyfish attributes. (334)

As artists, Stephen and Tarr position themselves like the god in this paradigm. We have only to recall Stephen's "artist, like the God of creation..." *P* 215).

I should like to take up the two principal women Tarr encounters in Lewis's novel, drawing some comparisons to Stephen's encounters with women to examine their respective attitudes toward the feminine. Tarr's encounters are much more tangible than Stephen's voyeuristic, internal renderings of women. There is some validity to Frederic Jameson's claim that Lewis is more richly dialogic than Joyce (39), though I would restrict this observation to their early stage of writing or to the strictest sense of dialog. Lewis's is a very restrained and protected dialog, compared with the exchanges eventually performed in *Finnegans Wake*. Though Tarr has a network of relationships, there is no depth or substance in any of them. Tarr wishes them to serve the process of his self-definition and his base needs. Lewis does achieve ironic distance from his protagonist—as Joyce does with Stephen—showing that Tarr does not succeed fully with his plan of artistic detachment and asceticism.

Bertha, a German and the first woman Tarr is involved with, is bourgeois, sentimental, vegetative; he insultingly calls her a "pumpkin." In short she is a safe venture for the artist wishing to preserve his energies because she is so alien and low. Through much of the novel, Tarr seeks ineffectually to rid himself of her attachment:

He had presumably been endowed with the power of awakening love in her. He had something to accuse himself of. He had been afraid of *giving up* or repudiating this particular madness. To give up another person's love is a mild suicide; like a very bad inoculation as compared to the full disease. His tenderness to Bertha was due to her having purloined some part of himself and cov-

ered herself superficially with it as a shield. Her skin at least
was Tarr. She had captured a bit of him, and held it as a hostage.
She was rapidly transforming herself, too, into a slavish depen-
dency. She worked with all the hypocrisy of a great instinct. (61)

Tarr has been implicated and incorporated into the feminine "madness" of love—a primordial plot perpetrated by female instinct. He
cannot get away cleanly with his skin. There is an appalling egotism
to the attachment—an admiration of skin or surface that is himself.
Repudiation of her is inoculation—an artificial, scientific antidote.
Bertha herself is the "full disease," the dangerous germs that lurk
in a female physical interior. The Bertha subplot also allows Lewis
to make cynical comments on the institution of marriage—an institution attacked in the more realistic writing of Edwardian ideologues
like George Bernard Shaw and H. G. Wells. Joyce has Stephen
Dedalus take up these arguments with another bourgeois female, E.
C., particularly in *Stephen Hero*.

Tarr encounters an alternate, more masculine woman in Anastasya, a figure Rebecca West described in her review of *Tarr* as "the
kitch Cleopatra from Dresden," though, in a more serious vein, she
also praised Lewis's Russian sensibilities. Unlike Stephen, who after
Stephen Hero has no serious discussion on gender or art with women,
Tarr has substantial dialogs with Anastasya. But he cannot figure out
how to have both sexual and intellectual relations with a woman:

> "What a big brute!" Tarr thought. She would be just as good
> as Bertha to kiss. And you get a respectable human being into
> the bargain! He was not intimately convinced that she would
> be as satisfactory. Let us see how it would be; he considered.
> This larger machine of repressed, moping senses, did attract. To
> take it to pieces, bit by bit, and penetrate to its intimacy, might
> give a similar pleasure to undressing Bertha! (218)

The sexual encounter anticipated here is destructive, dismembering.
Though Anastasya seems masculinely machinelike and self-possessed,
Tarr suspects that this is a bluff, and he fears for his art: "Surrender
to a woman was suicide for an artist. Nature, who never forgives an
artist, would never allow *her* to forgive" (219). In their dialogs,
Anastasya accuses Tarr of a "schoolboy" attitude toward women,
and tries to sell him on her blend of intelligence and deep sensuality.
She reassures all too blatantly,

> "Well, I have a cave! I've got all that, too. I promise you."
>   Her promise was slow and lisping. Tarr once more had to
> deal with himself. (313)

Anastasya has severely threatened Tarr's compartmented vision of femininity and creativity, and his own means of self-protection:

> He had always been sceptical about perfection. Did she and he need each other? His steadfast ideas of the flower surrounded by dung were challenged. She might be a monotonous abstraction, and if accepted, impoverish his life.... Irritants were useful though not beautiful. He reached back doubtfully toward his bourgeoise. But he was revolted as he touched that mess, with this clean and solid object beneath his eyes.

Though Tarr positions Anastasya ''above the line'' of messy femininity, Lewis fails to give her a creative role, beyond her efforts to educate Tarr. We find Tarr mentally working her into the cubist-vorticist, machinelike shapes of Lewis's own portraits, the hard factuality of things admired and promoted by Pound in Joyce as well as Lewis.

Stephen makes art of E. C. and the bird girl in *A Portrait*. He is moved partially by what he perceives as the messy, degrading aspects of womanhood to write his Villanelle: ''a tender compassion filled his heart as he remembered her frail pallor and her eyes, humbled and saddened by the dark shame of womanhood'' (P 222). The muck of menstruation humbles her in Stephen's imagination. It is not quite as severe an attitude as Lewis's scheme of placing women below the line, or Stephen's earlier labeling women ''marsupials'' in *Stephen Hero* (176, 210). Stephen thinks of his sinning—meaning primarily his consorting with prostitutes—as a comparable degradation he has experienced, a comparison that does not stand up logically when we consider the role of volition in his action versus female bodily function. As with Lewis, female sexuality is dangerously demeaning. But for Stephen, an early artistic work, the Villanelle, is produced out of a fantasy of fluid female engulfment that is described in vital, bright, mysterious terms:

> Her nakedness yielded to him, radiant, warm, odorous, and lavish-limbed, enfolded him like a shining cloud with a liquid life: and like a cloud of vapour or like waters circumfluent in space the liquid letters of speech, symbols of the element of mystery, flowed forth over his brain. (P 223)

With the prostitute, a younger Stephen had been touched physically on the lips, and metaphorically, upon the mind; he yielded and received a new language:

> He closed his eyes, surrendering himself to her, body and mind, conscious of nothing in the world but the dark pressure of her

softly parting lips. They pressed upon his brain as upon his lips as though they were the vehicle of a vague speech.... (*P* 101)

This primal encounter is echoed in the Villanelle scene. It suggests, as Lewis had, that the feminine threatens to capture the male, and to overcome his control. The Villanelle is one long appeal to a "temptress" to give up enchanting him; her powers include a religious dimension missing in Lewis's females. As in Tarr's formulation, the feminine is the foundation that Stephen's art arises from. More than that, Stephen discovers a feminine language of mystery and silence that has its own power and he does surrender.

Stephen had mentally rendered the bird girl he encountered in the previous chapter of *A Portrait* as a bird and an angel. She has her own liquid language, expressed in her action after "sufferance" of his "gaze" for some time, as she bent her eyes "towards the stream, gently stirring the water with her foot hither and thither. The first faint noise of gently moving water broke the silence, low and faint and whispering, faint as the bells of sleep..." (*P* 171). Stephen's response is orgasmic and ecstatic. He founds his artistic vocation on her appeal, and upon the murky realms Tarr seeks to avoid. "His soul was swooning into some new world, fantastic, dim, uncertain as under sea" (*P* 172). He is in the jellyfish realm.

Tarr, unlike *A Portrait*, does offer reactions of female characters to male aesthetics and actions. I have already introduced Tarr's dialogs with Anastasya. One of the most extraordinary moments in Lewis's novel comes when art and sensuality have a violent merger in Bertha's rape by a painter. The artist in this instance is not Tarr, but a fascist named Kreisler. Tarr dismisses Kreisler's painting as the product of an average man's sex instinct—more action than art, "embedded in sex, in fighting, in affairs" (320). Kreisler is as hopelessly engulfed in chaos as his female, bourgeois object. Woman is victim of such art, and Lewis allows us to experience Bertha's immediate reaction to rape in art. The rape is described in vorticist terms as the "whirlpool towards which they had, with a strange deliberateness and yet aimlessness, been steering" (195):

She saw side by side and unconnected, the silent figure drawing her and the other one full of blindness and violence. Then there were two other figures, one getting up from the chair, yawning, and the present lazy one at the window—four in all, that she could not bring together somehow, each in a complete compartment of its own. It would be impossible to make the present lazy one at the window interest itself in these others. A loathsome, senseless event, of no meaning, naturally to that figure there. (195)

Bertha and Kreisler both spend time in the uncontrolled, swirling region of the vortex. Bertha sees Kreisler in multiple spatial/temporal relations to the vortex as sexual arena—getting up to approach, reclining afterwards, and violently involved, as well as silently painting, the aloof artist. While she may no longer be swirled in the vortex, her consciousness retains its dizzying effect in these simultaneous images, and is far from the poised, calm view of the vorticist male artist. Perhaps as interesting as the fragmentation of Kreisler in Bertha's consciousness is her socialized assumption of responsibility for the incident: "the moral, heavily, too heavily, driven in by her no doubt German fate... What Tarr had laughed at her for... that silly and vulgar mush, was the cause of all this" (196). We never see Tarr painting Bertha; he is able to distance himself from this invasion of sexuality into art. Still, Lewis has made a powerful connection, and a statement on the victimization of woman as art object.

Lewis continued to define the feminine in art. His most coherent definitions concerning genders and modernism come in his chapter on Virginia Woolf in *Men Without Art*, where he claims to have taken the feminist "cow by the horns" (170). Here he dismisses Woolf's disputes with Arnold Bennett as petty disagreements between two orthodox writers, denying Woolf the eminence of the modernist revolutionary, and calling Bennett's realism a dead issue. As he shows with the "friskily feminine" character, Hobson in *Tarr* (5), Lewis is only too willing to dismiss most of his English colleagues of both sexes to the cultural realm of feminine mediocrity. Jeffrey Meyers's identification of Hobson as Clive Bell brings him into Bloomsbury territory (50). Lewis's theories of gender in writing are amusingly written; they have a satirical edge that may also have served a need to deny emotional involvement in such issues:

> Now there is one obvious division or opposition staring you in the face—and inviting you, on one side or the other, to drop into its pigeon hole and be at peace—that is the classification by gender: the Masculine and the Feminine depths of the universe. It is necessary for us to repeat here for the thousand and first time how illusory this division is found to be; to point out how many women are far more grenadiers or cave-men than they are

little balls of fluff...that a veneer of habit, and a little bit of
hair on chin and chest, is about all that fundamentally separates
one sex from the other? (*Men Without Art* 159)

Though Lewis is not deterministic about sex and gender in writing,
he dismissively assigns Woolf to the feminine category, along with
his Bloomsbury enemies like Lytton Strachey. The attributes of the
feminine are paleness, "a bogus sort of 'time' to take the place of
the real 'time'—to bring into being an imaginary 'time' small and
pale enough to accommodate their not very robust talents," a "salon
scale" (167). We are "invited...to install ourselves in a very dim
Venusberg indeed: but Venus has become an introverted matriarch,
brooding over a subterraneous 'stream of consciousness'—a feminine
phenomenon after all—and we are a pretty sorry set of knights
too" (167).

Lewis resents Woolf's use of Joyce's *Ulysses* to derive what he
considers a "feminine" description of modernism as "a little good
stuff by fits and starts, a sketch or a fragment" (164). To Lewis,
Ulysses is "robustly complete... It is not the half-work in short
'pale' and 'dischevelled' of a crippled interregnum" (167). He
explains, "Mrs. Woolf is merely confusing the becoming pallor and
uncertain untidiness of some of her own salon pieces with that of
Joyce's masterpiece" (166).

In *Time and Western Man* (1927) Lewis had begun to challenge
Joyce's feminine side. As a "time man" Joyce was falling into the
same pigeon hole as Woolf (86–88). In his essay "Satire and Fiction"
Lewis attacks Joyce's "internal method" regretting that it has "robbed
Joyce's work as a whole of linear properties—contour and definition
in fact":

> In contrast to the jelly-fish that floats in the center of the
> subterranean stream of the "dark" Unconscious, I much prefer,
> for my part, the shield of the tortoise, or the rigid stylistic
> articulations of the grasshopper.

Lewis locates creation in human, controlled, mechanical artistic production, disqualifying mimetic art and creation in nature, especially
in motherhood. It was the transparent envelope of the jelly-fish, the
darker, psychological Joyce that had won the admiration of that
female definer of modernism, Virginia Woolf (154).

Joyce provided deliberate responses to Lewis's brand of male
modernism in *Finnegans Wake*, as its annotators have consistently
recognized. Joyce's critique of gender in Lewis can perhaps be best

viewed at the end of the fable of "The Mookse and the Gripes," which rewrites Lewis's *Time and Western Man* as "Spice and Westend Woman" (*FW* 292.6).[1] While it still suggests that little girls are made of sugar and spice, and reminds us of the position of the London West End prostitute, this title is also subversive of Lewis's sexism, and makes his sort of blasting appear pseudo-revolutionary. Woman provides an end to the Western patriarchal values which have produced a literature of wasteland and fascism. Her "spice" presents a potent, exotic contrast to male modernist dullness of sensation, repetition, linear surface articulation, and sterility. "The Mookse and the Gripes" seems to end indecisively, with the two advocates of space and time (Lewis's space man, the Mookse; Joyce's time man, the Gripes) receding; they still carry on their tedious argument—"bullfolly andswered volleyball." They are watched by "Nuvoletta," but her coy flirtation (compounded of sugar and spice, perhaps) fails to distract them from their argumentative sports. Her sighed, "There are menner" (*FW* 157.8–158.5) seems an admission of hopelessness in gender. The scene continues, however, shifting to the omnipresent, feminine river, embodiment of the natural flow— if not the female modernist treacle—that Lewis scorned.

> The siss of the whisp of the sigh of the softzing at the stir of the ver grose O arundo of a long one in midias reeds: and shades began to glidder along the banks, greepsing, greepsing, duusk unto duusk, and it was glooming as gloaming could be in the waste of all peacable worlds (*FW* 158.6–10)

Into this setting of twilight waste and feminine lament come two mythical women (the washerwomen) who carry off the Mookse and the Gripes, metaphorically dealing death to their arguments. They challenge Lewis's position that God is male, since they suggest the cyclical role of the great goddess. It seems particularly damning that the woman who carries off the Mookse, the Lewis character, is described as a powerful black woman, a political entity that counters Lewis's classicism, sexism and racism.

> Then there came down to the thither bank a woman of no appearance (I believe she was a Black with chills at her feet) and she gatheredup his hoariness the Mookse motamourfully where he was spread and carried him away to her invisible dwelling... (*FW* 158.25–29)

The allusion to Oscar Wilde's *A Woman of No Importance* unsettles masculinity and heterosexuality in the scene. This final shift takes us to "mother spacies," a laundry, or a literary salon, and to writing that is comparable to the work of notable women modernists. I am reminded of the family allegories, the dark, carnivalesque landscapes and the sexual as well as animal metamorphoses of Djuna Barnes' *Ryder* and *Nightwood*. Gertrude Stein was engaged in a problematic working out of racism in her more realistic portrayal of the black woman of "Melanctha" in *Three Lives*. Virginia Woolf's last artist-heroine, Miss La Trobe of *Between the Acts*, ultimately rediscovered words in mud when she too faced "the waste of all peacable worlds." The mature Joyce was willing to yield control to the feminine in writing and in time. One of the "men of 1914" had failed Lewis as a male modernist and challenged him in "femaline" language (*FW* 251.21).

NOTES

1. A similar analysis of this passage of *Finnegans Wake* appears in my *James Joyce* (105–6).

WORKS CITED

Faulkner, Peter. *Modernism*. London: Methuen, 1977.
Gilbert, Sandra M., and Susan Gubar. "Sexual Linguistics: Gender, Language, Sexuality." *New Literary History* 16.3 (1985): 515–43.
Henke, Suzette. "Stephen Dedalus and Women: A Portrait of the Artist as a Young Misogynist." In *Women in Joyce*, edited by Suzette Henke and Elaine Unkeless, 82–107. Urbana: University of Illinois Press, 1982.
Jameson, Frederic. *Fables of Aggression*. Berkeley: University of California Press, 1979.
Kenner, Hugh. *Dublin's Joyce*. Bloomington: Indiana University Press, 1956.
———. *Gnomon: Essays on Contemporary Literature*. New York: McDowell, Obolensky, 1958.
———. *The Pound Era*. Berkeley: University of California Press, 1971.
———. *Wyndham Lewis*. Norfolk, Conn.: New Directions, 1954.
Levenson, Michael. "Form's Body: Wyndham Lewis' *Tarr*." *Modern Language Quarterly* 45.3 (1984): 241–62.
Lewis, Wyndham. *Blast* 1 (June 1914).
———. *Men without Art*. London: Cassell, 1934.
———. *Tarr*. New York: Knopf, 1926.
———. *Time and Western Man*. 1927; Boston: Beacon Press, 1957.
Lidderdale, Jane, and Mary Nicholson. *Dear Miss Weaver*. New York: Viking Press, 1970.
MacCabe, Colin. *James Joyce and the Revolution of the Word*. London: Macmillan, 1979.
Meyers, Jeffrey. *The Enemy: A Biography of Wyndham Lewis*. London: Routledge & Kegan Paul, 1980.

Parker, Valerie. "Enemies of the Absolute: Lewis, Art, and Women." In *Wyndham Lewis: A Revaluation,* edited by Jeffrey Meyers, 211–25. Montreal: McGill-Queens University Press, 1980.

Scott, Bonnie Kime. *James Joyce.* Feminist Readings Series. Sussex: Harvester Press, 1987.

Woolf, Virginia. "Modern Fiction." In *The Common Reader,* First Series, 150–58. New York: Harcourt, Brace & World, 1925.

12

The Letter Selfpenned to One's Other: Joyce's Writing, Deconstruction, Feminism

ELLEN CAROL JONES

1 coat of french polish
— Joyce, letter to Harriet Shaw Weaver

If we keep on speaking the same language together, we're going to reproduce the same history.

How can we shake off the chain of these terms, free ourselves from their categories, rid ourselves of their names? Disengage ourselves, alive, *from their concepts?*
— Irigaray, *This Sex Which Is Not One*

"The real metaphysical problem today is the word," Eugene Jolas proclaimed in his 1929 manifesto for *Work in Progress.* "The new artist of the word has recognized the autonomy of language" (79). In making the word "the real metaphysical problem today," James Joyce, like Nietzsche, challenges the assumptions underlying Western epistemology and metaphysics, including that of the phenomenalism of consciousness, by calling attention to their linguistic, rhetorical structures.[1] That undoing entails, as Paul de Man has argued, the undoing of cognition. Jolas claimed that "when the beginnings of this new age are seen in perspective, it will be found that the disintegration of words, and their subsequent reconstruction on other planes, constitute some of the most important acts of our epoch" (79). For in disintegrating and then reconstructing the language, the new artist of the word destabilizes meaning, calls into question the referentiality of language, exposes its arbitrariness, its materiality, its status as rhetoric.

Joyce's revolution of the word is part of the totality of our era, reflecting the revolutionary decentering of epistemology by nineteenth- and early twentieth-century thinkers; Jacques Derrida lists the most radical articulations of that decentering:

> the Nietzschean critique of metaphysics, the critique of the concepts of being and truth, for which were substituted the concepts of play, interpretation, and sign (sign without truth present); the Freudian critique of self-presence, that is, the cri-

tique of consciousness, of the subject, of self-identity and of self-proximity or self-possession; and, more radically, the Heidegger-ean destruction of metaphysics, of onto-theology, of the determination of being as presence. ("Structure, Sign, and Play" 250)

To that list Derrida adds James Joyce: Joyce "signs into a single work," he claims, "something like the necessity of an epoch," "the meaning of the *langue* of our time" (Panel, "Deconstructive Criticism of Joyce"). This rethinking of the concept of structure Derrida perceives as a "*rupture*" and a "*redoubling*":

> that in which language invaded the universal problematic; that in which, in the absence of a center or origin, everything became discourse...that is to say, when everything became a system where the central signified, the original or transcendental signified, is never absolutely present outside a system of differences. ("Structure, Sign, and Play" 249)

In this interminable play of language, the world is always already writing, "is, was and will be writing its own wrunes for ever."[2] And that world is a decentered one: "Is not the scene of writing," Hélène Cixous asks, "always decentered?" She claims that Joyce liberates signifiers from realism and from symbolism (the two poles Pound and Eliot prescribed, respectively, for Joyce's texts); he breaks the circle of what Barthes calls the "readable," the causal chain which guarantees the continuation of metaphysics (18, 21).

By emphasizing the politics of language as a material and social structure, Joyce effects a social revolution through his poetic revolution: "my action," he claims in a 1906 letter to Stanislaus Joyce, "is a virtual intellectual strike" (*SL* 125). His strike emanates from his position as colonized subject, as outsider, as exile: not only as social self-exile but also as linguistic alien. As Julia Kristeva notes, "To work on language, to labor in the materiality of that which society regards as a means of contact and understanding, isn't that at one stroke to declare oneself a stranger to language?" (*Sēmēiotikē* 1). Joyce's dislocutory and translating process of writing the English language—his transforming English to "unglish"—subverts linguistically the hegemony of British culture and its language. The transnationalism of *Finnegans Wake*, a text written in the wake of the Irish Free State, disarticulates, rearticulates, and at the same time annuls what Philippe Sollers terms the "maximum number of traces—linguistic, historical, mythological, religious. In what he writes, *nothing remains but differences,* and so he calls into question all and

every community. . ." (108). In challenging the epistemological pre-
suppositions of Western culture, in disrupting through his language
the received symbolic order,[3] Joyce exposes the ideologies of power
informing language and other symbolic constructs; his revolutionary
act is analogous to Catherine Clément's description of the feminist
action: "to change the imaginary in order then to be able to act on
the real, to change the very forms of language which by its structure
and history has been subject to a law that is patrilinear, therefore
masculine" (131).

   "The war is in words," Joyce proclaimed in *Finnegans Wake*
(98.34–35), and he wages "his penisolate war" in history, in writing,
with his pen and his slate—and his penis. In converting syntax to
"sintalks" (*FW* 269.3), does Joyce hope, as he wrote of the artist in
his Trieste Notebook, "that by sinning wholeheartedly his race might
come in him to the knowledge of herself" (Scholes and Kain 95)?
What is the significance of this conjunction of sexuality and writing
in the subversion of the symbolic order? What are the historical,
political, and psychoanalytical implications of marking that sexuality
by sexual difference? Michele Montrelay would argue that "orgasm
in discourse"—the breaking, the disjointing of discourse, the articulating of discourse through a meaning which endlessly escapes—
subverts such an order and that a specifically *feminine* sexual pleasure
and the literary text result from that war in words:

> Orgasm in discourse leads us to the point where feminine jouiss-
> ance can be understood as writing (*écriture*). To the point where
> it must appear that this jouissance and the literary text (which is
> also written like an orgasm produced from within discourse), are
> the effect of the same murder of the signifier. (234)

But the revolutionary subject, Julia Kristeva claims, is a subject—
whether masculine or feminine—able "to allow the *jouissance* of
semiotic motility to disrupt the strict symbolic order."[4] In disrupting
the symbolic order by disrupting language, the new artist of the word
calls into question the possibility, the very assumption, of knowledge—
and posits its impossibility.

   But all deconstructive discourses are necessarily inscribed within
the circle of a language based on the very metaphysical concepts they
intend to subvert. As Derrida points out, a metalanguage is a logical
and linguistic impossibility: "We have no language—no syntax and
no lexicon—"alien to the history of metaphysics: "We cannot utter
a single destructive proposition which has not already slipped into

the form, the logic, and the implicit postulations of precisely what it seeks to contest" ("Structure, Sign, and Play" 250).

Caught within the history of metaphysics, feminist critiques of phallogocentrism are thus necessarily determined by, frustratingly limited by, the dominant male discourse.[5] Phallogocentrism has traditionally stressed the principles of being as presence, of truth, of identity, of sameness, and of visibility as conditions for representation in language, assigning these principles to the male. Luce Irigaray critiques the power of the "master discourse," the philosophical *logos*, to eradicate the difference between the sexes in systems self-representative of a "masculine subject," to reduce all others to the economy of the same. The female is then defined within that logic "as nothing other than the complement, the other side, or the negative side, of the masculine" ("Women's Exile" 63). She is a void, a hole in representation. She is constituted as "not all": the phallic definition poses her as exclusion. As construct, "woman" exists "only as excluded by the nature of things which is the nature of words," according to Jacques Lacan; if she is excluded from the nature of things, "it is precisely that in being not all, she has, in relation to what the phallic function designates of *jouissance,* a supplementary *jouissance,*" an excess of which she cannot fully know or speak ("God and the *Jouissance*" 144–45). Yet it is in that very impossibility of acceding to the symbolic that Philippe Sollers places Joyce's power as a writer: "Joyce writes precisely from that radical negation of language. He writes and speaks in that impossible place where there ought not to be anything speaking or writing, and he brings it to a highly worked sublimation. In other words, Joyce gets something to come which in principle ought not to come." And Sollers claims that it is "this saturation of the polymorphic, polyphonic, polygraphic, polyglotic varieties of sexuality, this *unsettling* of sexuality, this devastating ironicalization of your most visceral, repeated desires which leaves you—admit it—troubled when faced with Joyce" (119, 120).

In a move similar to Joyce's reinscription of the sexual body into the language of literature, Irigaray first argues that women lack access to a language appropriate to the expression of their desire, that female sexuality cannot be articulated within Aristotelian logic: "language and the systems of representation," she says, "cannot 'translate' a woman's desire."[6] She therefore calls for a radical "disconcerting" of language and logic, a deconstruction of the binary logic that privileges the male, and for an opening of discourse to the sense of "nonsense,'' to the expression of what has always been constituted as other, as non-truth and non-being. Julia Kristeva believes that women *should* assume a negative function to the symbolic order: the revolutionary ''woman'' is any resistance to culture and language. And although Irigaray recognizes the necessity not to define ''woman,'' but to analyze how she is determined in discourse, she explores the possibility of a *parler femme* analogous to what she envisions as the multiplicity of female sexuality; its multiple tones and voices argue for no *one* female language, but for a plurality of languages. For Derrida, discourse that escapes the combinatory of the two sexes would be not a multiplicity of *only* female languages, but ''incalculable choreographies'' of sexually marked voices:

> ...I would like to believe in the multiplicity of sexually marked voices. I would like to believe in the masses, this indeterminable number of blended voices, this mobile of non-identified sexual marks whose choreography can carry, divide, multiply the body of each ''individual,'' whether he be classified as ''man'' or as ''woman'' according to the criteria of usage. Of course, it is not impossible that desire for a sexuality without number can still protect us, like a dream, from an implacable destiny which immures everything for life in the figure 2.... Tragedy would leave this strange sense...that we must affirm and learn to love instead of dreaming of the innumerable. Yes, perhaps; why not? But where would the ''dream'' of the innumerable come from, if it is indeed a dream? Does the dream itself not prove that what is dreamt of must be there in order for it to provide the dream? (''Choreographies'' 76)

Irigaray locates her writing within the ideological space of female desire, within the pre-Oedipal or the post-patriarchal, *as if* we could remember or imagine a space before or beyond the phallic economy. And Kristeva posits a language of the pre-Oedipal stage of the child's relation to the mother: ''semiotic discourse,'' the gestural, rhythmic, pre-referential language of female *jouissance*, a language not necessarily limited to the female speaker or writer. Indeed, she claims Joyce as an important practitioner of that semiotic discourse. Irigaray fancifully imagines a different syntactic system—one that allows the expression of female ''auto-affection,'' ''self-affection.''[7] But she recognizes that this different language, which would allow us to ''touch ourselves and be touched differently,''[8] will never definitively be found.

Irigaray's attempt to rethink the concept of woman without resorting to limiting or essentialist definitions enables her to critique the *conceptualization* of women in phallogocentric discourse, but also logically forces her to acknowledge as figurative and conceptualizing her *own* analogy between female sexuality and women's language. Since sexuality is not innate, but develops in response to a culture's symbolic system, much feminist theory about a female language can be criticized as what Ann Rosalind Jones calls "an ideal bound up through symmetrical opposition in the very ideological system it intends to destroy" (369). The feminist critique reverses the valuation of the binary poles, but still participates in that male-female opposition, with man as the determining referent. Historically, as Derrida points out, "the determination of sexual difference in opposition" has been "destined, designed, in truth, for truth; it is so in order to erase sexual difference. The dialectical opposition neutralizes or supersedes the difference. However,...one insures phallocentric mastery under the cover of neutralization every time" ("Choreographies" 72).

A deconstructive strategy would first reverse the binary opposition, calling into question the hierarchical valuation of the one pole over the other. It would move beyond the "positional"—difference determined as opposition—to a transformation or general deformation of logic. But such a strategy would also recognize that the reversal and displacement remain implicated in the very structure of privilege and power it critiques.

Does Joyce inscribe the female body in his text? Can such an inscription escape the phallic economy? Carl Jung, not quite knowing how to deal with the intractable *Ulysses*, felt he could at least praise Joyce for the final monologue of Molly Bloom: "The 40 pages of non stop run in the end is a string of veritable psychological peaches. I suppose the devil's grandmother knows so much about the real psychology of a woman, I didn't" (*JJII* 629). Nora Barnacle had a more cynical view of her husband: "He knows nothing at all about women" (*JJII* 629). Molly is the quintessential male representation of the other: she is "the unsurpassable expression of *the woman*, an imaginary of the female 'flesh-without-word,' the other who is assigned to that otherness, flesh, mystery, the inexpressible outside of the law and the speech of men, and is then asked to confirm, magically to say her reality as that" (Heath, "Language" 135). But as Christine van Boheemen points out, "A language of the essentially other, *alias écriture féminine*, is a logical impossibility, based on the hypothesis of an original other (female) identity, and the illusion of expressing that in language—which is after all the very instrument and constitution of the logos/logic of difference." Thus, although Molly Bloom is characterized as an emblem of "otherness" in *Ulysses,* a figure for the otherness of the text as a whole, she never does and never *can* speak for herself as other. Van Boheemen argues that "*Ulysses* seems *at once* to suggest the futility and logical impossibility of a language of the other, *and* to depend on the viability of the idea of making the other present in language for the coherence of its structure as fiction." And she sees the conflation of "subject and object, self and other, in *the idea of* the mother," in "*amor matris*: subjective and objective genitive" (*U-G* 9.842–43), as Joyce's usurpation of the role of the other as he signs himself at once as spiritual father and mother of his text.

Is Joyce's signature a "terrible mastering signature"—as Derrida phrased it (Panel, "Deconstructive Criticism of Joyce")—because he signs into a single work something like the necessity of an epoch? Or because he usurps the role of the (m)other to write that signature? In the "Oxen of the Sun" episode, Joyce parallels the birth of a male child with the birth of the English language—the English language, that is, as written by literary forefathers. In Stephen's envisioning of the postcreation, the corruptible flesh born of the mother is transformed by the (male) artist into the incorruptible logos: "In woman's womb word is made flesh but in the spirit of the maker all flesh that passes becomes the word that shall not pass away" (*U-G* 14.292–94). *Amor matris* may be the only true thing in life, but Stephen's proclamations about creation, whether of art or of life, either ignore—or incorporate into paternity itself—the necessary maternal matrix. "(Male) linguistic ontogeny recapitulates (male) linguistic phylogeny," Sandra Gilbert and Susan Gubar wittily note. "The borning 'Boyaboy' *is* his language, a patriarchal word made flesh in the extended *patrius sermo* of history, and though he is undoubtedly torn out of the prostrate *materna lingua* represented by silent Mrs. Purefoy, he is triumphantly flung, in a Carlylean birth passage, into 'God's air, the Allfather's air' " (534–35). But paternity itself is as artificial a construct as the *patrius sermo* of history. "Fatherhood," Stephen claims, "in the sense of conscious begetting, is unknown to man. It is a mystical estate, an apostolic succession," a parthenogenetic usurpation of the maternal function, moving—biblically, patriarchically—"from only begetter to only begotten'' (*U-G* 9.837-39). ''Creation from nothing,'' it is a mystery founded, like the world it both forms and informs, ''upon the void. Upon uncertitude, upon unlikelihood'' (*U-G* 3.35, 9.841). The ''attribution of procreation to the father,'' according to Lacan, ''can only be the effect of a pure signifier, of a recognition not of a real father, but of what religion has taught us to refer to as the Name-of-the-Father'' (*Écrits* 199). Or, as Joyce in the *Wake* phrases the relationship between paternity and the law: ''the farmer, his son and their homely codes'' (*FW* 614.31-32). In this realm of the symbolic Father, who authors and signifies the Law binding the subject, paternity may well indeed be a ''legal fiction,'' a metaphor, sanctioned by its own law, for what cannot be named. And as Derrida argues, the concept of the father is constituted by language:

> ...the father is not the generator or procreator in any ''real'' sense prior to or outside all relation to language.... Only a power of speech can have a father. The father is always father to a speaking/living being. In other words, it is precisely *logos* that enables us to perceive and investigate something like paternity. (*Dissemination* 80)

As Derrida reads Socrates' myth about writing in Plato's *Phaedrus*, the *logos*, the living, spoken word, depends on the father who engendered him—the *logos*—for his very presence: ''Without his father, he would be nothing but, in fact, writing.... The specificity of writing would thus be intimately bound to the absence of the father'' (*Dissemination* 77). A *logos* committed to writing, according to Plato, is a son who is lost, orphaned, expatriated from the fatherland, no longer able (or perhaps willing) to repeat his origin. Writing is also patricidal: it takes the place of the father, ''supplementing him and supplanting him in his absence and essential disappearance'' (*Dissemination* 89). Outside the law of the father, writing as supplement transgresses that law while always remaining external to it. In substituting ''the breathless sign for the living voice,'' in claiming to exist ''without the father (who is both living and life-giving),'' writing as supplement and transgressor is clearly connected with death (*Dissemination* 92). Writing, as Derrida asserts, ''menaces at once the breath, the spirit, and history as the spirit's relationship with itself. It is their end, their finitude, their paralysis....it is the principle of death and of difference in the becoming of being'' (*Grammatology* 25).

But the feminine subtends even the most phallogocentric theory of artistic creation. In Stephen Dedalus's myth about writing, where he "proves by algebra that Hamlet's grandson is Shakespeare's grandfather and that he himself is the ghost of his own father" (*U-G* 1.555–57), the absent father speaks through the son. Stephen will have it that *Hamlet* is a ghoststory. What is a ghost? He answers his own question: "One who has faded into impalpability through death, through absence, through change of manners" (*U-G* 9.147–49). A ghost by absence, a ghost by death, speaking his own words to his own son's name. A murdered father, an unquiet ghost, speaks; his son hears and, although never fully certain of the authority of the voice he hears (significantly, a point Stephen never mentions), he ultimately acts on its authority. The father's ghostly voice is "a voice heard only in the heart of him who is the substance of his shadow, the son consubstantial with the father" (*U-G* 9.480–81). The son's actions are predicated on the death of the father—and, ultimately, on his own death: "through the ghost of the unquiet father the image of the unliving son looks forth" (*U-G* 9.380–81). The dead father speaks; in a specular logic of the same, the *image* of the dead son looks forth through the ghost of the speaking father.

The law the father has revealed may the *lex eterna*—that which Stephen hopes to be "the divine substance wherein Father and Son are consubstantial": "Hamlet *père* and Hamlet *fils*. A king and a prince at last in death, with incidental music" (*U-G* 3.49–50; 9.1034–35). Or it may be the law of dissemination, a sowing of infinite repetition, proliferation, and supplementation. And is not symbolization possible only through loss, absence, repression? In Plato's myth of Thoth, the Egyptian god of writing is opposed to his other—the father, life, speech, origin—by both supplementing and supplanting that other. Yet the figure of Thoth takes its shape from the very thing it resists and for which it substitutes. As Derrida points out, "The god of writing is thus at once his father, his son, and himself" (*Dissemination* 93)—or, as Stephen's algebraic theory proves, "Hamlet's grandson is Shakespeare's grandfather and...he himself is the ghost of his own father." And in Plato's texts, this play of differences, this endless supplementation, is given a name: "The play of the other within being must needs be designated 'writing' by Plato in a discourse which would like to think of itself as spoken in essence, in truth, and which nevertheless is written" (*Dissemination* 163). Stephen describes something like this infinite play of differences, this double movement of the supplement, when he speaks of the moment of artistic creation:

>—As we, or mother Dana, weave and unweave our bodies... from day to day, their molecules shuttled to and fro, so does the artist weave and unweave his image. And as the mole on my right breast is where it was when I was born, though all my body has been woven of new stuff time after time, so through the ghost of the unquiet father the image of the unliving son looks forth. In the intense instant of the imagination, when the mind, Shelley says, is a fading coal, that which I was is that which I am and that which in possibility I may come to be. So in the future, the sister of the past, I may see myself as I sit here now but by reflection from that which then I shall be. (*U-G* 9.376–85)

That Stephen should present the creation of art in a Penelopean analogy, with mother Dana as the figure of the artist (the Celtic mother-fertility goddess Danu, AE's poem "Dana," and the magazine *Dana* edited by W. K. Magee [John Eglinton])—both female and writing—may seem out of place in a theory of artistic creation that privileges the relationship between father and son. And of course that the figure of the artist *is* female remains unspoken. Gilbert and Gubar postulate the primordial self/other couple as the mother/child rather than man/woman or father/son. "If this is so," they ask, "isn't it also possible that verbal signification arises not from a confrontation with the law of the father but from a consciousness of the lure and the lore of the mother?" (537). Is it possible Stephen's theory of artistic creation, of the sundering and reconciling of father and son, constructs an elaborate guard against the lure of the mother, the (m)other tongue? Although Stephen grounds his theory of Shakespeare in a certain origin and a certain identity, that grounding is destabilized, called into question, by the unknown, by what cannot be named, by the unconscious of the subject, by the discourse of the other. Is not this discourse of the other the discourse not only of writing and of death, but also of woman's *jouissance*?

His account of the experience of Shakespeare's life, the "experience" he has written, centers on one moment, the moment of maternal seduction. Although Shakespeare is "a lord of language," his belief in himself has been "untimely killed"; emasculated by Ann Hathaway's aggressive seduction, the artist is undone: "By cock, she was to blame. She put the comether on him, sweet and twentysix. The greyeyed goddess who bends over the boy Adonis, stooping to conquer, as prologue to the swelling act, is a boldfaced Stratford wench who tumbles in a cornfield a lover younger than herself'' (*U-G* 9.454, 257–60). Significantly, this moment of undoing—and artistic creation—entails the succumbing of the male body to sexuality, to female sexuality. As a fall into language, it acknowledges female *jouissance* as writing.[9] By centering Shakespeare's life on the ''first undoing''—''No later doing will undo the first undoing''(*U-G* 9.459)—Stephen places the genesis of his art in the womb of sin of the fallen Eve, of the mother whose ''strandentwining cable of all flesh'' (*U-G* 3.37) around her children signifies no beginning or end. The myth of paternity entails an origin, a first creation, a creation from nothing: the telephone number to Edenville, to our place of origin, after all, is ''Aleph, alpha: nought, nought, one'' (*U-G* 3.39–40). Eve's belly without blemish may be ''a buckler of taut vellum,'' an empty surface for writing, as Stephen hopes, on which he may inscribe his ''signs on a white field'' (*U-G* 3.42, 414). But, as Maud Ellmann argues, the navel—the ''scarletter on the belly''—tells another story, that has neither a beginning nor an end: ''that neither flesh nor words can ever say where they come from, or claim a unitary origin'' (101). Or, as the children query in *Finnegans Wake*, ''Where did thots come from?'' (*FW* 597.25), conflating the question of maternal creation with that of language and of knowledge.[10] Selfpenning a letter to one's other, then, is to recognize the limitation of the specular construct of the self as one, the coherence and mastery of ''I,'' and to acknowledge the scene on which that self is produced: the body of the woman (Heath, ''Language'' 137, 143).

Stephen would have it that the begetting of a son, the begetting of the *logos* and of the work of art, bypasses the maternal function. But in conflating writing with death, he unwittingly conflates it with the maternal. He centers Shakespeare's life on that ''first undoing,'' when Ann Hathaway hath a will: the ''lord of language'' is ''untimely killed'' by the seduction of the maternal lover. And yet the discourse of the other is the discourse of the female who uses her sexuality, her sexual desire and desirability—''woman's invisible weapon,'' Stephen names it—to drive Shakespeare to his greatest creativity: there is, Stephen says of Shakespeare, ''some goad of the flesh driving him into a new passion, a darker shadow of the first, darkening even his own understanding of himself'' (*U-G* 9.462–64). Socrates may privilege the living *logos*, the spoken word, over writing as supplement and as death, in a fable in which the ''play of the other within being must needs be designated 'writing'" (*Dissemination* 163). And Derrida may posit writing as absence, non-truth, non-essence, *différance*, and death against speech as presence, truth, essence, origin, and life as a pharmakon for "woman's invisible weapon." But Stephen realizes that even Socrates learned from the discourse of the other, from the (m)other tongue: "What useful discovery did Socrates learn from Xanthippe?" John Eglinton asks derisively.

—Dialectic, Stephen answered: and from his mother how to bring thoughts into the world. (*U-G* 9.233–36)

NOTES

1. Paul de Man defines what Nietzsche terms the "phenomenalism of consciousness" as "the tendency to describe mental events such as recollection or emotion in terms derived from the experience of the phenomenal world: sense perception, the interpretation of spatial structures, etc." (107). A critique of this metaphysical construct would prevent us from transforming "consciousness into an authoritative ontological category" (109). De Man further claims that the pattern of argument Nietzsche directs against the concept of consciousness is "the same pattern that underlies the critique of the main categories that make up traditional metaphysics: the concepts of identity, of causality, of the object and the subject, of truth, etc." (109).

2. *FW* 19.35–36. Stephen Heath makes this point in "Ambiviolences: Notes for Reading Joyce": "For Joyce's writing there is no break between world and book, for the world is always already writing ('is, was and will be writing its own wrunes for ever'); words and things move together in the ceaseless production of 'the world'" (67). And of the word.

3. In his Translator's Note to *Écrits*, Alan Sheridan defines Jacques Lacan's use of the term "symbolic" as designating "signifiers, in the sense developed by Saussure and Jakobson, extended into a generalized definition: differential elements, in themselves without meaning, which acquire value only in their mutual relations, and forming a closed order—the question is whether this order is or is not complete. . . . [I]t is the symbolic, not the imaginary, that is seen to be the determining order of the subject, and its effects are radical: the subject, in Lacan's sense, is himself an effect of the symbolic" (ix). Jane Gallop defines "the symbolic" in Lacan's work as the "register of language, social exchange, and radical intersubjectivity" (59).

Julia Kristeva posits two types of signifying processes: the "semiotic" and the "symbolic." The semiotic process relates to the *chora*, a term Plato describes in his *Timaeus* as a "receptacle": "an invisible and formless being which receives all things and in some mysterious way partakes of the intelligible, and is most incomprehensible" (51, quoted in *Desire* 6). In his Introduction to Kristeva's collection of translated essays, *Desire in Language*, Leon S. Roudiez adds that the *chora* is "anterior to any space, an economy of primary processes articulated by Freud's instinctual drives (*Triebe*) through condensation and displacement, and where social and family structures make their imprint through the mediation of the maternal body" (6). The *chora's* articulation is "uncertain, undetermined"; it lacks "thesis or position, unity or identity" (6). The symbolic process, on the other hand, refers to "the establishment of sign and syntax, paternal function, grammatical and social constraints, symbolic law" (6–7). The signifying process results from an articulation between the semiotic and the symbolic; the "speaking subject is engendered as belonging to both the semiotic *chora* and the symbolic device, and that accounts for its eventual split nature" (7).

4. Quoted in Moi 170. *Jouissance*, a term ubiquitous in recent French psychoanalytical, philosophical, critical, and feminist discourses, denotes ecstasy, both sexual and sublime; the enjoyment of rights and property; interest payable. Alan Sheridan distinguishes between "pleasure" (*plaisir*) and "*jouissance*" in his translation of Jacques Lacan's *Écrits*: " 'Pleasure' obeys the law of homeostasis that Freud evokes in 'Beyond the Pleasure Principle,' whereby, through discharge, the psyche seeks the lowest possible level of tension. '*Jouissance*' transgresses this law and, in that respect, it is *beyond* the pleasure principle" (x).

5. The neologism, "phallogocentrism," underscores the complicity between logocentrism and phallocentrism. Logocentrism is the desire for a first cause of being and meaning, for a central presence as the locus of coherence and authenticity, and for full self-consciousness ("thought thinking itself"); phallocentrism places the male-identified subject at the center of intellect, perception, experience, values, and language. As Derrida notes, "It is one and the same system: The erection of a paternal logos...and of the phallus as 'privileged signifier' (Lacan)" ("Avoir l'oreille de la philosophie" 311).

6. Irigaray, "Women's Exile" 71. See for this point Carolyn Burke, "Irigaray through the Looking Glass" 28.

7. *This Sex* 132–33. See Carolyn Burke, "Introduction to Luce Irigaray's 'When Our Lips Speak Together' " 67.

8. *This Sex* 147. See also Carolyn Burke's discussion of this point in "Irigaray through the Looking Glass."

9. "Orgasm in discourse leads us to the point where feminine jouissance can be understood as writing (*écriture*). To the point where it must appear that this jouissance and the literary text (which is also written like an orgasm produced from within discourse), are the effect of the same murder of the signifier." In defining writing as the jouissance of a woman, Montrelay argues that what the woman is writing is the name: both the *nom du père* (the name-of-the-father) and the *non* (not, nothing) (234).

10. In the 1905 "Three Essays on the Theory of Sexuality," Freud claims "we have learnt from psycho-analysis that the instinct for knowledge in children is attracted unexpectedly early and intensively to sexual problems and is in fact possibly first aroused by them.... And this history of the instinct's origin is in line with the fact that the first problem with which it deals is not the question of the distinction between the sexes but the riddle of where babies come from" (60, 61; his emphasis on the riddle of birth as predating the question of distinction between the sexes is qualified in "Some Psychical Consequences of the Anatomical Distinction between the Sexes," 1925). Freud argues in his 1909 "Analysis of a Phobia in a Five-Year-Old Boy" that "Thirst for knowledge seems to be inseparable from sexual curiosity" (51). Little Hans's sexual curiosity about male and female sexual organs and about how and where children originate "roused the spirit of inquiry in him and enabled him to arrive at genuine abstract knowledge" (51). Heath, MacCabe, and Ellmann all discuss the link between the origin of children—"tots"—and of knowledge—"thoughts"—in this passage from the *Wake*.

WORKS CITED

Burke, Carolyn. "Introduction to Luce Irigaray's 'When Our Lips Speak Together.' " *Signs: Journal of Women in Culture and Society* 6 (1980): 66–68.

———."Irigaray through the Looking Glass." *Feminist Studies* 7 (Summer 1981): 288–306.

Cixous, Hélène. "Joyce: The (r)use of writing." In *Post-structuralist Joyce: Essays from the French*, edited by Derek Attridge and Daniel Ferrer, 15–30. Cambridge: Cambridge University Press, 1984.

Clément, Catherine. "Enslaved Enclave." In *New French Feminisms: An Anthology*, edited by Elaine Marks and Isabelle de Courtivron, 130–36. New York: Schocken Books, 1981.

De Man, Paul. *Allegories of Reading: Figural Language in Rousseau, Nietzsche, Rilke, and Proust*. New Haven and London: Yale University Press, 1979.

Derrida, Jacques. "Avoir l'oreille de la philosophie." In *Écarts: Quatre essais à propos de Jacques Derrida*, edited by Lucette Finas et al., 301–12. Paris: Fayard, 1973.

———. "Choreographies." Interview with Christie V. McDonald. *Diacritics* 12 (Summer 1982): 66–76.

———. Contribution to panel "Deconstructive Criticism of Joyce." Ninth International James Joyce Symposium in Frankfurt, West Germany, June 1984.

———. *Dissemination*, translated by Barbara Johnson. Paris: Éditions du Seuil, 1972; Chicago: University of Chicago Press, 1981.

———. *Of Grammatology*, translated by Gayatri Chakravorty Spivak. Paris: Les Éditions de Minuit, 1967; Baltimore and London: Johns Hopkins University Press, 1976.

———. "Structure, Sign, and Play in the Discourse of the Human Sciences." In *The Structuralist Controversy: The Languages of Criticism and the Sciences of Man*, edited by Richard Macksey and Eugenio Donato, 247–72. Baltimore and London: Johns Hopkins University Press, 1972.

Ellmann, Maud. "Polytropic Man: Paternity, Identity and Naming in *The Odyssey* and *A Portrait of the Artist as a Young Man*." In *James Joyce: New Perspectives*, edited by Colin MacCabe, 73–104. Sussex: Harvester Press; Bloomington: Indiana University Press, 1982.

Freud, Sigmund. *The Sexual Enlightenment of Children*, edited by Philip Rieff. New York: Macmillan, 1963.

———. *Three Essays on the Theory of Sexuality*, translated and edited by James Strachey. New York: Basic Books, 1962.

Gallop, Jane. *Reading Lacan*. Ithaca and London: Cornell University Press, 1985.

Gilbert, Sandra M., and Susan Gubar. "Sexual Linguistics: Gender, Language, Sexuality." *New Literary History* 1985: 515–43.

Heath, Stephen. "Ambiviolences: Notes for Reading Joyce." In *Post-structuralist Joyce: Essays from the French*, edited by Derek Attridge and Daniel Ferrer, 31–68. Cambridge: Cambridge University Press, 1984.

———. "Joyce in Language." In *James Joyce: New Perspectives*, edited by Colin MacCabe, 129–48. Sussex: Harvester Press; Bloomington: Indiana University Press, 1982.

Irigaray, Luce. *This Sex Which Is Not One*, translated by Catherine Porter with Carolyn Burke. Ithaca: Cornell University Press, 1985.

————. "Women's Exile." *Ideology and Consciousness* 1 (1977): 57–76.

Jolas, Eugene. "The Revolution of Language and James Joyce." In *Our Exagmination Round His Factification for Incamination of* Work in Progress, edited by Samuel Beckett et al., 77–92. Paris: Shakespeare and Co., 1929; New York: New Directions, 1939, 1962.

Jones, Ann Rosalind. "Writing the Body: Toward an Understanding of *L'Écriture féminine*." In *The New Feminist Criticism: Essays on Women, Literature, and Theory,* edited by Elaine Showalter, 361–77. New York: Pantheon Books, 1985.

Kristeva, Julia. *Desire in Language: A Semiotic Approach to Literature and Art,* edited by Leon S. Roudiez; translated by Thomas Gora, Alice Jardine, and Leon S. Roudiez. New York: Columbia University Press, 1980.

————. *Semeiotike: Recherches pour une sémanalyse.* Paris: Seuil, 1969.

Lacan, Jacques. *Ecrits: A Selection,* translated by Alan Sheridan. Paris: Editions du Seuil, 1966; New York: W. W. Norton, 1977.

————. "God and the *Jouissance* of The Woman." In *Feminine Sexuality: Jacques Lacan and the école freudienne,* edited by Juliet Mitchell and Jacqueline Rose, 137–48. New York: W. W. Norton, 1982.

MacCabe, Colin. *James Joyce and the Revolution of the Word.* New York: Barnes & Noble, 1979.

Moi, Toril. *Sexual/Textual Politics: Feminist Literary Theory.* London and New York: Methuen, 1985.

Montrelay, Michele. "An Inquiry into Femininity," translated by Parveen Adams. *Semiotext(e)* 4 (1981): 228–35.

Scholes, Robert, and Richard M. Kain, eds. *The Workshop of Daedalus: James Joyce and the Raw Materials for* A Portrait of the Artist as a Young Man. Evanston: Northwestern University Press, 1965.

Sheridan, Alan. Translator's Note. In *Écrits: A Selection,* by Jacques Lacan, vii–xii. New York and London: W. W. Norton, 1977.

Sollers, Philippe. "Joyce & Co." In *In the Wake of the* Wake, edited by David Hayman and Elliott Anderson, 107–21. Madison: The University of Wisconsin Press, 1978.

Van Boheemen, Christine. "Joyce, Derrida, and the Language of the 'Other.'" Paper delivered for panel "Deconstructive Criticism of Joyce." Ninth International James Joyce Symposium in Frankfurt, West Germany, June 1984.

13

Simulation, Pluralism, and the Politics of Everyday Life

JULES DAVID LAW

Mortal! You found me in evil company
—Bloom's Nymph

The uniqueness of a work of art is inseparable from its being imbedded in the fabric of tradition. [. . .] An ancient statue of Venus, for example, stood in a different traditional context with the Greeks who made it an object of veneration, than with the clerics of the Middle Ages, who viewed it as an ominous idol. Both of them, however, were equally confronted with its uniqueness, that is, its aura.
—Benjamin, ''The Work of Art in the Age of Mechanical Reproduction''

In June of 1860, while browsing through the contents of an antiquarian street-stall in Florence, Robert Browning came across the quarto transcript of a seventeenth-century murder trial. The book, which Browning describes as ''pure crude fact / Secreted from man's life,'' was to become the basis for his verse novel, *The Ring and the Book*. What is of particular interest for us, in the context of Joyce, is Browning's description of the book's discovery, for it would appear to be a model of the discovery of history in the rhythms of the quotidian. At the beginning of the poem, Browning describes finding the book:

'Mongst odds and ends of ravage, picture-frames
White through the worn gilt, mirror-sconces chipped,
Bronze angel-heads once knobs attached to chests,
(Handled when ancient dames chose forth brocade)
Modern chalk drawings, studies from the nude,
Samples of stone, jet, breccia, porphyry
Polished and rough, sundry amazing busts
In baked earth, (broken, Providence be praised!)
A wreck of tapestry [. . .]
A pile of brown-etched prints, two *crazie* each,
Stopped by a conch atop from fluttering forth [. . .]
                                        [. . .] these
I picked the book from.   (Vol. 1, bk. 1, 35–36, 53–57)

Browning describes the discovery of the volume as a "restorative" event, and obviously he intends this in more than one sense. As he describes it, the "pure crude fact" of a Roman murder case, having originally been forged into history through its recording and transmission, and subsequently disappearing in the quotidian concreteness of a street-vendor's wares, has now been revivified before his very eyes. History steps forth from amongst odds and ends, to assert itself as an intensely personal fact, ostensibly eluding the tendential logic which has reduced it and its companion relics to objects of exchange in a street-vendor's booth. At the same time, this resurrection of history rescues Browning from the quotidian routine of his own life— the book's restoration is his as well.

The metamorphosis of the quotidian into the historic is one of the great themes of *Ulysses*, and though examples abound, one passage bears an intriguing, if parodic, resemblance to Browning's discovery of his restorative book. This analogous moment occurs when the Greek nymph represented in the erotic art-poster above Bloom's and Molly's bed steps forth on the stage of Nighttown to address Bloom:

([...] *Out of her oakframe a nymph with hair unbound, lightly clad in teabrown artcolours, descends from her grotto and passing under interlacing yews stands over Bloom.*)

· ·

THE NYMPH

Mortal! You found me in evil company, highkickers, coster picnic makers, pugilists, popular generals, immoral panto boys in flesh-tights and the nifty shimmy dancers, La Aurora and Karini, musical act, the hit of the century. I was hidden in cheap pink paper that smelt of rock oil. I was surrounded by the stale smut of clubmen, stories to disturb callow youth, ads for transparencies, truedup dice and bustpads, proprietary articles and why wear a truss with testimonial from ruptured gentleman. Useful hints to the married. (444–45)

Though Bloom interrupts momentarily here, the Nymph goes on compulsively to catalogue the commercial menagerie from which Bloom eventually "bore [her] away" and "framed [her] in oak and tinsel" (445). Though she has a sense of her own *context*, she is aware of no personal *history* prior to her magazine existence. This is entirely in keeping with the ethos of the "Circe" chapter which, as Franco Moretti has remarked, is the "unsurpassed literary representation of commodity fetishism" (*Signs Taken for Wonders* 185).

Like Browning, Bloom rescues a subject from amongst quotidian odds and ends, and frames it for his own purposes. The difference, of course, is that Bloom's nymph is only a *parody* of history and culture. Whereas Browning's *found art* needs only to be polished, or at best, catalyzed, to restore its historical and cultural resonances, Bloom's *found art* is truly the stuff of quotidian or everyday life—both reproducible and disposable. Despite the oak frame which Bloom provides for his "photo girl" from *Photo Bits*, he is fully convinced that her picture is not "art." Later in *Ulysses* he elaborates on the difference between "original" Greek statues and photographic reproductions:

> He dwelt, being a bit of an artist in his spare time, on the female form in general developmentally because, as it so happened, no later than that afternoon he had seen those Grecian statues, *perfectly developed as works of art*, in the National Museum. *Marble could give the original*, shoulders, back, all the symmetry, all the rest. Yes, puritanisme, it does though Saint Joseph's sovereign thievery alors (Bandez!) Figne toi trop. *Whereas no photo could because it simply wasn't art in a word.* (533, my emphasis)

Bloom here reproduces the traditional nineteenth-century assessment of the relationship between art and photography.[1] Nevertheless, his assumptions about aesthetic value are undermined by the larger tendency of *Ulysses* to juxtapose the mythic and the mechanical, and to evoke a "culture" of everyday life. The same logic which leads J. J. O'Molloy to pronounce "a postcard" as "publication" (264) is also at work in *Ulysses* preparing for photography to become "art," and for everyday life to achieve the status of an historical and aesthetic object.

The history and the culture of everyday life: are these parodic oxymorons, or modernist ideologies *par excellence*? And if it *is* possible to write the history and the culture of everyday life, is Joyce's work an authentic—or even, perhaps, a unique—contribution to that project? In order to approach these questions we might first note that Henri Lefebvre begins his ground-breaking study, *Everyday Life in the Modern World*, by designating June 16th, 1904, as the "momentous eruption of everyday life into literature" (2). *Ulysses*, writes Lefebvre, "rescues...each facet of the quotidian from anonymity." However, Lefebvre goes on to point out that *Ulysses* represents everyday life in a specifically *modernist* mode: as an exploration of subjectivity.

Ulysses is dominated by those details of subjective quotidian experience which now appear to us as modernist clichés: for instance, ordinary and private language, stream of consciousness, and the slips of tongue and mind mythologized by Freud in *The Psychopathology of Everyday Life*.[2] By contrast, argues Lefebvre, if one were to set out to write a novel about everyday life in the 1960s, under the shadow of post-modernism, one would begin with objects rather than with subjects (one thinks here of the novels of Robbe-Grillet).

Lefebvre's distinction between the modernist regime of the sub-ject and the postmodernist regime of the object, is by now a familiar one, perhaps even a cliché of its own. Nevertheless, to speak of a politics of narrative at this juncture in history without taking into account the notions of postmodernism, poststructuralism, and late capitalism which have intervened between us and Joyce, would be to deny our own positionality. In order properly to appreciate Joyce's revolutionary creation of a formal narrative from cultural bric-à-brac, it is necessary to emphasize how differently that bric-à-brac functioned in his time than in our own. Joyce assumes the inevitable structural presence of history and myth in everyday life—even in the patterns of commodity production. For Joyce, the fetishized commodities of everyday life hold and unsettle the consumer's gaze precisely because of the parodic dissonance between the cultural scenarios they gesture towards and the social situations in which they are actually exchanged. There is a dissonance too between commodities and their *represen-tation* in advertising, a dissonance that advertising counts on, para-doxically, both to "arrest" and to assist the "velocity of modern life." We can see this tension at work in two of Bloom's fantasies about the ultimate advertisement:

What also stimulated him in his cogitations?

[. . .] the infinite possibilities hitherto unexploited of the modern art of advertisement if condensed in trilateral monoidal symbols, vertically of maximum visibility (divined), horizontally of maxi-mum legibility (deciphered) and of *magnetising efficacy to arrest involuntary attention*, to interest, to convince, to decide. (559, my emphasis)

What were habitually his final meditations?

Of some one sole unique advertisement to cause passers to *stop in wonder*, a poster novelty, with all extraneous accretions ex-cluded, reduced to its simplest and most efficient terms *not exceeding the span of casual vision* and congruous with the *velocity of modern life*. (592, my emphasis)[3]

However, ours is no longer an era of commodity production, and the objects of commercial culture no longer arrest us as the nymph does Leopold Bloom. Whereas at the beginning of this century, advertising images were still novel enough to be recognized as (pleasant or threatening) distortions both of everyday life and of history, now advertising presents a self-generating simulation of reality, without any historical dissonance or uncanniness.[4] We like to think that if we scratched beneath the surface of contemporary everyday life, we would find the earthiness and uncanniness of Bloom's everyday life. But is this so?

In a critique of Western political economy not unrelated to Lefebvre's, Jean Baudrillard has described the shift from a traditional capitalist economy organized around the *commodity* to a late-capitalist economy organized around the *simulacrum* (*Simulations* 1–13, 26–30; *The Mirror of Production* 121–51). The commodity, though an exchange value, is not infinitely exchangeable. It is intended to be measured against something else, and therefore, in a sense, always has a residue of inadequacy, a value to be consummated later. The commodity is intended to be used as well as exchanged. Even if it is never actually used, the scenarios of its concrete use haunt it like a dream; its exchange only defers—without replacing—its essential use value.[5] (In this sense, the traditional commodity follows traditional art; Benjamin remarks that "One of the foremost tasks of art has always been the creation of a demand which could be fully satisfied only later" [237]). In the world of *Ulysses* commodities are rarely consumed instantaneously, or once and for all, but rather decay through a series of use values, as if possessed of a radioactive half-life: "huge webs of paper. Clank it. Clank it. Miles of it unreeled. What becomes of it after? O, wrap up meat, parcels: various uses, thousand and one things" (99).

The simulacrum, on the other hand, has no such uncanniness or sense of deferral about it; it exists to be experienced and used up at the same time, like a computer graphic, a television image, or a media event:

No more mirror of being and appearances, of the real and its concept. No more imaginary coextensivity: rather, genetic min-iaturisation is the dimension of simulation. The real is produced from miniaturised units, from matrices, memory banks and

command models—and with these it can be reproduced an
indefinite number of times. It no longer has to be rational,
since it is no longer measured against some ideal or negative
instance. It is nothing more than operational.
. . . .
It is no longer a question of imitation, nor of reduplication, nor
even of parody. It is rather a question of substituting signs of
the real for the real itself, that is, an operation to deter every
real process by its operational double, a metastable, program-
matic, perfect descriptive machine which provides all the signs
of the real. . . . Never again will the real have to be produced.
(Baudrillard, *Simulations* 3–4)

The simulacrum does not imitate or dissimulate a future use value;
it conjures up a reality with which it is then satisfyingly isomorphic.
The simulacrum is the fundamental unit of the information network,
the information revolution, and the information industry. It is purged
of both the history and the labor that creates it, and thus points to
a universe of objects without subjects.

The abolition of the subject and of the referent, which have
become the distinguishing and notorious features of both literary
and economic postmodernism, pose a challenge to our attempt to
recover the specific mode of representing everyday life which *Ulysses*
itself represents. In Browning's time, the increasing commodification
of everyday life was simply a stage for the contrastive and restorative
emergence of historical and mythical consciousness—thus Browning
discovered the material for his greatest artistic achievement in the
middle of an everyday life. Even if the possibility of an escape from
quotidian, commercial culture was really already a fiction, late
Victorian literature attested nonetheless to a very real and important
nostalgia for such transcendence in the form of myth and history.
For Joyce, everyday life—even if saturated in and by commercial
culture—was nevertheless the repository of history, meaning, and
myth. There was no need to extract the latter categories from the
former.[6] To read the productions of popular and commercial culture
was simultaneously to read the mythic history of mankind. This was,
of course, the only way for him to resolve the inherited nineteenth-
century contradiction between a "false" quotidian consciousness and
a "genuine" historical one.

But the apparent simultaneity, in Joyce's work, of the mythic
and the quotidian, of historicity and contemporaneity, is perhaps
the greatest obstacle to our historical—and thus our political—

understanding of *Ulysses*. Joyce seems to preempt the question of whether we read literature for historical or for contemporary ("relevant") experiences, precisely by demonstrating the inevitable structural presence of history and myth in everyday life. Thanks to Joyce, and to other early modernist thinkers, the very notion of "everyday life" now has a history, a psychological theory, and an unprecedented aesthetic evocation. Yet whose everyday life does Joyce represent? Everyday lives have changed so radically even in the short time between Joyce's life and our own that we are already in danger of misunderstanding what is meant for Joyce to have transformed the materials of everyday life into art. What if everyday life in the postmodern world in fact functions not merely to produce or reproduce its own history (for history is in a sense always "produced," "narrated," "constructed," etc.), but rather in doing so to discourage historical thinking?

Let me try to elaborate on this. If we were going to characterize Joyce's achievement, we would say that he exaggerates everyday life by making it denser and more complex than it "really" appears to the average consciousness. Thus it is his representation of subjectivity rather than of the physical world that we recognize as constituting his distinctive aesthetic deflection.[7] Despite Ortega y Gasset's perceptive comments about Joycean infrarealism (*The Dehumanization of Art* 35–36), it does not seem to us that Joyce distorted, or falsely represented the concrete objects of the quotidian world—he depicted them, after all, in all their obstinate and autonomous glory.[8] What he did was to de-center the perceiving mind. But the objects of the quotidian world are not quite so obstinate or resistant to consciousness today, in a society of controlled simulations, as they were at the beginning of the century in an awkward, transitional phase of consumer culture. If the quotidian bristles in *Ulysses*, that is not something we can recapture for our own culture simply by looking to Joyce for *new and fresh ways of seeing the world*.

It is precisely because we think of everyday life as an unproblematic notion—on a par with such concepts as the normal, the literal, and the ordinary—that we think of *Ulysses* as being every bit as democratic in its accessibility as it is radical in its inaccessibility. This myth of democratic accessibility ("all interpretations are valid") explains perhaps why critical pluralism (whose very mention generates endless lame controversies elsewhere in our profession) has never had to pay for, or fight for, its admission into Joycean circles. Elsewhere

in literary academia, the concept and the representation of everyday
life are uncritically rejected as popular culture; within Joyce circles
we are perhaps too uncritically receptive to the representations of
everyday life.

Why draw this connection between pluralism and everyday life?
Because what pluralism seems to deny, or at least to challenge, is
the very notion of a determining intentionality. And ever since Freud,
at least, we have considered *the quotidian to be the realm of the
unintentional.* The quotidian *is* the unintentional. Freudian everyday
life is defined precisely as that realm of experience in which our
actions and expressions are so habitual and un-thought-out at the
conscious level that their disruption by unconscious intentions is all
the more likely to be noticed. Joyce's grand mythification of the
quotidian reveals this "double life" of the everyday life, and has
become, simultaneously, the greatest evocation of intentionality *and*
of *un*intentionality in our language. The everyday life of *Ulysses*,
then, seems both to confirm and to challenge critical pluralism. But
in order to read politically, do we have to choose between a
conciliatory (and contemporizing) pluralism and a rigid (historicizing)
determinism?

I would like to say that our task is not to *choose* between
pluralism and its discontents, between Joyce, the chronicler of everyday life and Joyce, the mythmaker and esotericist, but rather to
see how this very choice arises out of an historically specific conception
of everyday life which *Ulysses* itself represents, and which contemporary criticism represents to us as still our own.[9] Seen in this light,
what *Ulysses* has to contribute to a politics of narrative is precisely
its hold on the fundamental tension between the intentional and
the unintentional, played out on the terrain of an increasingly
anachronistic everyday life, whose image is still familiar enough to
us to represent a powerful nostalgia. Cultivating this nostalgia cannot
protect us against the increasingly simulated nature of contemporary
existence and the disappearance of its historicity. But if we can learn
to treat *Ulysses* neither as a unified text nor as a pluralistic one, but
rather as a self-contradictory, overdetermined, and heterogeneous
one, we may be able to turn our nostalgia into a resistance to the
simulations of everyday life in our own world, simulations which
cannot endlessly fend off the massive social dislocations on our
horizon.[10]

NOTES

1. On the debate concerning photography and "art," see Benjamin (18–27).

2. On ordinary and private language, see Wittgenstein (*Philosophical Investigations*, especially paragraphs 97–133, 242–75).

3. Franco Moretti points to these two passages as evidence of the way in which Joyce conceives advertising as the new unconscious of the culture, "a form of persuasion based on unawareness" paralleling the "randomness, rapidity, discontinuity, uncontrollability and depth of the stream of consciousness" (*Signs Taken For Wonders* 196–97). However, Moretti's emphasis is less on discontinuities and disjunctions than on the fluid, subliminal effects of advertising, and this risks missing the difference between a modernist culture of commodities and the postmodernist culture of simulacra (which I shall discuss below). In Joyce's and Bloom's conception, advertising must somehow "arrest" and "stop" the consumer, even as it fits more or less "casual[ly]" into the flow of experience. The advertising image has not yet blended entirely with the fabric of everyday life, nor collapsed into an identity with the commodity which it represents.

4. See Jameson (*Marxism and Form*). In the early twentieth century, according to Jameson,

> Advertising, in the dimensions so familiar to us, is scarcely developed at all; indeed, the very ads themselves, whether *affiche*, the sandwich man of *Ulysses*, or that crude painting on a vacant wall which was Gertrude Stein's first introduction to the secret prestige of oil paints, can still be apprehended as objects of fascination in their own right. (104)

5. Jameson ("Postmodernism") points to the erasure of use value in the simulacrum: "Appropriately enough, the culture of the simulacrum comes to *life* in a society where exchange-value has been generalized to the point at which the very memory of use-value is effaced" (66).

6. Franco Moretti, like Adorno and Brecht in earlier debates with Lukács, defends Joyce against the charge of mystifying social experience by fetishizing its "mythic" aspects. In Joyce's work, according to Moretti,

> myth and history are *complementary*: they presuppose and neutralize each other, and it is impossible to establish a formal or ideological hierarchy between the two. In Joyce, myth is not identified with the aesthetic *form* (as in Eliot), and therefore cannot be the starting point for a new *cultural hegemony*. (192)

See also Lukács ("Realism in the Balance"), Brecht and Adorno ("Reconciliation Under Duress"), all in Bloch et al., *Aesthetics and Politics*.

7. Cf. Jameson (*Marxism and Form*):

> Think of the precariousness of the synthesis of Joyce, in which matter once again seems momentarily reconciled with spirit, all the objects and detritus of the city luminous and as though informed by subjectivity— except that the seams show [. . .].

8. Cf. Jameson ("Postmodernism"):

> Not only are Picasso and Joyce no longer ugly; they now strike us, on the whole, as rather "realistic"; and this is the result of a canonization

and an academic institutionalization of the modern movement generally, which can be traced to the late 1950s. (56)

9. Cf. Jameson ("Reflections in Conclusion," in *Aesthetics and Politics*):

> To take an attitude of partisanship towards key struggles of the recent past does not mean either choosing sides, or seeking to harmonize irreconcilable differences. [...] The fundamental contradiction is between history itself and the conceptual apparatus which, seeking to grasp its realities, only succeeds in reproducing their discord within itself in the form of an enigma for thought, an aporia. It is to this aporia that we must hold, which contains within its structure the crux of a history beyond which we have not yet passed. (213)

10. On the Marxist notions of ideological contradiction and overdetermination, see especially Althusser ("Contradiction and Overdetermination" 87–128) and Jean-Paul Sartre (*Search for a Method* 100–111, 140–66); on heterogeneity, see Derrida ("White Mythology," especially 214–15, 253–54; *Of Grammatology* 19–21).

WORKS CITED

Adorno, Theodor. "Reconciliation Under Duress," translated by Rodney Livingstone. In *Aesthetics and Politics,* by Ernst Bloch et al. London: Verso, 1980.

Althusser, Louis. *For Marx,* translated by Ben Brewster. New York: Vintage, 1969.

Baudrillard, Jean. *The Mirror of Production,* translated and with an introduction by Mark Poster. St. Louis: Telos Press, 1975.

———. *Simulations,* translated by Paul Foss, Paul Patton, and Philip Beitchman. New York: Semiotext[e], Inc., Foreign Agents Series, 1983.

Benjamin, Walter. "The Work of Art in the Age of Mechanical Reproduction." In *Illuminations,* edited and with an introduction by Hanna Arendt; translated by Harry Zohn. New York: Schocken, 1969.

Brecht, Bertolt. "The Essays of George Lukacs" and "On the Formalistic Character of the Theory of Narrative," translated by Stuart Hood. In *Aesthetics and Politics,* by Ernest Bloch et al. London: Verso, 1980.

Browning, Robert. *The Ring and the Book,* Vol. I. Boston: Houghton, Mifflin, 1884.

Derrida, Jacques. *Of Grammatology,* translated and with an introduction by Gayatri Chakravorty Spivak. Baltimore: Johns Hopkins University Press, 1976.

———. "White Mythology: Metaphor in the Text of Philosophy." In *Margins of Philosophy,* translated with additional notes by Alan Bass. Chicago: University of Chicago Press, 1982.

Jameson, Frederic. *Marxism and Form: Twentieth-Century Dialectical Theories of Literature.* Princeton: Princeton University Press, 1971.

———. "Postmodernism, or The Cultural Logic of Late Capitalism." *New Left Review* 146 (1984): 53–92.

———. "Reflections in Conclusion." In *Aesthetics and Politics,* by Ernest Bloch et al., 196–213. London: Verso, 1980.

Lefebvre, Henri. *Everyday Life in the Modern World,* translated by Sacha Rabinovitch, with a new introduction by Philip Wander. New Brunswick, N. J.: Transaction Books, 1971.

Lukács, Georg. "Realism in the Balance," translated by Rodney Livingstone. In *Aesthetics and Politics,* by Ernest Bloch et al., 28–59. London: Verso, 1980.

Moretti, Franco. *Signs Taken for Wonders: Essays in the Sociology of Literary Forms,* translated by Susan Fischer, David Forgacs, and David Miller. London: Verso, 1983.

Ortega y Gasset, José. *The Dehumanization of Art,* translated by Helene Weyl. Princeton: Princeton University Press, 1968.

Sartre, Jean-Paul. *Search for a Method,* translated and with an introduction by Hazel Barnes. New York: Random House, 1968.

Wittgenstein, Ludwig. *Philosophical Investigations,* translated by G. E. M. Anscombe. Oxford: Blackwell, 1958.

14

Joyce's Pedagogy:
Ulysses and *Finnegans Wake* as Theory
PATRICK MCGEE

Wyndham Lewis, to Joyce's somewhat irritated fascination, called *Ulysses* "an encyclopedia of english literary technique, as well as a general-knowledge paper. The schoolmaster in Joyce," he continued, "is in great evidence throughout its pages" (76). Although Lewis never appreciated what was most innovative in Joyce's teaching (indeed, he learned very little from Joyce), he was right to lay emphasis on the pedagogical effect of Joyce's work, on the way it sets out to inform and reshape the reading subject. Any work of literature or any writing can be said to produce this effect, but I want to argue that in Joyce's later work such an effect is primary. In relation to the issue of pedagogy, other questions about Joyce's work—whether *Ulysses* is a novel or what *Finnegans Wake* is about—become secondary; they are seen as questions posed and subsumed by Joyce's style.

In *A Portrait of the Artist as a Young Man,* the narrative events unfold in academic settings, often in the classroom, but more frequently in those places where we see Stephen Dedalus struggle against biological, spiritual, and academic fathers in order to achieve personal autonomy—the autonomy he demonstrates in chapter 5 by conveying his aesthetic theory to Lynch and by taking his imaginative life into his own hands in deciding to leave Ireland. Pedagogy is seen from the point of view of the student who uses his teachers and their teaching as Wittgenstein argued we should use his philosophical propositions—as a ladder to be climbed and then discarded. The teacher, like the father in Joyce, seems doomed to failure, especially for Stephen who, like his author, must teach himself to fly beyond the nets of language, nationality, and religion. Ironically, though, in the scene with Lynch in chapter 5, Stephen's own approach to knowledge and his method of conveying it are purely conventional, expository, magisterial. In advancing his aesthetic theory, Stephen takes into account neither himself as a desiring subject implicated in a web of words nor Lynch as a subject on whom the theory is intended to work and to produce an effect. The theory stands on its own as a cognition to which the teacher and the student, the voice and the ear, are only tangentially related. Ultimately, all that Stephen succeeds in proving is his quasi-mastery of the traditional thought associated with the names Aristotle, Aquinas, Ibsen, etc. He has a certain textual knowledge but no knowledge of the teaching process itself. Lynch would appear to have more understanding of that process in the way he carefully urges Stephen to speak by facetiously playing the part of the one who doesn't know and who has nothing better to do than to listen to the cogitations of genius. On the whole, the pedagogical effect in Joyce's book is not much more developed than in Stephen's demonstration. *A Portrait of the Artist* is *only* a novel; and, in spite of its complex ironies, it remains faithful to the convention of the novel and refuses to problematize the relation between the writer and the reader. It does not require the extensive restructuring of the reader through self-analysis and the overcoming in the reader of resistance to the act of reading.

Although such a restructuring is the pedagogical effect of Joyce's later work, the beginning of *Ulysses* is not greatly different from *A Portrait* in focusing on scenes of teaching. However, these scenes, as I will show, provide a critical view of pedagogy that the performative dimension of the entire book illustrates. In the "Nestor" episode, for example, Stephen at first epitomizes the awkward, bungling pedagogue who can hardly sustain the interest of his pupils. Based on what we see, he clearly fails as a teacher, at least in any normative sense of the word, although he does bring about the possibility of learning. He does this by exploiting the linguistic accident resulting from his pupil's attempt to identify the name Pyrrhus in a lesson on ancient history. Out of ignorance and frustration, young Armstrong associates the name of the ancient general with the word "pier"; and when Stephen asks for a definition of the latter, the boy says, "A kind of bridge. Kingstown pier, sir." Stephen cannot resist making a verbal joke: "Kingstown pier...Yes, a disappointed bridge" (*U-GP* 20–1).

If, as Derrida has suggested, education in its traditional forms "has as its ideal...the effacement of language" ("Living On" 93–94), then Stephen's teaching, in this instance, challenges such idealization by drawing attention to a use of language that resists

effacement. This use does not negate language's signifying or referential functions but shows to what extent these functions depend on
a rhetorical surface, to what extent the grammar and logic of reference
bring about their own displacement by uncovering the metonymic
links between apparently unrelated signifiers. Stephen's young pupils
are confused by his joke because they cannot see through the phrase
"a disappointed bridge" to the referent that would yield an objective
meaning and, thus, stop the play of words. They don't know how
to respond to the joke because they don't know how to repeat it. As
Freud stressed, a joke is only understood when it can be repeated;
even our initial response has less to do with grasping its meaning
than with grasping the logic of its construction, the way it capitalizes
on linguistic coincidence. The troubled gaze of Stephen's students
after hearing the joke is a symptom of their traditional education, of
their lack of knowledge about language as language, about its rhetorical dimension. Knowledge of such a dimension entails the ability
not only to tell jokes but to make the figures of speech that are
crucial to the construction of both literary texts and persuasive arguments. Indeed, ignorance of rhetoric blocks the process of invention
itself, prevents the subject from being able to take a position from
within language and to assert its linguistic independence in the process
of self-representation.

Just in case his students did not grasp the point about language
the first time, Stephen decides to give them a second chance. He
tells them a riddle: "*The cock crew, / The sky was blue: / The bells
in heaven / Were striking eleven. / 'Tis time for this poor soul / To
go to heaven.*" When no one guesses the answer, Stephen reveals it
himself: "The fox burying his grandmother under a hollybush" (*U-
GP* 22). Stephen lays a trap with this unanswerable riddle in order
to teach his pupils a lesson. Precisely because the rhetorical force of
language surpasses its power of signification, it can always be used to
mystify, to create the illusion of a positive referent where there is
none. The riddle creates the illusion of meaning, but the answer
subverts that illusion (and hides the private meaning known only to
Stephen, i.e., the reference to his dead mother) by insisting on the
arbitrariness of its relation to the riddle. This forces us to see what
we frequently do not see when we read formulations as different as
an intelligence quotient or a political slogan: the gap between the
raw signifier and the set of interpretive constraints that produce
meaning and social value. However, Stephen can convey this knowl-

edge only by risking failure as a teacher insofar as nothing guarantees that either we or his pupils will "get the message" or be able to repeat the performance.

In other words, Stephen, whatever his intention, teaches his students that understanding involves more than effacing words in order to grasp a referent. In involves seeing or hearing words as iterative, as self-reflexive. If we are blind or deaf to this dimension of language, then we become susceptible to every kind of mystification and block our own capacity for creative self-transformation. We surrender our positions as subjects and become the objects of another's subjectivity, instead of subsuming subject and object, through the critical use of language, within the collective being of the social symbolic. Stephen's pupils are confused because they have heard language that refuses to be effaced and demands to be repeated—a language that must be repeated in order to be understood. But what purpose exactly does this confusion serve? Is it possible to learn from confusion? After Stephen's pupils have fled the classroom for the hockey field, Stephen remains behind to teach Cyril Sargent how to solve some math problems. Mr. Deasy has told Sargent to copy the problems off the board, but Stephen wants to know if the boy can do them himself. When he says no, Stephen sits down and works out a problem in front of him. Demystifying his own knowledge by refusing to give Cyril an overly complicated explanation, Stephen simply performs and then asks Cyril to repeat the performance on a different problem. Cyril copies the data and then, "Waiting always for a word of help his hand moved faithfully the unsteady symbols, a faint hue of shame flickering behind his dull skin" (*U-GP* 23). Cyril, however, awkwardly, manages to repeat Stephen's performance which is not the same thing as copying something off the board. Cyril succeeds, but he might have failed. By any measurable standard, Stephen's pedagogy does not succeed; he does not illuminate the boy's darkness or fill the void of his ignorance or dissolve his shame. If Cyril were asked, he would not know what Stephen had done to teach him. And yet Cyril learns something from Stephen in learning not to fear the problem—not to fear a certain language. Stephen's refusal to finalize knowledge on the blackboard forces Cyril to teach himself. It forces him to repeat Stephen's repetition since, contrary to what Cyril thinks, Stephen is not the one who knows but the one who repeats the steps of a formula that were already a repetition in the first place.

The ''Scylla and Charybdis'' episode dramatizes a related aspect of Joyce's pedagogy. Stephen presents a theory of Shakespeare's life and work that impresses the small collection of Dublin intellectuals in the library in the same way the ''grandmother'' riddle impresses the pupils in ''Nestor.'' Stephen faces an audience that not only resists the knowledge he conveys but also questions the authority with which he speaks. Rather than working to legitimate himself before these archons of Irish letters, Stephen plays a game of intellectual brinksmanship, which collapses, at the end of his discussion, in the following dialogue: ''You are a delusion, said roundly John Eglinton to Stephen. You have brought us all this way to show us a French triangle. Do you believe your own theory?—No, Stephen said promptly'' (*U-GP* 175). Contrary to what Eglinton asserts, Stephen probably never intended to compel belief but to show a problem. In ''Telemachus,'' Mulligan said that he ''proves by algebra that Hamlet's grandson is Shakespeare's grandfather and that he himself is the ghost of his own father'' (*U-GP* 15); but Eglinton comes closer to the truth in identifying Stephen's performance as a kind of geometrical demonstration. Stephen does not teach his audience the truth about Shakespeare; he shows them the shape of the desire for truth, a French triangle. This geometry underlies not only Stephen's story of Shakespeare's quest for an identity which is perpetually complicated by the triangular structure of desire in the relation between self and other, Shakespeare and Ann Hathaway. It also underlies Stephen's own performance as a speaking subject in relation to the audience as other. This geometry of desire destabilizes the relation between self and other by insisting on the structural possibility of a third position (which may or may not take the form of a third party), the position of the other as subject or the subject as other. This third position is what Jacques Lacan calls the desire of the capital Other, which is a desire inherent in the use of language. Stephen's pedagogy makes him into a delusion or a ghost in that it destabilizes the position of authority from which he only pretends to speak; it foregrounds the rhetorical dimension to such an extent that it forecloses the possibility of any stable referent as the object of his thought. As a result, in speaking his thought, Stephen articulates speech *as desire*—a desire that appears to be collective in that it exceeds the intention of the autonomous subject. The French triangle Stephen constructs in front of the librarians and Mulligan, like the math problem he solves in front of Cyril Sargent, is useless knowledge until it is repeated with a difference, until the audience draws it out of their own experience as linguistic beings. Nothing, of course, insures that they will.

The whole of *Ulysses,* I would suggest, possesses the structure of a French triangle. It has this structure in the obvious way that it is a novel of adultery and in the more subtle way that it triangulates the desire of writer and reader by foregrounding language itself, by perpetually undoing the grammar of narrative and the logic of content through rhetorical displacement. The book's pedagogical effect derives from this stylistic emphasis, and thus it goes against the grain of Western education which privileges logic and grammar over rhetoric. As Derrida remarks in ''Ulysses Gramophone,'' ''Joyce laid stakes on the modern university, but he challenges it to reconstitute itself after him.'' The first step of that reconstitution involves a reading of *Ulysses* that would require as its condition the reeducation of the reader. Of course, in this first step, Joyce takes the resistance of the reader into account by providing a relatively coherent narrative structure and logical content in spite of the rhetorical forces that pull against them in the second half of the novel. In the actual marketing of the book, he initiated a seduction of the reader by encouraging and participating in the construction of a pedagogical apparatus, which includes criticism, source studies, notes, schemata, plot summaries, etc. The spectacular history of this apparatus in the formation of the ''Joyce industry'' testifies to the book's resistance both to reading and to teaching. In effect, the book must be taught in order to be read; reading must become self-teaching.

In this respect, Joyce's work anticipates and supports Paul de Man's speculation on the pedagogical implications of the resistance to theory. According to de Man, the resistance to theory is ''a resistance to the use of language about language,'' that is to say, ''a resistance to language itself or to the possibility that language contains factors or functions that cannot be reduced to intuition'' (13). Traditional historical scholarship, for example, takes for granted that one is able to see through language to the truth, whether the truth is the referent, the historical context, the author's intention, etc. Such an intuitive view of reading foregrounds logic and grammar over rhetoric for the simple reason that logic and grammar are allied to the referential function of language, its truth function, while rhetoric studies figures of speech or tropes which ''pertain primordially to language." As de Man points out, in the medieval *trivium*, tropes, officially considered a part of grammatical study, actually occupied a disputed borderline between rhetoric and grammar, since they were and are "text-producing functions that are not necessarily patterned on a nonverbal entity." Grammar, on the other hand, is "by definition capable of extra-linguistic generalization" (15). The reading of any text precipitates the tension between rhetoric and grammar in such a way that grammar (along with its conceptual cohort, logic) finds the order of knowledge it postulates destabilized by the figurative power of language. "The resistance to theory," therefore, as de Man writes in yet another formulation, "is a resistance to the rhetorical or tropological dimension of language, a dimension which is perhaps more explicitly in the foreground in literature (broadly conceived) than in other verbal manifestations or—to be somewhat less vague—which can be revealed in any textual event when it is read textually" (17). It is no accident that Joyce's work has lent itself so frequently to theoretical formulations, most notably in the work of Lacan and Derrida. For to the extent that Joyce's work capitalizes on the tension between the referential function and the rhetorical dimension of language, it operates like a theory, that is, as language about language forcing us to recognize reference as one function of the rhetorical. In other words, the pedagogical effect of Joyce's writing constitutes it as a theoretical discourse.

Ulysses is, as I am placing it, the first step in Joyce's reconstitution of the university, and *Finnegans Wake* is the second. To an extent, Joyce merely continues the pedagogical experiment of *Ulysses* by radicalizing it; he challenges the reader's resistance by blurring plot and diffusing content to an unprecedented degree. But ultimately the extent of this radicalization produces a pedagogical effect of such magnitude that it becomes almost impossible to teach the book within the frame of the university—not only as presently constituted but as fundamentally conceived. In other words, *Finnegans Wake* tends to resist any institutional framework—no matter how radical— founded on the principle of reason. I say that it resists, not that it opposes. Joyce's last work is not a celebration of the irrational— which, in any case, would only submit it to the principle of reason; it offers no alternative, no counterculture, no counter university. I don't believe that it is unreadable or unteachable, though its resistance to teaching and reading exceeds that of any other book in our culture, including *Ulysses*. Finally, this resistance to reading is what we teach; the purpose of *Wake* pedagogy is to show our students how to recognize, manage, and write about this resistance. Every time *Finnegans Wake* breaks into the space of the university, it calls that space into question by drawing attention to what the university only assimilates as a problem it cannot solve, unlike *Ulysses* which creates the illusion that the university can solve any problem. It is no accident that the *Wake* usually appears in the margins of the university—that it has been so frequently taught in the living rooms of professors, during the evening hours, without university credit.

I would like to think of *Finnegans Wake* as an extension course on the French triangle. It extends the lessons of Stephen in "Scylla and Charybdis" and of Joyce in *Ulysses;* but only with difficulty can it be appropriated to the official "core" curriculum. In *Ulysses,* Stephen explores the French triangle within the house of reason, the library, whose boundaries he more or less respects. In *Finnegans Wake,* the library is engulfed by the triangle, an opening to the abyss that the principle of reason desperately tries to fill. The triangle is the sigla of ALP, the mother, and the outline of her sexual organs, the hole into which the critic tries to insert the principle of reason. Of course, such a critic is at least figuratively male, like the Shaun figure, Professor Jones, modeled on Wyndham Lewis, in the chapter of riddles and answers that recall Stephen's "grandmother" riddle. The professor, reasoning against brotherly love, reveals a form of domination inherent in magisterial pedagogy: "My unchanging Word is sacred," he says. "The word is my Wife, to expone and expound, to vend and velnerate, and may the curlews crown our nuptias! Til Breath us depart! Wamen." The professor describes himself and his discourse as "The ring man in the rong shop but the rite words in the rote order!" (*FW* 167.28–33). Roughly translated: the man married to reason in the place of unreason with the sacred words of tradition memorized by rote. The patriarchal professor impresses with his knowledge and threatens with his authority; but, fortunately for us, his words, asserting their own autonomy, refuse the system he wants to instill in them.

Shem's approach to the triangle, though more circular, is less indirect. In the pedagogical chapter of *Finnegans Wake,* "Night Lessons," Shem, in the guise of Dolph, teaches his brother Shaun, in the guise of Kev, to construct an equilateral triangle within intersecting circles, another chapter in the geometry of desire. In doing so, Dolph figuratively lifts his mother's "maidsapron" (*FW*

297.11); and Kev, beginning to get a confused notion of what the triangle is all about, remarks: "Mother of us all! O, dear me, look at that now! I don't know is it your spictre or my omination but I'm glad you dimentioned it!" (*FW* 299.3–6). Dolph thinks Kev too stupid to follow his demonstration (at first, Kev is more interested in his mother's navel than in her genitals); but the problem is stated more accurately by saying that Kev doesn't know what his language knows—i.e., the triangle has to do with his mother or generation through sex. Kev's words, "mother of us all," answer the question he is afraid to ask about his own desire (for his mother or rather for her desire), while a rhetorical reading of the interjection undoes that answer in the same gesture. Kev doesn't know if he has followed the logic of Dolph's demonstration, if what he knows is the product of Dolph's "spectre," a Blakean word for the principle of reason. He doesn't know if his knowledge is rational or if it comes from his "omination," that is, his imagination or his prophetic sense and ability to recognize omens. He is glad Dolph "dimentioned" it, though he resists the knowledge of what those dimensions signify.

Language defines its own dimensions in the pun "dimention." For in the "dimentioning" of language, in doubling it so that we read it grammatically and logically (however ungrammatical and illogical it may be) even as we undo its "grammatical cognition" through a rhetorical reading of its figurative play—in this double speech or double writing, we discover the dimensions of language, its materiality or spacing. To use the distinction from speech act theory that Derrida likes to play with, language oscillates between "use" and "mention." In the *Wake,* Shem-Dolph mentions and Shaun-Kev tries to put what he mentions to use; but in that very act Shaun stumbles or stammers like his father and everything he says doubles back or, in Derrida's terminology, "invaginates." "My Lourde! My Lourde!" Kev further remarks, "If that aint just the beatenest lay I ever see! And a superpbosition! Quoint a quincidence!" (*FW* 299.6–8). Kev puns away without the slightest knowledge of what he is saying. My lord and master is also the miracle of Lourdes which had to do with a virgin mother; but Kev's mother, "the beatenest lay" he ever saw, is no virgin. And neither is his language with its superpositions, one word on top of another, one word inside of another, and everywhere coincidences, including the one revealed by the superposition of the early English word "queynt," which was a vulgar name for the vagina, on the phrase "Quite a coincidence.'' ''Quoint a quincidence!''—such coincidences are the invaginations of the rhetorical dimension.

This dimension of Joyce's writing resonates with what Lacanian psychoanalysis calls ''la bêtise.'' In the *Encore* seminar, Lacan notes that ''le signifiant est bête,'' the signifier is stupid, beastly, animalistic. Beyond those meanings inscribed within the imaginary register, language is *en corps* (a pun on the title of the seminar), ''in or of the body''; and Lacan considers this relation to be ''the foundation of the symbolic dimension that alone permits us to isolate analytic discourse as such'' (24). *La bêtise* can also mean ''nonsense''; and language at its most substantial is nonsense. Lacanian theory, like Joyce's art, depends for its content and its effect on linguistic play and coincidence—for example, when Lacan directs our attention to the substantial dimension of language by rewriting the French word ''dimension as ''dit-mension'' (25). Whereas Joyce changes the *s* of the English ''dimension'' to *t* to signify the double-mentioning or iterative dimension of language, Lacan adds a *t* to the first syllable of the French ''dimension'' to signify the priority of the signifier over the signified in speech. Both Joyce and Lacan use the pun to collapse the distinction between ''use'' and ''mention'' into a single rhetorical act. Insofar as the pun can be said to signify, it has been used to produce a semantic effect; however, insofar as the puns of both Joyce and Lacan illustrate the very thing they signify, which is the always possible subversion of meaning through rhetorical displacement, they are mentioned or cited as examples of the impossibility of meaning in the absolute sense. Grammar and logic, or the order of signification, are subsumed by the rhetorical dimension; yet without the grasp of grammar and logic in the act of reading it is virtually impossible to grasp the rhetorical dimension in the full scope of its cognitive function.

To carry the comparison between Lacan and Joyce a step further, the pedagogical effect of Lacan's writing is directly related to what many consider to be the eccentricity of his style. As Shoshana Felman eloquently argues, pedagogy is not a theme in psychoanalysis but a rhetoric, an utterance, an action, and finally a style. Lacan was ''the first to understand that the psychoanalytic discipline is an unprecedented one in that its *teaching* does not just reflect upon itself, but turns back upon itself so as to *subvert itself,* and truly *teaches* only insofar as its subverts itself'' (39). In support of this assertion, Felman cites a passage from Lacan from which she makes a curious omission:

"Any return to Freud founding a teaching worthy of the name will occur only on that pathway where truth...becomes manifest in the revolutions of culture. That pathway is the only training we can claim to transmit to those who follow us. It is called—a style" (39). Felman omits the superlative adjective modifying the word for "truth" in Lacan's text, which speaks of "la verité la plus caché," the most hidden truth becoming manifest in cultural revolutions (*Écrits* 458). What is the most hidden truth that any teaching worthy of the name discloses? After Lacan's seminar on "The Purloined Letter," we should be able to guess that the most hidden truth of psychoanalysis is out in the open where everyone is free to misconstrue it. It is language itself, or rather the rhetorical dimension of language, the field of operation of what Lacan calls the Unconscious. Lacan, like Joyce, theorizes by giving play to the Unconscious in the disfigurations or dislocutions of style.

In the "Night Lessons" episode of *Finnegans Wake,* Dolph disfigures language and thus illustrates Paul de Man's formula for pedagogy which says that "it is better to fail in teaching what should not be taught than to succeed in teaching what is not true" (de Man 4). Dolph tries to teach Kev the truth about his mother by problematizing the relation to truth, the distinction between the literal and the figurative. He teaches what should not be taught not only in exposing the private parts of his mother's anatomy but also in showing that even anatomy has its rhetorical dimension and ideological function. But this strange geometry lesson fails in teaching Kev the truth that language, like sex, is not a mystery—that language invaginates not because it is feminine but because it is rhetorical. It fails because the truth cannot be simply communicated; it can only be shown. Dolph shows Kev "figuratleavely the whome of your eternal geomater" (*FW* 296.30–297.1) It is not that Dolph, Kev, or the reader sees the womb/home of the eternal earth mother figuratively as opposed to literally but rather that the figurative, or the rhetorical, and the ideological frames must limit any possible vision of home, womb, or mother. In "Night Lessons," the closer Dolph gets to describing the facts of sex the more abstract and mathematical his language becomes, reducing feminine sexuality to the "power of empthood," that is, a logarithmic value of nought. To these male-centered rationalizations of sex balanced against the puritanical ignorance of Shaun-Kev, Issy retorts in the footnotes with a language whose rhetoric lies in its simplicity: "I enjoy as good as anyone" (*FW* 298.F1).

Issy's enjoyment undoes the principle of reason Joyce caricatures in Dolph; she constitutes the third side of the triangle pointing toward an invisible fourth position, "beyond." In the summary of his demonstration, Dolph nearly says as much himself: "there are trist sigheds to everysing but ichs on the freed brings euchs to the feared" (*FW* 299.1–3). Stated simply, there are three sides to Shem-Dolph's triangle: I, you, and s/he. When the *I*s are freed, including the "I" in Issy, *you* will move to the fourth position beyond the triangle. The word for "you" here, the German *euch* with an English *s*-ending, could be taken as a pun on the word "us": euchs is us. As Professor Jones says parenthetically, "I am speaking to us in the second person" (*FW* 161.5–6). In the liberation of the feminine subject through the assertion of feminine desire and pleasure, you, that is, all of us, will move to the fourth position, the position of the collective where there is no contradiction between the first and second persons, between the singular and the plural. As the diagram on page 293 of *Finnegans Wake* shows, the fourth position is generated out of the first three as the second triangle is generated out of the first. The triangle is the structure of desire that constantly repeats in displacing itself. It is the structure of desire in language or the rhetorical dimension.

Clive Hart noted long ago that "The primary energy which maintains the highly charged polarities of *Finnegans Wake* is generated by cycles of constantly varied repetition—'The seim anew', as Joyce puts it [*FW* 215.23]" (31). Hart says explicitly what Joyce says implicitly in writing *Finnegans Wake* as a repetition, with a difference, of *Ulysses*. (To continue the parallel with Lacan, the title of *Encore*, meaning "still" and "once again," emphasizes the repetition with a difference characteristic of his teaching.) Of course, this function of repetition in Joyce could be taken as an impasse, perhaps even the poststructuralist impasse. As many have stressed, Joyce's work anticipates poststructuralism, anticipates the impasse of repetition that poststructuralism identifies as its first principle. But I think there is a way of reading Joyce that goes beyond the impasse, beyond poststructuralism—though I don't mean to say that poststructuralism itself is without knowledge of this "beyond."

Derrida, in his meditation on the university, remarks that " 'Thought' requires *both* the principle of reason *and* what is beyond the principle of reason, the *arkhe* and an-archy. Between the two, the difference of a breath or an accent, only the *enactment* of this 'thought' can decide. That decision is always risky, it always risks the worst. To claim to eliminate that risk by an institutional program is quite simply to erect a barricade against the future'' (''Principle of Reason'' 18–19). The pedagogy that emerges out of Joyce's work, particularly *Finnegans Wake,* is the pedagogy of enactment. It is a pedagogy that constantly risks itself in undoing the so-called objective knowledge we inject into our students and in capitalizing on the function of desire in the language we derive our knowledge from. This pedagogy is rhetorical because it teaches knowledge not merely as content but as enactment. At its limit, in teaching *Finnegans Wake* for example, this pedagogy actually challenges the foundation of the university; it offers itself as a form of resistance to the university's totalizing functions, to the encyclopedic unity of its knowledge, to the social and intellectual hierarchies into which it is organized. This does not mean, however, that such a pedagogy is opposed to the university in principle since it has no principle beyond the university. It challenges the university by exploring the thought of what lies beyond the principle of reason, both in the future and in the present. It also insists that the university can never contain knowledge in its totality and that teaching is never simply a matter for the university. For Joyce, the only teaching worthy of the name is self-teaching in the radical way I have indicated. But, as every reader of Joyce knows, teaching oneself is a collective act. Such a pedagogy, *as theory,* points beyond its own institutional framework, even beyond poststructuralism as the still-emerging critical institution of our time. We should not be afraid to go beyond poststructuralism or to fail in teaching it. As Joyce urges, we should not be afraid to teach ourselves or, like Issy in *Finnegans Wake,* be ashamed to be ''selfthought'' (*FW* 147.9).

WORKS CITED

de Man, Paul. ''The Resistance to Theory.'' *Yale French Studies* 63 (1982): 3–20.
Derrida, Jacques. ''Living On: Borderlines.'' In *Deconstruction and Criticism,* edited by Harold Bloom, 75–175. New York: Seabury Press, 1979.
————. ''The Principle of Reason: The University in the Eyes of Its Pupils.'' *Diacritics* 13 (Fall 1983): 3–20.
————. ''Ulysses Gramophone: Hear say yes in Joyce.'' Forthcoming in *James Joyce: The Augmented Ninth,* edited by Bernard Benstock. Baltimore: Johns Hopkins University Press.
Felman, Shoshana. ''Psychoanalysis and Education: Teaching Terminable and Interminable.'' *Yale French Studies* 63 (1982): 21–44.

Hart, Clive. *Structure and Motif in* Finnegans Wake. Evanston, Ill.: Northwestern University Press, 1962.

Lacan, Jacques. *Écrits*. Paris: Éditions du Seuil, 1966.

————. *Le séminaire, livre xx: Encore,* edited by Jacques Alain-Miller. Paris: Éditions du Seuil, 1975.

Lewis, Wyndham. *Time and Western Man*. Boston: Beacon Press, 1957.

15

From Catechism to Catachresis:
Aspects of Joycean Pedagogy in
Ulysses and *Finnegans Wake*

LORRAINE WEIR

> *...there is nothing more wonderful than a list, instrument of wondrous hypotyposis.*
> —Eco, *The Name of the Rose*

Catachresis, catafalque, cataglottism: tropes of the Fall in Derrida's *Glas*, signs of the inevitability of the author, of authority, and of the interrogation of sign and signature which the text both provokes and inscribes.

> *Catachresis*...n. 1. Trope wherein a word is diverted from its proper sense and is taken up in common language to designate another thing with some analogy to the object initially expressed; for example, a tongue [langue], since the tongue is the chief organ of spoken language; a looking glass...a leaf of paper...It is also a catachresis to say: ironclad with gold; to ride a hobbyhorse....2. Musical term. Harsh and unfamiliar dissonance.
> E. Κατάχρησις, abuse, from κατά, against, χρῆσις, usage. (2)

Cataglottism, the "use of abstruse words," becomes catafalque, bearer of the corpse of language and authorial *imprimatur*, becomes catachresis, the transformation of language through the trope of cataglottism enshrined through the agency of death upon a catafalque (author, book, reader, arche-text, writing) which is the Fall, tomb (*tombe*) and tome of the catachretic text. Thus Derrida encodes not only the cycle of *Finnegans Wake* from Tim Finnegan's fall to ᴍ's rise but of the "phall" (FW 4.15) of language across the Joyce system from catachresis to catechism, from syllogism to epiphany, by way of the glassy medium of the medieval *speculum*, a dream with a death-knell built into it. *Glas*.

If *Portrait*, *Ulysses*, and *Finnegans Wake*—the major components of the Joyce system—constitute a *specula/*tive text (a text, in other words, which operates according to the textual program characteristic of the medieval *speculum* or "mirror" form), those glyphic devices or sigla,[1] which serve in the *Wake* as metonymic operators of marked data, may be found in varying forms elsewhere within the system, functioning in similar ways. Thus where a reader like S. L. Goldberg in *The Classical Temper* sees the Joyce system as an essentially Realist one moving toward glyphic disintegration, we may also see a predominantly *specula/*tive pedagogy which teaches readerly modes of programmed iteration as a strategy of world-building in and for itself; a "Gothic pedagogy"[2] with what Kenneth Burke refers to in *The Rhetoric of Religion* as the "god-term" disseminated among the semes and sigla of the work, from SD and LB to ⋔ and Δ, among others; a learning system which segments its materials sequentially into questions and answers, and simultaneously into epiphanies, puns, and riddles. Throughout, the diachronic serves as vehicle for the synchronic which is its goal: ironically, a *Tunc* strategy, "then" and "now" always having the significance of macrocosmic statement, in the *Book of Kells* with its optical interlacing (to use Vinaver's term) as in the *speculum* and the liturgy with their topoi and rituals of declension and gesture.

This paper takes three of Joyce's system's major technics—syllogism, catechism, and the kernel trope of catachresis—and provides a necessarily brief account of some of their interactions and functions.[3] My intention here is primarily to suggest some of these semiotic operations in terms of *Ulysses* as focal text rather than to demonstrate their workings across the whole system. Readers uncomfortable with the assumptions and lexicon of Eco-ian semiotics and information theory may find that *Ulysses* disappears in the process. My point, however, is precisely that *Ulysses* is programmed process—in other words, that the text encodes specific processual moves—, and that we encounter the " 'finished' text merging with its own development," as Michael Groden puts it (157–58), not only when we work with the Gabler edition of the text but whenever we take up *Ulysses* in whichever edition we use.[4]

1. Syllogism

In the midst of a catechetically structured recital of the ills to which life is subject, "Ithaca" 's narrator asks, Did Stephen participate in his dejection?

> He affirmed his significance as a conscious rational animal proceeding syllogistically from the known to the unknown and a conscious rational reagent between a micro and a macrocosm

ineluctably construed upon the incertitude of the void. (*U-G* 1535)

The unknown macrocosm, the void, is a place, a locus on a memory chain, a destination attainable through the exercise of the syllogism. A vehicle of parallax and of parallactic enactment of the text, SD's syllogism is grounded in the act of reading as root paradigm. "Signatures of all things I am here to read" says SD (*U-G* 75). Like LB, he erodes any distinction between animate and inanimate in his quest for understanding of the substance, the mode of operation and being of all creation. "[S]easpawn and seawrack, the nearing tide, that rusty boot. Snotgreen, bluesilver, rust: coloured signs. . .": like the Ballast office clock, already catalogued, *significant,* waiting to "be epiphanized," followed by a "dog's bark" (*U-G* 93) and a dead dog, by SD's lips which "lipped and mouthed fleshless lips of air: mouth to her moomb. Oomb, allwombing tomb" (*U-G* 97).

Death woven into the possibility of life creates the end-term: infinity, the end of the catalogue, no supplement possible; the defining term of the Joycean syllogism in *Ulysses.* "See now. There all the time without you: and ever shall be, world without end" (*U* 75), the doxology with its end-term suppressed ("Amain" as *Finnegans Wake* gives it—*FW* 81.08). The end is the book itself, graphically represented in Ithaca by the transcoding of LB through the language of sleep and into punctuation:

> Going to dark bed there was a square round Sinbad the Sailor
> roc's awk's egg in the right of the bed of all the awks of the
> rocs of Darkinbad the Brightdayler"
> Where? (*U-G* 1633)

Thus the middle term is suppressed within the system, leaving the first and last terms, SD and MB, Telemachia and Nostos, in balance.

In this transsignifying, syllogistic process, SD is the reagent, LB the field of enactment, and MB the occasion of transsignification. If, at the referential mimetic level, incertitude is what is being enacted throughout 16 June 1904, at the processual mimetic one it is the point of parallactic infinity, the naming of all the parts of this "world without end." At the end of "Circe," the ghostly Rudy is bound in speculary reading paradigmatic of the transience of performance as well as of text and reader, and of their illusory nature. Later, in the "Ithaca" chapter, LB arrives at a similar point from a different trajectory:

Was this affirmation apprehended by Bloom?

Not verbally. Substantially. (*U-G* 1535)

—not understanding, not cognition but *apprehension* and apprehension which moves a stage beyond LB's inaudible speaking of Rudy's name during the vision. Here there are no words: apprehension has reached its ulti-mate form as substance. The very stuff of being, the wholeness and particularity of SD's statement, is consumed in this Joussean eating of the book. So LB models the reception of the performance-text in his role as "conscious reactor against the void of incertitude" (*U-G* 1625). But, in contrast to SD's emphasis on the void, LB's on incertitude character-izes the reader's primary analytic task in the Joyce system: to submit to textual programming, thereby reducing the incertitude occasioned by the bias of referential mimesis toward kerygmatic reading. Beginning to move beyond the surfaces of plot and character (to the extent that these devices are used in *Portrait, Ulysses,* and the *Wake*) as a means of reader orientation, the apprentice reader approaches the different surfaces of the system's processual mimetic techne. In other words, the referential micro-structure serves the primary purpose of situating the competent reader within the textual syllogism which requires the response demanded by all performative discourse: enactment of the weaving of the macro-structure according to textual program. When our sense of readerly balance falters and what Kenneth Burke refers to in *Language as Symbolic Action* as the "terministic screen" (44) of the microstructure dominates our reading, the system contains us within a complexity of semiosis for which the referential cannot begin to account.

Motivation, then, or the intratextual factoring of the text by such elements as parallax (in the Formalist sense of motiv: a recurrent unit acquiring meaning beyond its basic semantic value as a result of repetition across the text or any portion of it)—or "looking back... in a retrospective kind of arrangement" (*U-G* 1423)—mimes the semiotic operations of the system as a whole. Through the co/incidence of units comprising the motiv, the system finds one agent of synchrony or the achievement of, as it were, the strengthening of its paradigmatic axis. This operation is what "Oxen of the Sun" refers to as "retro-gressive metamorphosis" (*U-G* 849) since such readerly cognitive processing must always be the consequence of rereading, reflection, analysis. "*Da capo*," as the instruction puts it in "Sirens" (*U-G* 627). In this mnemonic exercise, "Ithaca" provides rhythmo-catechetic training[5], the response paradigms generated by its techne (that is, by its encoded performative directives) hypostatizing what Michel Beaujour has referred to as "topo-logy," the logic and logospecificity of topos and place, troping the performative discourse of the text and modeling its most basic semiotic operations.

2. Catechism

In the course of his study of the Gospels as "a narrative semiotics," Louis Marin reflects on the meaning of locus, "place," in the context of the discovery of Christ's empty tomb:

> The fact that this place (locus) is a tomb and that the absence is that of a disappeared cadavre introduces into the semantic dimension of history the transformation of topography into topos, of locus of space into locus of speech (*parole*).[6]

Marcel Jousse's concept of the "rhythmo-catechizing" process encoded within the Gospels here intersects with Marin's theory at the point where catechism takes over from event for with the disappearance of the body comes the disappearance of authority. As the medieval cliché puts it, there can be no *auctoritas* without the divine *auctor* whose presence suffuses the text with meaning.[7] Thus the necessarily parallactic enactment of the catechetical techne mimes not the recovery of the author but the recovery of the topoi in the process of readerly enactment of the performance-text. Like the holistic gestural enactment of the Gospels in the liturgy, the processing of Joycean performative discourse requires a training process in the recognition of what "is epiphanised" (*SH* 211) within the text at the motivic level as well as at other levels of patterning across each component of the system. Thus the parallactic "topo-logy" of "Ithaca" with its catechetical response paradigms becomes a massive review exercise and we are put through our dramatistic paces.

Central to that catechistic process is an accommodation of typography to topography epitomized in the rhetorical figure of *topographia*,[8] a semantic correlative of what modern physics epitomizes as spacetime. Joycean *topographia* is, however, very different from Marin's understanding of the topographic transformation from "locus of space into locus of speech" since the Joyce system rejects the reification of "speech/parole" as powerfully as it does that of "space," and teaches us only itself.

What we learn in "Ithaca"—as in the rest of *Ulysses*—is neither scientific nor encyclopedic but *specula*/tive, which is to say modeled upon the medieval *speculum* with its hyperbole of systems and elaboration of components bound not by referential or scientific codes of origination—as, say, the *Britannica* is—but only by the logic of their own composition and semiotic relation to other systems. Compare the status of the encyclopedia with its relentless struggle to "keep abreast of the latest knowledge," as the cliché has it; a struggle which evidences the drive toward the fullness of sequentiality, of "fact," in the face of the equally relentless incursion of mystery. As Vincent Descombes puts it:

> On the one hand, the name of Encyclopedia excludes the supplement, for this title announces that the book is meant to have a comprehensive coverage of its subject from A to Z. On the other hand, in order to be what it claims to be, the Encyclopedia must allow the possibility of a supplement, an exposition beyond Z...." (56)

"Beyond Z" is that condition which Gilles Deleuze refers to as the "rhizome" and Umberto Eco as the "inconceivable globality" (*Semiotics and the Philosophy of Language* 83), a global plenitude of knowledge which is beyond the rational powers of the human brain.

The encyclopedia, in other words, is grounded—in sheer violation of its apparent epistemology—in the possibility of finally writing Truth, of inscribing the Logos and thereby, for a moment, suppressing mystery. The medieval *speculum,* in contrast, is free of this burden precisely because what Barthes refers to in *Sade/Fourier/ Loyola* (3) as the logothetic ambition is denied to it. The perfection of the god-term is precisely what it may not inscribe except in the sense that catalogues grounded in the rhetorical strategy of *elaboratio* are ultimately acts of homage to the creator of such frequently enumerated groups as, to quote Michel Beaujour's list (32), "the nine heavenly spheres, the nine angelic orders, the four elements, the four humours of the body and the soul, the four ages of the world, the seven ages of man, the seven virtues and the seven deadly sins." If we allow for the performative nature of both liturgy and Joyce system, we are not far here from the world of Plumtree— "Peatmot. Trumplee. Moutpat. Plamtroo" (*U-G* 1501) or "Old Ollebo, M.P." (*U-G* 1487) or any of the response paradigms across the system. In performance, in enunciation, the text becomes what it is. As Eco puts it in *The Aesthetics of Chaosmos* (7), "If you take away the transcendent God from the symbolic world of the Middle Ages, you have the world of Joyce," a "world" or system to which Kenneth Burke's strategy of "logologizing" is applicable.

"If we defined 'theology' as 'words about God,' " Burke writes in *The Rhetoric of Religion* (1), "then, by 'logology' we should mean 'words about words.' " In contrast to Eco's procedure of subtraction, logology is a strategy of conservation and has the great advantage of enabling us to consider that theological statements "about the nature of 'God'...[may] be adapted *mutatis mutandis* for use as purely secular observations on the nature of *words.*" This is a crucial maneuver since, for Burke, "men's thoughts on the Divine embody the principles of verbalization" (1). Logologically speaking, then, the *speculum* directs its inquiry toward the celebration of language in itself, a goal which can be achieved only through the "rhythmo-catechizing" of response paradigms whose ever-increasing complexity inscribes the polysemy of language itself.

In the Joyce system, these response paradigms are mnemonic events in part because neither component of the catechetical paradigm is necessarily predictable within the sequence of which it is a part. Precisely because so much of what we learn through this mode will strike us as being—rather like the nine angelic orders—non/sense outside the system, the catechetical act is grounded in strict, paradigmatic order and syntagmatic processing. Its sense, in other words, is defined by and within the system. Not referential value but mnemonic placing within the topography of the whole is the criterion for Joycean inscription of data. Consider LB's catechized conclusion about the nature of the heavens:

> That it was not a heaventree, not a heavengrot, not a heavenbeast,
> not a heavenman. That it was a Utopia, there being no known
> method from the known to the unknown....(*U-G* 1545)

—a statement which we know to be only part of the paradigm since, two pages later, LB adapts SD's syllogistic procedure in the sacramental elucidation of MB as "invisible attractive person...denoted by a visible splendid sign" (*U-G* 1547). All of which leads us to the traditional, coincidentally oppositive conclusion that MB is either a Utopian being who enables the movement from known to unknown or that she is the missing term of an incomplete syllogism. More likely, she is— like Δ in the *Wake*—aligned with the celestial sphere, given "Ithaca" 's earlier assertion of "The heaventree of stars hung with humid nightblue fruit" (*U-G* 1537) as the "spectacle" which confronts SD and LB as they emerge into the garden to urinate in tandem. If the association of MB with urine seems unlikely, we have only to think of the various chamber pot references in *Ulysses* and of the extension of this topos in *Finnegans Wake,* "Fanny Urinia" (*FW* 171.28), to confirm the outlines of this response paradigm within the Joycean *speculum.*[9]

If tree, grot, beast, man, and water make neither a heaven nor a Utopia, it is clear that they are at least elements of a knowable, cataloguable system, a *speculum mundi* which inevitably includes both love and hate as well. They are terms on LB's memory wheel: 'Hate. Love. Those are names. Rudy. Soon I am old" (*U-G* 615). Fulfilling Emile Benveniste's principle that "an utterance is performative insofar as it *names* the act performed.... The utterance *is* the act; the utterer performs the act by naming it" (274), this present-tense naming performs the act it utters but the performance is a complex one for we can respond adequately to such dramatistic demands only to the extent that we have acquired performance-competence.[10] Catachresis serves to assist our achievement of that pedagogical goal.

3. *Catachresis*

However ekphrastic the moment, however recapitulative the motiv/ation, the textual performance must end.[11] And that end must be inscribed within the system as well, inscribed so fully that the moment of semantic infinity—the moment when parallax at last accepts the intersection of its lines—will also be part of the gestural repertoire. This is the function of the pun, a form of catachresis or "misuse" which epitomizes the Joyce system's defiance of the ontological primacy of sequentiality in the act of reading. Where catechism is structurally dialogical, catachresis in its punning form is syllogistic, its middle term dispersed from the immediate occasion across the system. A device of segregation and dissociation in Joyce, catachresis mimes the Babel of all language, temporarily hazarding a creative aphasia. But used within a system characterized by a high degree of redundancy and motivic patterning, and itself inscribed within the text's motiv/ation, catachresis has the effect of ictus, a term whose neurological meaning is as useful here as its poetic one. Ictus refers to that brief pause which comes before the beginning of certain kinds of epileptic seizure, a pause which stands in double relation to the ensuing event for it is both warning of a time of disruption to be suffered within the neurological system and last brief space of clear, sometimes heightened awareness before interruption of consciousness occurs. In the language of poetics, ictus denotes the stress falling on the long syllable of a metrical foot but, as the *Princeton Encyclopedia of Poetry and Poetics* reminds us, the term was also used by Horace and Quintilian "to describe the movement of the foot or the hand in keeping time with the rhythm of a verse," (362) a kinesic gesture associated with Joussean rhythmo-catechizing.

In a system characterized by processual mimesis, ictus mimes the moment of death or semantic infinity within the "double gesture" (to use Derrida's term from "The Double Session") of catachresis. Like epiphany, catachresis serves to clear an opening in language, to interrupt the relentlessness of inscription and enact the absence of name. As a single event, catachresis attempts to subvert the memory system built up through enactment of catechetical performative discourse while retaining the place of mnemonics within the semiosis of the system. Attempting to sustain the instant of transsignification by intensifying the polyvalence of that operation, catachresis refuses to accede to the semantic demands of conversion and remains grounded in the iterability of the word and in its status within the logothetic economy of performative utterance. Analogous to Freudian dreamwork, catachresis synthesizes question and response, past and future, manifest and latent, catalyzing dichotomies into polyvalent units within the memory system. But this analogy is a partial one at best for Joycean catachresis, as a strategy of the *specula/*tive mode, works in triumphant rejection of mystery—or, in terms of Freud's ontotheology, of the "unconscious" with its claims to encyclopedic rather than *specula/*tive operation.[12] Like parody, catachresis functions in this context as a device of programmed enunciation and sometimes of homage, rather than of kerygmatic proclamation. And like epiphany, catachresis epitomizes the system's defiance of the ontological primacy of sequentiality in the act of reading, attempting through the dissemination and re/collection of its terms to test the memory system built up in the course of its own enactment in performance.

While "Ithaca" provides an extended initiation into the catechetical mode and a rigorous exercising of dialogical procedures present in elementary form since the beginning of the *Portrait,*[13] *Finnegans Wake* develops catachresis by way of Vico's "Mental Dictionary" in *The New Science* (par. 482) and his concepts of poetic geography and poetic etymology (par. 527). To those concepts both geometry and hieroglyphics are essential in the *Science Nuova* and in the *Wake* where in II.ii the catechetical exercise of schoolboy lessons is repeatedly fractured, first by $\perp$'s interjections which mime the effect of catachresis, and later by the geomater diagram or catachresis in Euclidean glyphic form. Elsewhere I have argued that it is the Vichian principle of morphogenesis—that is, of textual decomposition, deconstruction and code-generation—which governs the performative discourse of the *Wake*. In the case of the geomater diagram, the "keys to" (*FW* 628.15) this process are not only given but displayed topographically through a double gesture conjoining catechism and catachresis across that anatomically discursive space which has been particularly involved in the production of what Vico refers to as "interpatratio" (par. 448), the father's interpretation.

In the *Wake*, then, catachresis is concerned with "scribings scrawled on eggs" (*FW* 615.10): the inscription of language through the body, in terms of it, and upon it, whether the flesh in question be Δ's, $\sqsubset$'s, or the "hides and hints and misses in prints" (*FW* 20.11) of the "mamafesta." Logologically considered, sacramental transformation is syllogistic transsignification (in becoming word, flesh decays into process). The result: "silents selfloud" (*FW* 267.17), the *Wake's* resolution of catachresis into Vico's highest form of language: the silence of the gods before the first thunderword provoking human experience of fear, marriage, warfare, organized religion, and the modern state. Taking Vico's catalogue as one basis for its *specula/*tive history, the *Wake* inscribes the moment of ictus—of that instant of suspended comprehension which is the syllogistic moment of catachresis as trope—at the center of the system. In doing so, the system moves constantly toward its own closure in response, its own opening in surprise and silence.

NOTES

1. Cf. Roland McHugh's use of this term in *The Sigla of* Finnegans Wake to signify a mode of "personality condensation" (10 ff.). I extend the use of the term here to the other components of the Joyce system, an application for which Joycean precedent may be found in, for example, Buffalo Notebook VI.C.7 in *The James Joyce Archive*, vol. 27.

2. I owe this phrase to my colleague Patricia Merivale who uses it in a very different sense in her article, "Learning the Hard Way: Gothic Pedagogy in the Modern Romantic Quest."

3. This paper is a portion of a book on the poetics of the Joyce system. I am grateful to the Social Sciences and Humanities Research Council of Canada for funding in support of this project and for a grant in aid of my participation in the Tenth International James Joyce Symposium in Copenhagen, June 1986.

4. With the semiotic concept of process used here, compare John Paul Riquelme's phenomenological approach to the "oscillating perspective" of the reader, and Wolfgang Iser's of the shifting "pictures" presented by the narrative.

5. On Marcel Jousse's concepts of rhythmo-catechizing and mnemonic gesture, see Weir, "The Choreography of Gesture: Marcel Jousse and *Finnegans Wake*."

6. Louis Marin "Du corps au texte: propositions métaphysiques sur l'origine du récit" *Esprit* 423 (1973): 925, quoted in Beaujour, 308.

7. See A.J. Minnis (10 ff.) on *auctor* and *auctoritas*.

8. See Gerard Le Coat *The Rhetoric of the Arts, 1550–1650,* 49.

9. Among the many studies of this element, see Solomon, 77–80.

10. On the catechetical "method of narration," compare Shari Benstock and Bernard Benstock, "The Benstock Principle," 19.

11. See Krieger, 105–28.

12. For a development of this argument, see Weir, "Performing the Dreamwork: Vichian Morphogenesis in *Finnegans Wake*," forthcoming.

13. A detailed discussion of this part of the system will be found in Weir, "Barthes' *Loyola* / Joyce's *Portrait* (Taxonomy and Paradigm)."

WORKS CITED

Barthes, Roland. *Sade/Fourier/Loyola,* translated by Richard Miller. New York: Hill & Wang, 1976.

Beaujour, Michel. *Miroirs d'encre — Rhétorique de l'autoportrait.* Paris: Seuil, 1980.

Benstock, Shari, and Bernard Benstock. "The Benstock Principle." In *The Seventh of Joyce,* edited by Bernard Benstock, 10–21. Bloomington: Indiana University Press, 1982.

Benveniste, Emile. *Problémes de linguistique gènèrale.* Paris: Gallimard, 1966.

Burke, Kenneth. *Language as Symbolic Action.* Berkeley: University of California Press, 1966.

———. *The Rhetoric of Religion—Studies in Logology.* Berkeley: University of California Press, 1970.

Deleuze, Gilles, and Fèlix Guattari. *Rhizome.* Paris: Minuit, 1976.

Derrida, Jacques. *Glas,* translated by John P. Leavey, Jr., and Richard Rand. Lincoln and London: University of Nebraska Press, 1986.

———. "The Double Session." In *Dissemination,* translated by Barbara Johnson, 173–286. Chicago: University of Chicago Press, 1981.

Descombes, Vincent. "Variations on the Subject of the Encyclopedic Book." *Oxford Literary Review* 3 (1978): 54–60.

Eco, Umberto. *Semiotics and the Philosophy of Language.* Bloomington: Indiana University Press, 1984.

———. *The Aesthetics of Chaosmos: The Middle Ages of James Joyce,* translated by Ellen Esrock. Tulsa, Okla.: University of Tulsa Monograph, 1982.

———. *The Name of the Rose,* translated by William Weaver. New York: Warner Books, 1984.

Goldberg, S.K. *The Classical Temper.* New York: Barnes & Noble, 1961.

Groden, Michael. "Foostering over Those Changes: The New *Ulysses.*" *James Joyce Quarterly* 22 (1985): 137–59.

Iser, Wolfgang. *The Implied Reader.* Baltimore and London: Johns Hopkins University Press, 1974.

Joyce, James. *The James Joyce Archive,* Vol. 27, edited by Danis Rose. New York and London: Garland, 1978.

Krieger, Murray. "The Ekphrastic Principle and the Still Movement of Poetry; or *Laokoon* Revisited." In *The Play and Place of Criticism*, 105–28. Baltimore: Johns Hopkins University Press, 1967.

Le Coat, Gerard. *The Rhetoric of the Arts, 1550–1650.* European University Papers, Series 18, Vol. 3. Bern: Herbert Lang, 1975.

McHugh, Roland. *The Sigla of* Finnegans Wake. Austin: University of Texas Press, 1976.

Merivale, Patricia. "Learning the Hard Way: Gothic Pedagogy in the Modern Romantic Quest." *Comparative Literature* 36 (1984): 146–61.

Minnis, A.J. *Medieval Theory of Authorship — Scholastic Literary Attitudes in the Later Middle Ages.* London: Scolar Press, 1984.

Preminger, Alex, Frank J. Warnke, and O.B. Hardison, Jr. *Princeton Encyclopedia of Poetry and Poetics.* Enlarged ed. Princeton: Princeton University Press, 1974.

Riquelme, John Paul. *Teller and Tale in Joyce's Fiction.* Baltimore: Johns Hopkins University Press, 1983.

Solomon, Margaret C. *Eternal Geomater: The Sexual Universe of* Finnegans Wake. Carbondale: Southern Illinois University Press, 1969.

Vico, Giambattista. *The New Science,* translated by Thomas Goddard Bergin and Max Harold Fisch. Ithaca: Cornell University Press, 1968.

Vinaver, E. *The Rise of Romance.* Oxford: Clarendon Press, 1971.

Weir, Lorraine. "Barthes' *Loyola* / Joyce's *Portrait* (Taxonomy and Paradigm)." *Texte* 4 (1987).

———. "Performing the Dreamwork: Vichian Morphogenesis in *Finnegans Wake.*" forthcoming.

———. "The Choreography of Gesture: Marcel Jousse and *Finnegans Wake.*" *James Joyce Quarterly* 14 (1977): 313–25.

16

ALP's Final Monologue in *Finnegans Wake:* The Dialectical Logic of Joyce's Dream Text

KIMBERLY DEVLIN

The female in *Finnegans Wake* assumes a number of representational forms within the dream text: verbal object, the topic of the washerwomen's gossip (*FW* I.8); visual object, the geometrical diagram studied during the math lesson (II.2); writing subject, a hypothetical author of the letter (I.5); and speaking subject, an imagined witness at the deposition (III.3). In their respective essays on Issy and ALP in *Women in Joyce,* Shari Benstock and Margot Norris both convincingly argue that the images of the female in the *Wake* are dialectically structured, a series of psychological reversals and oppositions, shaped by the male dreamer's fears and desires. The female emerges as an enigmatic "other," as a being whose nature is finally only speculative, as a perspectival abyss that the dreamer recurrently tries to plumb ("First he was living to feel what the eldest daughter she was panseying and last he was dying to know what old Madre Patriack does be up to" [*FW* 408]). As an elusive element, she appropriately finds her correlative in nature in the mobile and protean river, whose essence can never quite be captured and contained, and whose imagined babbling voice cannot always be clearly understood ("With lipth she lithpeth to him all to time of thuch on thuch and thow on thow. She he she ho she ha to la. Hairfluke, if he could bad twig her! Impalpabunt, he abhears. The soundwaves are his buffeteers; they trompe him with their trompes" [*FW* 23]). The larger dialectical representation of the female as speaking or writing subject, on the one hand, and as viewed or discussed object, on the other, may reflect the dreamer's attempt to envision this "other" point of view, countered by a recognition of its inaccessibility, its remoteness.

ALP's closing monologue seems to mitigate the uncompromising otherness of the female principle in the *Wake:* critics suggest that here we finally hear the actual voice of ALP, even those who elsewhere in their analyses take into account the dream's unmistakably male subjectivity. Benstock, for example, suggests that ALP's monologue is divorced from the rest of the *Wake,* providing "an alternate vision against which Earwicker's dream vision can be measured" (177), and discusses the final pages of the dream as if they were not colored by male wishes and fears, as if their narrative status were comparable to that of Molly's soliloquy at the close of *Ulysses:* "It is left to Anna Livia, who has the final 'word' in the novel, to confirm the future for her daughter...ALP's hints seem to suggest that diverse and flighty Issy will grow into the calm and unified mother/wife that Anna Livia now is" (190–191). Clive Hart describes the final pages of the book as "the closest thing to 'interior monologue' in *Finnegans Wake,*" as a "stream of almost unmodified Dublin speech" (55). In *The Decentered Universe of* Finnegans Wake, Norris grants the speech a similar standing, implying that we actually hear "leafy speafing" (*FW* 619), the feminine voice unmediated by the dreamer's consciousness (96–97). In her more recent essay in *Women in Joyce,* she emphasizes the interpretive obstacles raised by the book's ending, though without resolving them:

> We must understand the dreaming male figure in order to understand the female figure. Yet Joyce, paradoxically, sets up a hermeneutical spiral in *Finnegans Wake* through which the best insights into the condition of HCE (presumably the male dreamer) are given by Anna Livia in her final monologue. This interpretive doubling is a bit like Lewis Carroll's *Through the Looking Glass,* where we are momentarily in doubt whether Alice dreams the Red Knight or the Red Knight dreams Alice [sic]. (199)

This "hermeneutical spiral," I would argue, characterizes the structure of not simply the final monologue, but the entire dream text: although HCE does envision himself speaking at several points, most of the information (or misinformation) we are given about him is mediated, delivered via imagined others. Within this narrative constructed around the hypothetical viewpoints of other, HCE is logically identified as the dreamer not because he is the central "speaker," but rather because he is the central "spoken of"—all narrative roads seem to lead to him. The final speech, I think, is a continuation of this ex-centric dream text, the female voice imagined yet again, the fantasized voice of a fantasized other, discoursing primarily upon the dream's favorite subject—the dreamer himself. The *Wake* critics who imply the voice is "real" overlook the fact that the closing monologue contains reversals and contraries which make little sense on the level of realistic or waking narrative, and that it generates multilayered images typical of condensed, overdetermined visions of dream. The verbal and visual ambiguities of the speech, moreover, work dialectically, following the logic seen elsewhere in the *Wake,* expressing connected anxieties and desires.

Elsewhere I have argued that the dream text of the *Wake* betrays a male fear of the female "eye" (the literal visual organ and the alien perspective it represents) as an unwelcome critical vantage point, as an agency of potential exposure ("The Female Eye" passim). In the final monologue, though, ALP is imagined tactfully censoring her visual field, reassuring her spouse that she will not look at him in his fallen state, that she will think instead of how he looked when young:

> Maybe that's why you hold your hodd as if. And people thinks you missed the scaffold. Of fell design. I'll close me eyes. So not to see. Or see only a youth in his florizel, a boy in innocence, peeling a twig, a child beside a weenywhite steed. (*FW* 621)

This image of the politely veiled female eye, blocking out unpleasant sights and replacing them with happier ones, provides an apt correlative for the dominant discourse of the final monologue: the kindly, optimistic, and circumlocutory speech is the verbal equivalent of ALP's censored gaze. As constituted by her language here, ALP is endowed with many of the trappings of a fantasy woman, a male ideal of the perfect wife—adoring, soothing, forgiving, and redemptive (although this is only one extreme of a dialectical image). Her mellifluous voice becomes the agent of renewal in itself, bidding HCE to rise and giving him the encouragement to do so. The close of the dream, I would like to suggest, represents an invalid's vision of being revived from a coma by a caring mate, of suddenly waking up from a deathlike state—a sort of plausible version of the "Tim Finnegan's Wake" song. It is surely a wishful vision, but also a fearful one, the dreamer imagining not simply revival, but also how he might be treated and spoken to upon his return to the world of the waking—the pictured situation is not altogether heartening.

During the first part of the monologue, ALP is represented performing a series of nurturing and redemptive activities for HCE: laying out clean laundry, boosting his ego, taking him on a rejuvenatory outing, speaking to him with fondness and optimism. But her monologue generates a double discourse, the surface statement often contrasting with the insinuation, the sanguine circumlocution with the sad implication. ALP's inventory of HCE's apparel, for instance ("Here is your shirt, the day one, come back. The stock, your collar. Also your double brogues. A comforter as well" [*FW* 619]), may evoke a simple domestic image of a wife picking out her husband's clothes, or a sadder vision of her helping an invalid get dressed, perhaps even trying to reteach him the names of common objects. Indeed, the emphasis on identification, naming, and basic recall at many points in the speech may imply an assumption (on her part) of a derangement in the mental faculties that control such abilities: HCE envisions himself being addressed as a victim of senility, as a person well into his second childhood. Her offer to hold her spouse's "great bearspaw" (*FW* 621) when they go on their imagined walk is a gesture that can be construed as affectionate, romantic even, or utterly humiliating: it may reveal the dreamer's anticipated unsteadiness and his need of guidance, for at points in this closing dream vision he does not seem to know where he is ("You know where I am bringing you? You remember?" [*FW* 622]). ALP's remarks on the locales that they pass sound, on one level, like idle and friendly conversation, but betray, on another, HCE's possible disorientation. He seems to envision himself in a situation identical to Rip van Winkle's, returning to a world suspiciously unfamiliar to him, awakening from what he feels has been a single night's sleep only to find his environs have drastically changed. The dream woman is heard passing off this change as perfectly natural and plausible, pretending that cities can literally spring up over night, presumably in order to circumvent the truth of the dreamer's prolonged slumber: "Why, them's the muchrooms, come up during the night. Look, agres of roofs in parshes. Dom on dam, dim in dym. And a capital part for olympics to ply at" (*FW* 625). When one inquires into the logical motives behind the imagined speech acts that comprise the final monologue disturbing possibilities frequently emerge, creating a subtext that bespeaks all too clearly the dreamer's dread of his own potential helplessness and subsequent infantilization.

The proposed rejuvenatory outing is envisioned as a return to a romantic spot on Howth from ALP's and HCE's earlier days together ("You'll know our way from there surely. Flura's way. Where once we led so many car couples have follied since" [*FW* 623]), with the young courting couple represented as primordial lovers, succeeded by countless others, including no doubt Molly and Leopold Bloom

("All quiet on Howth now. The distant hills seem. Where we. The rhododendrons...All that old hill has seen. Names change: that's all. Lovers: yum yum" [*U* 377]). At the end of the *Wake,* as at the end of *Ulysses,* sexual reminiscence provides a means of psychic rejuvenation, though ALP uses it to revive the other rather than the self, recalling for HCE his gentler moments as a lover as well as his fiercer ones ("One time you'd stand fornenst me, fairly laughing, in your bark and tan billows of branches for to fan me coolly. And I'd lie as quiet as a moss. And one time you'd rush upon me, darkly roaring, like a great black shadow with a sheeny stare to perce me rawly" [*FW* 626]). The ensuing fond recollection of their marriage vows, however, turns suddenly sad as ALP realizes that the death described then as the remote and hypothetical condition of separation has become a not-so-distant reality ("How you said how you'd give me the keys of me heart. And we'd be married till delth to uspart. And though dev do espart. O mine!...And can it be it's nnow fforvell?" [*FW* 626]). The nostalgic return to the past in *Finnegans Wake* has a very different associative and affective end point than in *Ulysses,* the return evoking not simply memories of initial union but also the projected moment of parting.

The most disturbing ambiguity of the outing lies in the way it is described, ALP referring to it as a "journee saintomichael" (*FW* 621)—a journey sentimental or a journey to Saint Michael, whom Adaline Glasheen identifies as "the receiver of the souls of the dead" (193). The thought of being escorted to the spot of a romantic tryst becomes confused with the thought of being escorted to the grave, as in a funeral ritual, sexual "death" perhaps being associated with actual death, the first sexual fall with the final physical fall into mortality. The implied psychological linking of different types of "falls" here has clear precedent in "Circe": when the nannygoat present at the Blooms' lovemaking on Howth enters the parade of phantasms, a vision immediately ensues of Bloom falling "*from the Lion's Head cliff into the purple waiting waters*" (*U* 550). In *Finnegans Wake* the association is synchronic rather than diachronic, the envisioned journey emerging as a dual-layered image, like a picture produced from two negatives. The dreamer imagines his wife leading him to the tip of Howth Head or to the outermost bourne, the afterlife, to the house of the Earl of Howth or to the house of God:

> We might call on the Old Lord, what do you say? There's
> something tells me. He is a fine sport. Like the score and a
> moighty went before him. And a proper old promnentory. His
> door always open. For a newera's day. Much as your own is.
> You invoiced him last Eatster so he ought to give us hockockles
> and everything. Remember to take off your white hat, ech?
> When we come in the presence. And say hoothoothoo, ithmu-
> thisthy! His is house of laws. (*FW* 623)

Previously in the dream, HCE has had explicit visions of his wife
not only interring him, loaming him from head to foot, but also
actually weaving his grim fate, like an implacable goddess of destiny:
"Now she's borrid his head under Hatesbury's Hatch and loamed
his fate to old Love Lane" (*FW* 578). In the final monologue the
image of the woman burying the dead male is more strongly repressed,
carefully hidden beneath an antithetical screen vision, an image of
her trying to rejuvenate him.

As the couple travel in the dreamer's mind from inland out
towards the open sea, ALP eventually acknowledges her own fatigue
("For I feel I could near to faint away. Into the deeps") and the
increasing frailty of her own senses: "Illas! I wisht I had better
glances to peer to you through this baylight's growing. But you're
changing, acoolsha, you're changing from me, I can feel. Or is it
me is? I'm getting mixed" (*FW* 626). ALP's concessions of personal
debility and her sudden confusion as to who is "changing" signal
a major reversal, a key switching of roles, providing the first definite
hints that it is the female—and not the male—who is ultimately
envisioned as dying. Shortly afterwards, however, ALP insinuates that
she is not actually dying, but rather is sneaking off, running away
from the family she has become disgusted with, tired of their failure
to take an interest in her concerns or to appreciate her sacrifices:

> A hundred cares, a tithe of troubles and is there one who
> understands me? One in a thousand of years of the nights? All
> me life I have been lived among them but now they are becoming
> lothed to me. And I am lothing their little warm tricks. And
> lothing their mean cosy turns. And all the greedy gushes out
> through their small souls. And all the lazy leaks down over their
> brash bodies. How small it's all!...I'll slip away before they're
> up. They'll never see. Nor know. Nor miss me. (*FW* 627)

The final vision of the *Wake* reflect's the male's fear of being
abandoned by his weary mate—a fear, according to Richard Ellmann,

Just as the *Wake* suggests that ALP's flight is motivated by maternal fatigue, by "a hundred cares, a tithe of troubles," "Eveline" similarly hints that Mrs. Hill's death is precipitated by the day-to-day demands placed on her as mother and wife: she has led "that life of commonplace sacrifice closing in final craziness" (*D* 40), a final craziness that ALP shares, conceding that she has grown "loonely in me loneness"(*FW* 627)—not only lonely but also loony. In both works the departing mother expects that the dutiful daughter will take her place. Young Eveline must raise "the two young children who had been left to her charge" (*D* 38), having given her ailing mother "her promise to keep the home together as long as she could" (*D* 40). ALP also expresses a hope that her family will stay together—"Try not to part! Be happy, dear ones!"—and leaves in her wake "a daughterwife from the hills again" (*FW* 627—note the allusion to Eveline's last name). The father's desire for the daughter, blatant in the dreamworld, finds a more devious and sinister outlet in the waking reality of *Dubliners*. Eveline lives in fear of her father's violence, afraid that he might "go for her," even though she is nineteen, well beyond the age when children are reprimanded through physical punishments: "she knew that it was that that had given her the palpitations" (*D* 38). The aggressive father in the *Wake* has a similar effect on the daughter, or so he imagines, Issy glossing "the backslapping gladhander" in her footnotes with the remark, "He gives me pulpititions..." (*FW* 276).

The palpitations of the young woman signify fear and loathing but also their opposite—unacknowledged desire. A repressed Electra complex lies at the heart of Eveline's story, a complex unwittingly encouraged by the defeated mother, reinforced by the bullying father, and unconsciously acceded to by the passive and paralyzed daughter, who implicitly opts for the stultifying bond to Mr. Hill over a union with someone her own age, a new life with Frank, however ambiguous and uncertain that new life may be. In *Finnegans Wake*, of course, this incestuous drama is played out not within a waking narrative of the daughter's thoughts, but rather in a dream narrative of the father's. In accordance with the perspectival shift from conscious to unconscious psychic life, Joyce foregrounds the taboo desire only hinted at in "Eveline," bringing it to the surface. Shifting from the daughter's to the father's point of view, Joyce also represents a very different dialectic of anxiety and desire, significantly revising the outcome of the earlier short story. Although the dreaming father of the *Wake* hopes that the daughter will dutifully replace his spouse, he suspects and fears simultaneously that she will not stay with him, that like the mother, she will abandon him. He imagines the fleeing ALP offering her pity, gently hinting that he will have to compete with a younger generation of men for the daughter's loyalties and affections: "I pity your oldself I was used to. Now a younger's there" (*FW* 627). Running counter to the father's incestuous desire for the daughter throughout the dream is the grim epiphany of normal generational cycles, children ineluctably replacing parents rather than bonding with them.

The mother's disillusioned leavetaking at the end of the dream is foreshadowed much earlier, in the daughter's devious commentary on the grammar book in the homework lesson (*FW* II.2). Appended to the instruction that counsels Issy to "mind your genderous towards his reflexives such that I was to your grappa...when him was me hedon" is an exclamatory footnote that reads, "Frech devil in red hairing! So that's why you ran away to sea, Mrs Lappy. Leap me, locklaun, for you have sensed!" (*FW* 268). The apparent incongruity between the text counseling female deference to the male and the marginal comment recording female disloyalty and abandonment can be resolved by stressing the latter's interpretive status. The daughter is imagined here reading between the lines of "gramma's grammar" (*FW* 268) and finding in the conventional wisdom of the maternal text—in its ostensible endorsement of stereotypical sex roles—an epiphanic explanation for ALP's flight. The subversive notation assumes that the older woman has in fact grown tired of acting "genderous" towards male "reflexives," weary of playing the wife who caters selflessly to her husband's whims. Although her ensuing departure may be a sin, it may also reflect her good sense ("Mrs Lappy...you have sensed!"). Issy is envisioned as understanding a silent discourse of the female text, detecting the dissatisfaction inherent in its advice, hearing in it not a complacent admission of male superiority but rather a veiled complaint against male egotism.

This footnote is interesting to consider in the context of "Eveline," for Eveline too reads and understands an alternate discourse of the mother. Mrs. Hill's implied request to the daughter to assume her role and responsibilities is subverted by her final mad and incoherent exclamations, the specific plea qualified by the larger behavioral statement. The daughter perceives a sad logic behind the mother's retreat into lunacy and death, just as Issy intuits the logic

behind ALP's analogous departure in the *Wake:* Eveline's thought of
her mother's "life of commonplace sacrifices closing in final craziness"
puts selfless maternal duty and ultimate insanity into a disturbing
cause-and-effect progression, an alarming sequence of inevitability. She
decides to break the promise to the mother because she interprets her
crazed demise as a counterstatement to the request, as an admonition
of what that elicited promise may lead to. Her "sudden impulse of
terror" (*D* 40) can be best accounted for if one assumes that Eveline
recognizes unconsciously in her mother's death a premonition of her
own possible fate, the memory ultimately fortifying not her sense of
duty but rather her resolve to leave. The daughter vows an active
physical escape from her oppressed position—a contrast to the mother's
passive psychological escape into madness—though she is pathetically
unable to carry through her resolve, apparently forgetting the warning
embedded in the earlier recollection. That closing scene of "Eveline"
in which the young woman stands suspended between flight and duty
reappears at the very end of the *Wake,* I would like to suggest, albeit
in a much altered and complicated guise.

The final vision of the dream is a highly ambiguous one, one
that expresses both a desire and a fear through a rapid alternation
of images. ALP's union with her "cold mad feary father" (*FW* 628)
reduplicates the previously envisioned union of HCE and his "daughterwife" Issy, providing an overdetermined expression of the desire
for father-daughter incest and of the implicit attendant wish for
recaptured youth, for eternal renewal through a bonding with the
female child who is reminiscent of the wife when young. In this
protean vision of human roles so typical to the dream, Issy is not
only wishfully imagined as spouse, but ALP is also seen as daughter,
and it is in this capacity that her final gestures—both physical and
verbal—become most equivocal. One moment ALP is the obedient
daughter dutifully returning to the father, but in the next she is
the rebellious daughter, turning away from the father towards the
younger lover, the lover whom she sees as a means of escape from
patriarchal oppression: "it's sad and weary I go back to *you,* my
cold father, my cold mad father, my cold mad feary father, till the
near sight of mere size of *him,* the moyles and moyles of it,
moananoaning, makes me seasilt saltsick and I rush, my only, into
your arms. I see them rising! Save me from those therrble prongs!"
(*FW* 627–628, my emphasis). The intensifying vision of the father's
wrath ("my cold father, my cold mad father, my cold mad feary

father'') and the interesting pronominal shift that follows can be logically connected. At first ALP addresses the father himself (as a ''you''), but then after envisioning his increasingly threatening mien, she suddenly refers to him more distantly, in the third person (''the mere size of him''), so that she is now imagined talking about the father to someone else. This second addressee is the lover to whom she ultimately turns for a saving embrace (''I rush, my only, into your arms...Save me from those therrble prongs!''), like Eveline fantasizing about Frank before she leaves home (''Frank would take her in his arms, fold her in his arms. He would save her'' [*D* 40]). At the end of the earlier short story, the lover is associated with the sea, envisioned as the element that will drown the self (''All the seas of the world tumbled about her heart. He was drawing her into them: he would drown her'' [*D* 41]); at the end of the *Wake* the father himself plays this annihilating role, cast as he is as ''Old Father Ocean'' (*U* 50), as both the Irish and Greek sea gods, Mananaan (''moananoaning'') and Poseidon, the latter's threatening trident providing a rough imagistic variant of Mr. Hill's threatening blackthorn stick.

The frightening image of the violent father reverses itself in the subsequent image of the protective father gently carrying the daughter along as he did when she was a child (''Carry me along, taddy, like you done through the toy fair!'' [*FW* 628]). The dialectical structure of this mediated self-image is anticipated when ALP is envisioned remembering her father ambivalently (''I'm sure he squirted juice in his eyes to make them flash for flightening me. Still and all he was awful fond to me'' [*FW* 626]), like Eveline recalling both her father's violence and his kindness. The double resonance of the phrase ''Far calls. Coming, far!'' (*FW* 628) reintrojects into the dream text the uncertainty of ALP's imagined response to the patriarch, the ambiguity of her nature—either fond, submissive, and childlike, or fearful, mistrusting, and defiant: she may be responding dutifully to the voice of the ''far,'' the distant unknown Eveline is tempted by but ultimately rejects. In his mapping of the verbal correspondence between the end of ''Eveline'' and that of the *Wake,* Hart juxtaposes one of Frank's last words to Eveline—''Come!'' (*D* 41)—with this ''Coming, far!'' spoken by ALP (54). The two cries make sense, though, not as verbal analogies or parallelisms but as an entreaty and a response, as a plea and an answer. What is heard here on the final page of the dream, in short, are the words Eveline

is unable to speak. In this ambiguous rerendering of the close of
the earlier short story, the daughter is imagined acquiescing obediently
to the demands of the father *or* responding fervently to the cry of
the lover, depending upon what one chooses to hear in that final
equivocal "far."

The two visions of the daughter that emerge through the rapidly
shifting images and various verbal ambiguities are incompatible within
the framework of a realistic narrative—the daughter cannot return to
the father and abandon him simultaneously—but they do make sense
as a dialectical narrative of dream. In fact I would argue that the
logic of the *Wake's* seemingly contradictory ending can be best
understood if one imagines the dreamer at this point as Mr. Hill
and then speculates about what he might have dreamed about after
reading Eveline's letter on the night she attempts to leave her family.[2]
The possibility of the daughter's departure, made clear by the letter,
would logically produce an intensified unconscious desire for her
loyalty, that desire expressed in such clear and overdetermined form
at the close of the dream. Mr. Hill's probable conscious response to
the attempted escape is anger and violence, a response apparently
recalled in the image of the "cold mad feary father" authoritatively
brandishing his trident or blackthorn stick: the dream text here may
provide us with a disquieting hint of what Eveline encountered upon
her return to the home. But the very threat of the daughter's
departure would probably awaken in the father not only feelings of
outrage, but also ones of vulnerability and weakness, a sense of
uncertain control over the daughter he needs: hence the opposite
and fearful dream vision of her opting for the lover over the father,
defiantly breaking the familial bond. Indeed, in that final vision of
the daughter turning away from him—both verbally and physically—
at the sight of his "therrble prongs," the father recognizes his
violence not as the means of controlling the daughter, but as the
very thing that frightens her away from him: she is not simply lured
away by another but also driven away by his aggression. If earlier in
the *Wake* the daughter is envisioned as understanding a silent and
subversive discourse of the mother, here she is imagined (on one
level of the dialectic) as acting upon that wisdom of the malcontent,
seeing the sense and not the sin in running away to sea, realizing
the danger inherent in staying with the father and the attraction of
that mysterious "far."

At the end of her monologue ALP embraces the sexual, imagining her own erotic surrender: "If I seen him bearing down on me now under whitespread wings like he'd come from Arkangels, I sink I'd die down over his feet, humbly, dumbly, only to washup" (*FW* 628). The image stands in opposition to one of Eveline's closing visions at the station, her "glimpse of the black mass of the boat" (*D* 40), inverting color (black/white), religious association (Black Mass/Annunciation, demonic/angelic), and implicit emotional effect (fright/acceptance), while maintaining the linking impression of massiveness. The "black mass of the boat" may embody a vague sexual threat and contribute to Eveline's distress and hesitation (in *Finnegans Wake* boats often become explicitly phallic—"with his runagate bowmpriss he roade and borst her bar" [*FW* 197]); at the end of the dream, however, the daughter is represented overcoming all sexual fears, envisioning not only her sexual surrender but also her survival, seeing erotic "death" as leading inevitably to self-renewal, resurrection ("I sink I'd die down over his feet, humbly, dumbly, only to washup"). The man ALP gives herself to remains characteristically equivocal, the resonances of the Annunciation suggesting the father-lover, but the allusion to "Arkangels" suggesting the younger lover as well: as B.J. Tysdahl points out, the conclusion to the *Wake* enfolds a reference to Ibsen's *Lady from the Sea* (178, 210), the lover "from Arkangels" being the Stranger in the play, the sailor-lover who (as in "Eveline") serves as the father-lover's rival.

In "Eveline" the mother's death and the daughter's possible flight are separate narrative events; in the dreamworld they are conflated, intermingled, recognized as analogous departures with similar causalities—weariness over female roles within the patriarchial family. ALP's dual status as both dying mother and fleeing daughter leaves the ultimate vision of female journeying and bequeathal of keys ambiguously suspended. Although there is a logical critical tendency to interpret ALP's keys symbolically, their more literal and mundane significance should not be forgotten: they may simply be house keys, like those in anyone's pocket or purse. On one level these keys left behind at the final decision to depart ("Lps. The keys to. Given!" [*FW* 628]) are perhaps passed from ALP-as-mother to Issy-as-daughter, in a wishful vision of dutiful female succession; but in her capacity as daughter, ALP may be returning those keys of the house back to the master himself—they are the keys which may have logically accompanied Eveline's farewell letter, keys perhaps associated with domestic responsibility.

What happens after the female return in "Eveline" can be imagined and is indeed explored from a new perspective in the final dream vision of the *Wake;* what happens after the female departure projected within this dream vision on the other level of the dialectic cannot, in contrast, be so easily conjectured. In an ending that resonates of Ibsen's *A Doll House,* the leave-taking female relinquishes the keys of her safe but oppressive domestic position to embrace an unknown that defies conception, resists articulation, arrests the flow of the dream language in midstream. When Joyce revisits and revises "Eveline" from its inherent male point of view, he adumbrates its abyss, that region beyond envisioning: that region is surely death itself, but also the female other who eludes the dreamer both physically and psychically, perhaps coursing fatalistically towards "that other world," perhaps ecstatically towards freedom.

NOTES

1. For an account of Nora's threatened departures, see Ellmann's *James Joyce,* 687–688.

2. This is not to suggest that Mr. Hill is the dreamer, that I pretend to have solved the riddle of HCE's identity (which ultimately, of course, remains indeterminate). What I am suggesting in a larger study of *Finnegans Wake* (of which this essay forms a part) is roughly this: in constructing the dream of a dying "anyman," who relives the successive phases of his life in the dream text, Joyce uses a lot of the content of his earlier works—content both psychical (states of mind) and concrete (material, situational details)—to express the desires and fears encountered in and attached to these successive phases. HCE is a composite figure, created from figures not only from history, myth, and earlier works of literature, but also from Joyce's own canon.

WORKS CITED

Benstock, Shari. "The Genuine Christine: Psychodynamics of Issy." In *Women in Joyce,* edited by Suzette Henke and Elaine Unkeless, 169–96. Urbana: University of Illinois Press, 1982.

Devlin, Kimberly. "The Female Eye: Joyce's Voyeuristic Narcissists." Forthcoming in *New Alliances in Joyce Studies: "When it's Aped to Foul a Delfian."* Newark: University of Delaware Press.

Ellmann, Richard. *James Joyce.* Oxford: Oxford University Press, 1982.

Freud, Sigmund. *The Interpretation of Dreams,* translated by James Strachey. New York: Avon Books, 1965.

Glasheen, Adaline. *A Third Census of* Finnegans Wake. Berkeley: University of California Press, 1977.

Hart, Clive. *Structure and Motif in* Finnegans Wake. London: Faber & Faber, 1962.

McHugh, Roland. *Annotations to* Finnegans Wake. Baltimore: Johns Hopkins University Press, 1980.

Norris, Margot. "Anna Livia Plurabelle: The Dream Woman." In *Women in Joyce,* edited by Suzette Henke and Elaine Unkeless, 197–213. Urbana: University of Illinois Press, 1982.

———. *The Decentered Universe of* Finnegans Wake. Baltimore: Johns Hopkins University Press, 1976.

Tysdahl, B.J. *Joyce and Ibsen: A Study in Literary Influence.* New York: Humanities Press, 1968.

17

Shahrazade, Turko the Terrible, and Shem: The Reader as Voyeur in *Finnegans Wake*

HENRIETTE LAZARIDIS POWER

Finnegans Wake contains a number of references to *The Thousand and One Nights*; and the number of those *Arabian Nights* provides a model both for the proliferation of accounts of HCE's fall, and for the structure of cycle and *ricorso* which Joyce has borrowed from Vico. Like the "one thousand and one stories, all told, of the same" (*FW* 5.28) in Joyce's text, *The Thousand and One Nights* suggest the completion of one cycle (or millenium) and the beginning of another. Certainly, the *Arabian Nights* is a text known for its numbers and for its sex—as is *Finnegans Wake*. Yet Joyce has taken another more obscure element from the *Arabian Nights,* and applied it to his own "nightynovel." Among other narrative structures, the tales and fables of the *Arabian Nights* involve a traditional feature of medieval Arabic literature known as the "witnessing system"—a convention which validates a particular saying (often by Mohammed) by locating it in a chain of witnesses who testify to the authority of the text (Gerhardt 378). Joyce, too, uses a witnessing system. Yet, as the third chapter of the *Wake* indicates (with the conflicting and confusing accounts of passersby and pub customers), Joyce's intent is not to validate but to devalue authority. The chain of witnesses provides not an accurate testimony, but what Colin McCabe has described in Joyce's work as an "infinite regress of meta-languages"—these meta-languages being, more simply, the discourses which attempt to certify and specify the meaning of a given prior text, yet which become themselves discourses to be specified—or questioned—by another witness (14).

The key here to the unraveling of the chain of witnesses and to the devaluation of authority is Joyce's treatment of voyeurism as he relates it to the narration and the reading of the *Wake*. And it is here—with regard to the positions of watcher and actor, reader and narrator—that the *Arabian Nights* provides perhaps its most significant contribution to Joyce's redefinition of narrative in the *Wake*. For, like Joyce's narrative tactics in the *Wake*, Shahrazade's strategy in the narration of the *Arabian Nights* uses forms of voyeurism to subvert the balance of authority between teller and listener (or reader), and to redefine traditional concepts of textual and sexual mastery.

Though there are several scenes of voyeurism to consider in the *Wake*, and though there are references to the *Arabian Nights* throughout Joyce's text, I will concentrate my discussion here on the tale of Willingdone, the Lipoleum(s), and the two jinnies (*FW* 8.9–10.23)—a tale which contains no overt allusions to the *Arabian Nights*, yet which provides an example of the kinds of narrative subversion that both Shahrazade and Joyce are engaged in. For my conclusion, I will turn to "The Mime of Mick, Nick, and the Maggies" (*FW* II.i) where we can watch the aesthetic subversion taking place in the "Magnificent Transformation Scene" (*FW* 222.17) of a pantomime. Before I discuss these texts from the *Wake*, however, I would like to look at the overall structure of the *Arabian Nights;* and, particularly, I'd like to look at the uses of looking in the text.

Shahrazade's use of narrative as an act of survival and liberation is a familiar literary topos. Later on, I will comment on the remarks Michel Foucault has made on this subject. But, for the moment, I would like to consider certain other elements of narrative structure which emerge in the *Arabian Nights* before Shahrazade arrives at her lifesaving narration. The frame narrative which establishes Shahrazade's position as the teller of the tales to King Shahryar, as well as the tales she tells, involves a complex series of betrayals, assertions of authority, and, significantly, episodes of voyeurism. Margot Norris's suggestion of a primal scene or primal sin as the source of the various episodes of voyeurism in the *Wake* is appropriate here. In the *Wake*, the primal scene involves the exposure or betrayal which results from the children's viewing of their parents' sexual activity (Norris 44–45). The primal scene of the *Arabian Nights*, however, involves the witnessing of one's own sexual betrayal—a scene which is repeatedly revised in the rivalry between King Shahryar and his younger brother.

While sibling rivalry is prominent in both the *Arabian Nights* and the *Wake*, a more significant rivalry which emerges in the former text is that between men and women. Shahryar asserts his own superior position in this relationship by enacting a vicarious and sexual revenge on his unfaithful wife: he violates a different virgin each night, and

orders her to be beheaded the next morning. It is Shahrazade who
volunteers to be the next—and, she hopes, the last—virgin, and who
manages to halt this series of violations by telling the King part of
a tale each night after sex. Significantly, Shahrazade invites her sister
Donyahzade to become the ostensible audience of her tales; the two
sisters share both female imprisonment and female narration. In the
rivalry between male master and female subject, Shahrazade has
challenged the male-centered hierarchy of elder and younger kings
with a perhaps female concept of balance and cooperation.[1]

The frame of the *Arabian Nights,* then, provides us with certain
distinct narrative elements: the notion of witnessing associated with
betrayal; a rivalry in which witnessing figures as an element in the
exchange of power; and a configuration of the female pair. These
elements emerge from a fairly traditional narrative politics. At the
outset of the *Arabian Nights,* the male is the master of the female
subject; he commands the woman to entertain him—as domestic
servant, and/or as sexual object. (One of the many titles of *The
Thousand and One Nights* is, appropriately, *The Arabian Nights'
Entertainments.*) To put this situation in textual terms, as the reader
of the woman's performance, the man reserves the right to judge,
interpret, and determine her text. He provides the meta-language for
her discourse. However, the master is subject to two betrayals here—
both engineered by women. Initially, with the King's betrayal by his
wife, his power as a reader is subverted; he is forced to read his own
vulnerability in the Queen's assertion of her own sexual freedom. His
meta-language, then, becomes implicated in the infinite regression of
languages which Joyce later turns into *Finnegans Wake.* As a reader,
the King has become not so much a reader, a judge, but a passive
witness to a female rebel's text. However, though the Queen's subversion of her master has exposed the fallibility of the master's power,
the subversion continues to sustain a traditional concept of authority;
the Queen has simply now put the male, not the female, in the
position of passivity.

Significantly, both Shahrazade and Joyce take the Queen's subversion one step further as they subject the master to a second betrayal.
If the Queen has turned the authoritative reader into a passive *witness,*
Shahrazade turns the witness into a *voyeur*—a figure whose position
involves both passivity and activity, both detachment or concealment
and participation. This is clear in the King's position regarding
Shahrazade's narrative. With the presence of Donyahzade in what

becomes a narrative *ménage à trois,* the King loses direct control over
the text. His reading of Shahrazade's performance is mediated by the
other woman who shares and undermines his position as the sole
reader/critic. The reader, then, is no longer a detached judge who
can determine the content of a text with his own interpretive text;
nor is he a passive witness who is determined by another text (as he
is while he witnesses his sexual betrayal). If we were to ascribe a
single position to this reader in the narrative dynamics of Shahrazade's
revisionary text, we would place him on the margin—not outside,
but on the edge—of the circle in which the women's narrative is
enacted. Yet the reader/King's position is not a static one. Rather,
like a *voyeur,* the reader is in a compromised position—in two senses
of the word: not only is he caught in his vicarious enjoyment of the
sexuality of Shahrazade's tales, but he is also caught between the two
postures of the supposedly authoritative audience of the tales, and
the performer *in* them. (The King's performance consists of the nightly
sex with Shahrazade which serves as a physical counterpart to the sex
of her narrative.)

Shahrazade's revision of the traditional dynamics of reading and
writing depends largely on the fusion of these two functions. In
reference to Joyce's work, Hélène Cixous has suggested that an understanding of the text demands a "lecture-écriture" (419–32)—a
simultaneous reading and writing. I would add, then, that the text
is the product, to begin with, of a "lecteur-écrivain"—a reader-writer.
The same is true of the *Arabian Nights,* and of the formulation of
the *voyeur.* For if the King, as reader, has no stable or static position
with regard to the text, this is so because the writer of the text is
also unstable. The King shifts from master to victim because Shahrazade, too, moves from subject of a dictator to dictator of a tale.
Like the King, Shahrazade is a *voyeur* who produces her narrative in
a compromised position.

Shahrazade's compromised position is, however, to her advantage. She shares her stance with Turko the Terrible of *Ulysses* and of
the Gaiety Theatre's first Christmas pantomime (McHugh 132)—a
voyeuristic figure who, as the song goes, is "the boy / that can enjoy /
invisibility" (*U* 10) precisely because he can proclaim that invisibility
in the text of his song while he himself remains safely hidden.
Shahrazade's mobility and invisibility engage her reader in a kind of
shell game; each time the reader attempts to reveal her under a
particular cover, he finds that she is elsewhere. It is this ability to be

always elsewhere which is essential to the role of the *voyeur* and to Shahrazade's survival as a storyteller. Foucault's remarks on narrative and survival are relevant here.

In "What is an Author?", Foucault asserts that the writer "must assume the role of the dead man in the game of writing": in order to assert himself in his text, the writer must efface himself as well. Foucault excludes Shahrazade from this category of writers, saying that, rather than enact death, her text avoids it (by seducing the King away from murder into marriage) (102–3). Yet I would argue here that Shahrazade avoids death precisely because she does play dead in her text; in fact, her seduction is part of her strategic self-effacement. She prevents the division of her speaking head from her subjected body by presenting herself as an already divided woman. While, on the other hand, Donyahzade may divide the King's share of power over the tales, she also appeases the King by helping to create the illusion of a divided and dependent woman. Shahrazade's use of Donyahzade, then, creates a visible mask of invisibility and vulnerability for the elusive and manipulative speaker.

In a sense, Shahrazade's narrative strategy allows her to conduct her own *Wake*. For the Irish, a wake involves a raucous ceremony of game-playing, story-telling, singing, and drinking intended to protect the mourning household from the spirits of death. Shahrazade fends off similar spirits which take the form of the King and his violent power. Significantly, she does so not by emphasizing her own activity (as do the celebrants described by the ballad of "Finnegan's Wake," for instance), but by presenting herself as a passive victim, figured in the fragmented image of the two sisters.

Through her treatment of doubles and halves, and her redirection of the lines of narrative vision, Shahrazade has subverted the traditional formulation of authority, with its suggestion of usurpation and rivalry. Yet, as we move from Shahrazade's to *Finnegans Wake,* we see that Joyce's text is full of rivalries—between Willingdone and the Lipoleum(s), Buckley and the Russian General, the Cad and HCE, Mutt and Jute, and Shaun and Shem, to name a few. And while the *Arabian Nights* moves eventually towards reconciliation, the *Wake* moves along a series of antagonisms whose constant realignment propels the text. Nevertheless, the nature of these realignments suggests that, like Shahrazade, Joyce locates (or dislocates) the authority of the reader in the figure of the *voyeur* who is both victor and victim, usurper and usurped. In fact, we can see these realignments as part of what Norris has called the "maternal salvage" of ALP—like Shahrazade, another revisionary female. Though Norris opposes ALP's redistribution and exchange to the "unlawful appropriations" of the rival males, I would like to suggest that this male rivalry, and its constant *im*-balancing of power, is subject to transformation by the redistributive aesthetic of ALP (64, 67–68).

As with the initial configurations of power in the *Arabian Nights*, the tale of Willingdone and the Lipoleum(s) seems to indicate that authority is determined by one's position as viewer or performer. "[F]einting to read in their handmade's book of stralegy," the jinnies create a performance, "a cooin her hand" and "a ravin her hair" (*FW* 8.31–34). Like the King who watches the narration dramatized as the performance of two women, Willingdone is the reader of the two jinnies' calculated self-exposure. But the jinnies are not the only performers here. For, as he "git the band up" (*FW* 8.34), Willingdone becomes a *voyeur* who participates vicariously in the sexuality of the scene before him.[2] His erection here parallels the King's nightly sex with Shahrazade; it represents an enactment of the narrative, preventing the reader from determining the text from a position of detachment—or from any single position at all. Willingdone is forced into a simultaneous observation and involvement.

It might appear that Willingdone maintains a position of mastery over the two jinnies. After all, his sexual and martial authority is affirmed as "sexcaliber hrosspower" (*FW* 8.36) just as the power of the King's sword is concentrated in, and replaced by, his phallus. Yet the potential authority of Willingdone's erection is undermined by an emblem of perception: the "tallowscoop" (*FW* 8.35, 9.34) which falls "on the flanks of the jinnies" (*FW* 8.35–36). Both phallic and optic, the tallowscoop implicates the role of the reader with that of the *voyeur*. Even its optic qualities alone suggest the dual role of the reader/*voyeur* as the tallowscoop fuses immediacy and distance, detachment and participation. As with the regression of meta-languages and of witnesses throughout the *Wake*, here in particular, the *voyeur* joins a chain of viewers and exposers which dislocates rather than defines authority.

As becomes evident when the three rival Lipoleum(s) condense into the "hindoo seeboy" (or the "cursigan Shimar Shin") (*FW* 10.14, 10.18), the *voyeur* himself is exposed, seen by another *voyeur* who, unlike Willingdone, appears to remain "hindoo" or hidden.

Instead of a chain of witnesses who authorize their own and each preceding text, Joyce produces a chain of *voyeurs* who keep the text suspended in indeterminacy. One critic of the *Arabian Nights* has pointed out that Shahrazade's survival and narrative success depends on her replacement of the signified with the signifier, a strategy which allows for the development of an unlimited number of discourses or of witnesses (Ghazoul 43). The same occurs in the *Wake*—a text which remains "lapse but not leashed" (*FW* 62.24), falling, with neither origin nor anchor, from one signifier to the next, from one act of voyeurism to another.

Joyce's narrative strategy here makes possible both a plurality of discourses and a plurality of readings or of positions for the reader/*voyeur* to adopt. Perhaps because of this plurality, neither *and* each side emerges as a single victor from the battle for power between Willingdone and the Lipoleum(s). Willingdone wins the division of his three rivals who are represented by the "triplewon hat" (*FW* 8.15); and the Lipoleum(s), realigned three-in-one as Shimar Shin, win their own survival and partial retaliation by blowing up both Willingdone's "harse" and the triplewon hat that Willing-done has hung on the "harse"'s tail (*FW* 10.2). Since the positions of power are determined by the dynamics of both combat and voyeurism, the victory here must be a pyrrhic one—in two ways—as each master is necessarily made subject to vision and division.

The pyrrhic or peer-ic victory is essentially the creation of the Lipoleum(s) who unsettle the apparently monumental power of "Stonewall Willingdone" (*FW* 10.2) with their fractious and fractured presence, "grouching down in the living detch" (*FW* 8.22). While the jinnies read their strategy against Willingdone from a "hand-made's book" (*FW* 8.32), so, in a sense, do the Lipoleum(s): they take their strategy from Shahrazade's book of tales. As Shahrazade has done, the Lipoleum(s) present themselves to their supposed master as already divided; in this way, they survive their division into "half of the threefoiled hat" (*FW* 10.8). The Lipoleum(s) center their threesome on one soldier—Shimar Shin—whose name suggests the antagonistic twins of the *Wake*, and whose identity appears to be constituted in two opposing halves. Joyce has, in a way, prepared us for this reading of the Lipoleum(s) through his allusion to Giambattista della Porta (as "Gambariste della porca"—*FW* 9.35–36), the author of "I Due Fratelli Rivali." Through Shimar Shin, the Lipoleum(s) preserve Shahrazade's illusion of a binary and hierarchical structure while they subvert the mastery of the nominal authority—an authority which remains, like its putative subject, always elsewhere. After all, with their shifting between a double and a triple configuration, the Lipoleum(s) elude both defeat and victory; neither Willingdone's sexcaliber, nor the reader's interpretive penetration will succeed in articulating (that is, in both dividing and determining) their position. Male rivalry has been feminized, in a sense, transformed into the redistributive tactics of the Prankquean who turns Tristopher and Hilary (*FW* 21.12) into Larryhill and Toughertrees (*FW* 22.19, 22.24), and who turns a binary opposition like this one (sad/glad) into a triple configuration with her fairy-tale pattern of three returns.

Appropriately, Joyce derives the names of the two "jiminies" in the Prankquean episode from Bruno's motto, itself a compromise of contraries: "In tristitia hilaris hilaritate tristis" (McHugh 21). It would appear that Bruno and Shahrazade have the same function in Joyce's text. Both figures represent a breakdown of oppositions into reunion or compromise. Nevertheless, there is a difference here, suggested in part by the difference in gender. For instance, Shahrazade's function relates more specifically to oppositions in the dynamics of reading and writing. And her manipulation of these oppositions suggests the figure of the *voyeur* as reader-writer—a figure, after all, who takes a prominent part in this text about sexual exposure and sexually motivated observation. Finally, Shahrazade's strategy is a subversive one which involves the concealment inherent to the *voyeur*. Shahrazade's subversion prompts a reconsideration of Julia Kristeva's distinction between the rhetorician and the stylist with regard to the issue of gender in the *Wake*. In *Desire and Language,* Kristeva argues cogently that symbolic language is distinct from (and, perhaps, in opposition to) semiotic language. The one involves a repressive attribution of meaning and fixity, while the other operates in the area—or the *chora*—of the unnameable, of the unstable, and of desire; symbolic language belongs to the father, while semiotic language is the mother's or the woman's discourse. Yet Kristeva goes on to ascribe semiotic (or poetic) language to the "stylist" who challenges that father's discourse with a new one of his or her own. The "rhetorician," meanwhile, remains fascinated with paternal discourse, "miming a father" in his or her symbolic language (133–39, 138). I would argue that, in certain respects, the stylist simply continues the possessive and repressive behavior of

fathers and sons, and of male discourse. It is the rhetorician, on the
other hand, who adopts Shahrazade's distinctly female strategies of
subversion and transformation. As Shahrazade has done, the rhetorician mimes the father, at the same time, "seducing" him away
from paternal discourse towards the hybrid and elusive language of
the *chora* (or body) he has intended to master (138).

Shem, too, is a rhetorician, functioning in the *Wake* like the
hidden seeboy Shimar Shin. Shahrazade, Shimar Shin, and Shem
are all *voyeurs* who announce their power from a position of disguise
or concealment, and whose discourse both mimes and defies their
opponents. Joyce makes Shem's dual function clear in his revision
of the Biblical family which gives Shem his name. Shem's Biblical
antecedent is known for covering his drunken father Noah without
taking a glance at Noah's exposed body. His brother Ham, on the
other hand, is known for both watching and proclaiming his father's
physical vulnerability. Yet, in Joyce's condensation of Ham, Shem,
and Japhet into Shem and Shaun, Shem adopts the roles of both
brothers at once. For, when he writes, Shem's text both covers and
reveals—proclaims his identity and obscures it. As Shem puts it
himself, his writing is a "squirtscreen" to detail and disguise a
"squidself" (*FW* 186.6–7). As becomes clear in Shem's self-inscrip-
tion with his own excrement, Joyce suggests here that writing involves
disguise and self-compromise; narrative is a form of *de-scription*—
the unwriting of any particular subject of any particular text. And
it is this *de-scription* as a transformation of both self and master,
and as an act of survival, which makes the writer a *voyeur*, a hidden
seeboy.

As I have pointed out, the gaze of the *voyeur* sets in operation
a continuing exchange between the positions of reader and writer,
master and subject. The exchange continues until the two positions
combine, and until subjection becomes an element of mastery. This
fusion of opposites is apparent, certainly, in Joyce's frequent allusions
to Bruno and his theories, and in his use of the Prankquean and
her threes. In "The Mime of Mick, Nick, and the Maggies," as
well, where pantomimic transformation and combination is the rule,
we see HCE, "cap-a-pipe" (*FW* 220.26), turning into his Shem-like
rival the Cad; a fallen Shem/Glugg turning into HCE, caught in
the complex of "Herzog van Vellentam," "Bohnaparts," and "jen-
nyjos" (*FW* 238.24–26, 238.33); and the Lipoleum(s) or Bohnaparts

turning from male to female as they become "la pau'Leonie" to "Josephinus and Mario-Louis" (*FW* 246.16–17). Of course, these transformations have been taking place from the very beginning of a text which forces us to redefine reading. Margot Norris has pointed out Heidegger's observation that reading and gathering are etymologically related. The German *lesen*, which denotes both activities, recasts reading as "not the rapid, automatic decoding to which we are accustomed, but a slow, patient, bringing together, putting one thing with another" (69). In other words, reading *Finnegans Wake* is a participation in the semiotic, not the symbolic, discourse of a *voyeur* as we confront a language that cannot be decoded or named. Moreover, the fixed meta-language of a master has given way to the work of a female rhetorician, and to ALP's gathering and redistribution. We can see this transformation of narrative dynamics in the "Mime," where the Prankquean and her numbers appear, and where "tempt-in-two will stroll at venture and hunt-by-threes strut musketeering" (*FW* 245.19–20) in yet another version of the "baffle of Whatalose" (*FW* 246.27).

In the gestural language of the "Mime," Joyce offers us a dramatization of Shem/Glugg's change from authoritative writer *and* reader to reader-writer (to use Cixous's terms again) or *voyeur*. Somewhere in this pantomime scenario lurks the invisible Turko the Terrible of *Ulysses* and of the Gaiety.[3] Here it is Izod, with her "grateful sister reflection in a mirror" (*FW* 220.9) who takes the role(s) of Shahrazade and Donyahzade, and who becomes an agent of Shem/Glugg's transformation.[4] Joyce's diction leads us to associate Shem's search for the answer to the flower-girls' riddle with Willingdone's observation of the jinnies; both men are engaged in some sort of visual prying. Shem's "gazework" recalls Willingdone's "Wounderworker" tallowscoop (*FW* 224.26, 8.35); and the slang "bander" occurs again in reference to both Shem who must "fand for himself," and Shaun who "bandished it with his hand the hold time" (*FW* 224.26, 224.34). Even without linguistic parallels, the episode is the same: the male figure looks at the female temptresses who resist him as they expose themselves to his gaze. Significantly, the context for this resistance has shifted now from warfare to interpretation as Shem tries literally to read Izod and her flowergirls. Yet, as the King has done in his intended reading of Shahrazade, Shem fails in his attempt. Before we consider the cause for Shem's failure, it will be helpful to look at his response to it.

Shem answers his failure to provide an answer to the riddle of color with an act of revenge: he writes. In his anger, "He do big squeal" and he will "set it up all writhefully rate in blotch and void" (FW 228.6, 229.27). Like his attempt at interpretation, Shem's self-expression participates in the male discourse of "unlawful appropriation." His reading has been an unsuccessful exercise in determination—in fixing the elusive text of the flower-girls with his authoritative meta-language. To Shem's one-track questions,[5] the flower-girls and/or Izod respond with only negatives and movement—forms of verbal and physical evasion. Shem's written corrective for the girls' indeterminacy involves another attempted declaration of authority: his "squeal" is a meta-language of aggressive retaliation. Nevertheless, though he may intend to state the case against the vagueness of heliotrope in the apparent clarity of black and white, Shem ends up writing in "blotch and void," "reading off his fleshskin and writing with his quillbone" (FW 229.30). In other words, whether he likes it or not, Shem resorts to the voyeuristic reading-writing of a hidden seeboy. As I.vii has suggested, writing involves the *de-scription* of both the writing subject and the subject of the writing.

I have pointed out that transformations are the rule in *Finnegans Wake*. The conventions of pantomime theatre shed some light on the particular type of transformation at work in Joyce's "Mime." The "Harley Quinn" (FW 221.25) of traditional pantomime is endowed with a slapstick or bat which has the ability to transform his surroundings and to convert his enemies. The slapstick has the magic power we see in Shem's "lifewand" (FW 195.5), and perhaps, in Stephen's ashplant (U 432).[6] Yet, for all its phallic power, Harlequin's wand fails him, and he must be rescued by a "benevolent agent" who is traditionally female. What has taken place here is an assertion of female power and of a female aesthetic—one which replaces combat with reconciliation and reunion.[7] In Shem's case, it is the combined figures of Izod, the flower-girls, the Prankquean, and ALP who transform the phallic mastery of both sex and text.

As a *voyeur*, Shem must both read and write with an "eyetrompit" (FW 247.32–33), and so must accept the error inherent in every attempt to see or describe the truth. After all, throughout the riddling of the "Mime," Shem can presumably *see* the colors of the rainbow girls ("eye seize heaven!"—FW 247.31), but he cannot articulate those colors in a text. Even his eventual solution of the riddle remains unverbalized. The text tells us simply "Wink's the winning word!" and "Luck!"; later on, we are told "There lies her word, you reder!" and the letters appear as architectural and anatomical pieces (*FW* 249.4–5, 249.13–14, 249.16–17). Again, a fixed text is impossible; even Izod's word (of honor) will lie to us. As with the signs of window, hedge, prong, hand, and so on, the letters of Izod's text remain scattered throughout the equally scattered text of the *Wake*. In order for Shem, or any reader, to discover either text, he or she cannot simply decode the signs into a meta-language. Instead, the reader must gather the letters together, redistribute them, and rearrange them. Writing in a voyeuristic mode, Izod has concealed the answer to her riddle in her question (*FW* 248.11–14); in order to see it, we must read in the same way.

For all that it is a pantomime, Joyce's "Mime of Mick, Nick, and the Maggies" has its share of sound and words.[8] Nevertheless, silence has the *last* word: "Mummum" (*FW* 259.10). Yet this is not a literal, but a figurative silence. Unlike the "Mum's" and the "Silanse" (*FW* 228.15, 228.17) which precede Shem's verbal revenge on the flower-girls, this silence suggests the ability of this voyeuristic text to remain outside the limiting and determining framework of a meta-language. Both the "Mime" and the *Wake* leave their reader able to see the scattered signs of the text, able to gather them together in some way, but unable to articulate and master them in a language of his or her own.

In my discussion, I have suggested the possibility that Shahrazade offers Joyce a model for the reader redefined as a *voyeur* who simultaneously holds the reader's power of judgment and the writer's power of expression, who both discriminates and generates. Like a witness in the infinitely regressing chain of Joycean and voyeuristic testifiers, Joyce's model has created a model of her own as a counterpart to the King. Among her tales in the *Arabian Nights* are some which concern Haroun al Raschid, the Caliph of Baghdad during the ninth or tenth century, and the supposedly beloved "Commander of the Faithful." The Caliph is also a *voyeur* who masks himself to maintain his form of mastery; disguised as a commoner, the Caliph investigates the welfare of his kingdom. He becomes, then, a "commander" or dictator who both watches and prescribes, who is both passive witness and active teller. In his wanderings around Baghdad, the Caliph suggests the *Wake*'s HCE—

a suggestion which Joyce hints at through the image of HCE "stambuling haround Dumbaling" (*FW* 33.36–34.1). Together, HCE and Haroun al Raschid suggest a new position for interpretive and/ or narrative authority in the configuration of reader, writer, and text. The position is, in fact, a lack of position, a lack of any fixed site from which a fixed claim to power can be made. In the *Wake,* the identification of place must coincide with disinformation; for instance, when we ask where ALP is, the answer must be "we nowhere she lives" (*FW* 10.26). After all, we are forced to look for her through an "eyetrompit."

As the stories about HCE, Willingdone, and others multiply in the *Wake,* the text warns us that we will be unable to distinguish an origin or an individual at all: "since in this scherzarade of one's thousand one nightinesses that sword of certainty which would identifide the body never falls" (*FW* 51.4–6). If it *were* to fall, that sword would divide head from body, teller from text, or teller from listener. And such a divisive and decisive falling would put a stop to the somewhat different falling—the linguistic lapsing—which is the substance of the *Wake.* In a sense, the text's principle is to conduct a wake for itself—to keep at bay the evil spirits of a traditional hermeneutics which determines an origin and an ending for its subject, and which produces the final utterance of a meta-language. One way in which Joyce has kept the traditionalists at bay is to transform the sword of certainty—not into the proverbial ploughshare, but, as a *voyeur* would, into a tallowscoop.

NOTES

1. Though neither the sisters nor the brothers are twins, the mirroring configuration of the women as they share in the presentation of the tales suggests a form of equality that the two brothers lack.

2. As McHugh points out, "bander" is French slang for "to have an erection" (8).

3. He lurks elsewhere in the *Wake* as well, as "Turk of the Theater," "Thorker the Tourable," and "turgoes the turrible" (*FW* 98.10, 132.18, 205.29).

4. Henceforward, Shem/Glugg will be, simply, Shem.

5. The first series of questions concerns only gems, and the second, only yellow (*FW* 225, 223).

6. Appropriately, Stephen uses his ashplant dramatically, "shattering light over the world," in the pantomime-influenced play of "Circe" where he ponders gesture as a "universal language" (*U* 432).

7. With her more powerful wand, the benevolent agent might be a version of what Suzette Henke has called the "phallic mother" in Joyce (117–18).

8. This is only fitting since, after the Regency, pantomimes ceased to be completely silent (Mayer 19).

WORKS CITED

Cixous, Hélène. "Joyce, la ruse de l'écriture." *Poétique* 4 (1970), 419–32.

Foucault, Michel. *The Foucault Reader,* edited by Paul Rabinow. New York: Pantheon Books, 1984.

Gerhardt, Mia I. *The Art of Storytelling: A Literary Study of the Thousand and One Nights.* Leiden: E.J. Brill, 1963.

Ghazoul, Ferial Jabouri. The Arabian Nights: *A Structural Analysis.* Cairo: Cairo Associated Institution for the Study and Presentation of Arab Cultural Values, 1980.

Henke, Suzette. "James Joyce and Women: The Matriarchal Muse." In *Work in Progress: Joyce Centenary Essays,* edited by Richard F. Peterson, Alan M. Cohn, and Edmund L. Epstein, 117–131. Carbondale: Southern Illinois University Press, 1983.

Kristeva, Julia. *Desire in Language: A Semiotic Approach to Literature and Art,* edited by Leon Roudiez. Ithaca: Cornell University Press, 1980.

Mayer, David, III. *Harlequin in His Element: The English Pantomime, 1806–1836.* Cambridge: Harvard University Press, 1969.

McCabe, Colin. *James Joyce and the Revolution of the Word.* London: Macmillan, 1979.

McHugh, Roland. *Annotations to* Finnegans Wake. Baltimore: Johns Hopkins University Press, 1980.

Norris, Margot. *The Decentered Universe of* Finnegans Wake. Baltimore: Johns Hopkins University Press, 1976.

18

The *Wake*'s Confounded Language

DEREK ATTRIDGE

Not far from the venue of the Tenth International James Joyce Symposium is a church, Vor Frelsers Kirke, with a superb eighteenth-century spire, so constructed that around the outside of it a stair spirals disconcertingly to the top. There is no truth, my guidebook reassures me while inviting me to make the ascent (''in good weather only''), in the legend that the builder fell to an untimely death from his newly completed but not entirely stable tower. But if the story is untrue, how has it gained sufficient currency to merit an official denial in a guidebook? And why, in any case, should a guidebook, whose function is to enhance my pleasure by giving me facts about the objects I see, waste its space with a legend I am told to dismiss as false?

Evidently, the story of the hapless builder, irrespective of its historical accuracy, has a vivid appeal which strongly colors the sight-seer's experience of the fantastic spire—an appeal that springs no doubt from its connection with the wide-ranging family of mythic and literary texts that work and rework the motif of the building of the tower and the consequent fall. (Leaving James Joyce out of it for the moment, two texts we might think of are the eleventh chapter of Genesis and the ballad of Tim Finnegan.) One way of representing the force of this motif is to see it as a parable which teaches the virtue of humility: to build a tower, or to climb a ladder, is to attempt to rise above one's proper station, and the dizziness that seizes the mortal who ascends to such heights is the voice of a god— a jealous god, no doubt—who feels his mastery threatened; or, in more modern terms, it is the inner voice that whispers to us, just at the fatal moment, that our technology can never be adequate to our desires.

But we must remind ourselves of the alternative construction which could be placed upon the myth. The tower from which the builder falls is one which has reached the very limits of human capacity; one from which the builder did *not* fall would, by virtue of that fact, be less lofty than it might be. Part of the attractiveness of these stories about builders—the sons of Noah, Tim Finnegan, the builder of the spire of Vor Frelsers Kirke—is that they invite us to take pleasure in humanity's capacity to arouse the envy of the gods, in the fact that our desires can always outstrip our technology. From this perspective, the Fall is necessarily fortunate, not, as the Christian tradition would have it, because it brings forth otherwise unattested Divine mercy but because by its own daring it makes manifest the prohibition it transgresses against, and in doing so exposes the hidden power structure—whether we call it the force of God or the force of Nature—within which humanity is obliged to operate.

One of the significant differences between the myth of the first Fall and that of Babel is that the latter is the story of a collective struggle with Divine power, not an individual one. And what the myth identifies as the source of strength of the collective is *language;* it is this that makes possible the development of the technology of brickmaking, described in some detail in Genesis Chapter 11, which leads in turn to the plan to "build a city and a tower, whose top may reach unto heaven" (Authorized Version, 11.4). But this, interestingly, is not the ultimate aim; we seem to circle back to the power of language, since the purpose of the magnificent city (Hebrew "Babel" is, of course, Greek "Babylon") is to "make us a name, lest we be scattered abroad upon the face of the whole earth" (11.4). Their fears are, it turns out, quite justified: the Lord reflects on the power that a shared language gives to a community, and is not happy with the prospect. "Behold, the people is one, and they have all one language; and this they begin to do: and now nothing will be restrained from them, which they have imagined to do" (11.6). He therefore confounds the language of the people, and thus fragments the collective and takes away its power. They do indeed make a name for themselves, but the name is "Babel," which the Yahwist associates punningly with Hebrew "balal," or confusion.[1]

The myth of Babel expresses a yearning for a condition of perfect mutual intelligibility, for a language of total communication shared by all humanity; a utopian community in which no misunderstanding could occur and therefore no strife. Humankind is prevented from attaining such a state not by its own weakness but by a law imposed from outside; to be thus would be to be as gods. Language is therefore our bane when it could be our salvation. Babel signifies both the imaginable possibilities and the actual limitations of collective existence; the word "Babel" in English has come to mean both "a visionary scheme" and "a confused medley of sounds."

It's a commonplace that our post-Babelian condition is more fully evinced in *Finnegans Wake* than in any other linguistic artifact; one of its most notorious features is the cacophony of various languages, sometimes miraculously chiming but more often multiplying dissonant meanings in a confusion of noises. The tireless work of explicators has reduced that dissonance by showing that what at first sight seems an array of discordant meanings is often an elaborate harmony, and one might say that the vision that (consciously or unconsciously) has encouraged *Wake* explication over the years has been the same one that underlies the Babel myth: the dream of achieving a reading in which all the languages of the *Wake* will speak to one another lucidly and comprehensibly, and thus become one language, a new super-language that will unite divided humanity once more, at least in the aesthetic realm. This vision, the explicatory enterprise assumes, was Joyce's vision: *Finnegans Wake* is his tower of anti-Babel, designed and built to counter the destructive act of the jealous god who drove the nations apart, and to bequeath to the world an artifact which, by making out of the kaleidoscope of languages a new tongue and a new name to hold humanity together, will succeed where the sons of Noah failed. If much of the *Wake* sounds to us as Babelian confusion, this must be—so it is assumed—because we are still locked in our monoglot cultural prisons, lacking the energy and enterprise to follow Joyce in his multilingual architectural feat of total unification.

We are not, of course, talking only about the interpretation of *Finnegans Wake;* what is at issue is the hermeneutic drive itself, the urge to translate what is apparently "confused" into a language which will be entirely transparent, to unweave the polyglot textual fabric into the monoglot thread. The hermeneutic hope is that the Lord will be more lenient this time, and allow the city of mutual intelligibility to be built by means of the new technologies of interpretation and translation (which are, of course, closely related activities). The Babelian texture of the *Wake* offers the greatest possible challenge to the interpreter and translator, one fundamental problem being, as Jacques Derrida has pointed out in discussing Joyce's use of the Babel myth ("Two Words" 155, "Des Tours de

Babel'' 170–71, and ''Table Ronde'' 132–33), that the most successful
translation / interpretation of Wakean words will, by definition, be
the least successful at relaying a fundamental property of the text:
its being in more than one language at once. But as long as Joyce's
book is seen, like every other book, as intended for, and amenable
to, complete explication, the hermeneutic faith will doubtless survive.

We find, then, that there are two competing uses to which the
myth of the fall from the tower might be put; it could be taken as
an encouragement to accept the imperfections that surround us
(including the impossibility of perfect communication) as the justly
imposed and unavoidable condition of our existence, or a call to
regard them as something unjustly willed upon us (or culpably
allowed by us to come into being) which it is our prime duty as a
human collective to overcome. I could respond to my guidebook
entry by lamenting the sad tale of architectural ambition outstripping
technical capability or by admiring the sacrifice that taught others
the way forward to more solidly constructed towers. (Among the
larger systems of belief that would tend, respectively, in these
directions would be some kinds of Christianity and some kinds of
Marxism.) From the first perspective, the language of *Finnegans Wake*
produces an ironic comedy inviting laughter at our shared ridicu-
lousness and mutual incomprehension (if not an unreadable tragedy
reflecting despair at our hopeless condition); from the second, it
constitutes a celebratory comedy demonstrating our potential for
imaginative fertility and mutual understanding.

Faced with these two opposing views, we might—following the
spirit if not the exact method of Fredric Jameson in *The Political
Unconscious*—look for a more comprehensive perspective which will
at once explain the contradicting positions and, without rejecting
them, move beyond them. They both, it seems to me, arise from
the same conception of language, a conception that cannot be made
to cohere with the way language works in practice. Language is
widely seen, in both popular and scientific understanding, as fundamentally and constitutively a matter of intersubjective communication: a procedure of coding and decoding preexisting mental
contents, which, if the linguistic machine is working properly, remain
unchanged by the passage from one mind to another. The efficiency
of the procedure depends on the arbitrariness of the relation between
signifier and signified: what matters is that the code is sufficiently
complex and subtle to encapsulate all the details of the mental

contents, and iconic or symbolic relationships would only interfere with this. It is arbitrariness that makes possible the existence of more than one language (since there is no signifier more or less appropriate for any given signified), but it is also arbitrariness that makes possible all types of translation (including interpretation, which translates one text into another more readable text), since the mental contents are assumed to remain constant, and only the way they are encoded varies.

To hold this view of the nature of language is, of course, to be puzzled and disappointed by the empirical evidence, which suggests that the communicative procedure fails more often than it succeeds; there always seems to be some contingent reason why a given utterance is unable to yield wholly and truly its burden of meaning. (I leave aside the vexed problem of how one would ascertain that anything that could be called a completely successful act of communication had in fact occurred.) Particularly unsatisfactory in its failure to communicate a stable preexisting meaning is the written utterance, and most of all what is called the "literary text"— with *Finnegans Wake* as the worst offender of all. Hence the two attitudes I've sketched: resignation at the necessary imperfections of a nonideal world, or hope that technological improvements (better languages, more efficient channels of communication) or sociopolitical advances (increased human solidarity, perhaps) might eventually reveal to us language in its true form, as it should always have been.

A different view of language, however, would not produce this disparity between the idea and the experience, a view that I won't expatiate on now since it's become familiar, in various versions, in the writing of a number of philosophers and literary theorists, but could be broadly described in terms of its rejection of the communication model and its emphasis instead on language's constituting and conditioning force. Not just an instrument neutrally serving objects and intentions, language operates in and upon the world in a host of different ways, and is already implied in any possible mental content. The literary text, far from being the most aberrant instance of language, is the instance that reveals its nature most clearly, as an endlessly retranslatable complex of signifiers, existing as part of a set of public, and political, institutions, themselves caught in a process of constant transformation. And, in this respect, *Finnegans Wake* is the most typical and the most revealing of all literary texts.

The myth of Babel, from this wider perspective, is a story western culture tells itself to account for the failure of its own model of language to match up to the reality it experiences; language has to be judged as fallen from its true self, whether necessarily or unnecessarily, if the belief in this model is to be sustained. (The difference between intralingual and interlingual failure of comprehension is not a significant one; we can take the story of Babel as referring to the institution of several languages or to the making imperfect of the communicative processes within any single language.) But *Finnegans Wake* retells the myth, a number of times, from a different perspective: neither lamenting language's fall nor trying to secure its recovery, it finds its pleasures in the knowledge that language, by its very nature, is unstable and ambiguous. (The irreverent treatment of artificial world languages like Esperanto and Volapük in the *Wake* functions in a similar way.) Once the belief in a pure communicative language has been abandoned, the sharp difference between monoglot and polyglot discourse disappears; any language is many languages—a Babel of registers, dialects, older and newer forms, slang and borrowed items, accents and idiosyncracies— and all that the *Wake* does is to extend this logic to its comic extreme. True, no single reader could assimiliate all the *Wake's* languages; but no single hearer could assimilate all the languages— no doubt confused and contradictory languages—that I give utterance to, knowingly or unknowingly, each time I produce an everyday statement.

As Laurent Milesi points out in an informative article entitled "The Babelian Idiom of *Finnegans Wake*," there is a reference early in the *Wake* to the traditional number of nations—and hence languages—on earth, a reference which reminds us that a linguistic item will have as many meanings as there exist codes in which to place it:

> So you need hardly spell me how every word will be bound
> over to carry three score and ten toptypsical readings throughout
> the book of Doublends Jined. (20.13–18)

But this, of course, is true of every word of every book, not just of our circular story of Dublin's giant. Babel is a condition of all language, not just that of the *Wake,* and it is this that provides language with its power to give pleasure and to change the world (by no means incompatible functions). In Joyce's text, the myth of the fall from the shaky tower of Babel may be read, like all the many falls in the book, not as a moral lesson in humility, not as a symbol of defeated human aspiration, but as an instance—comically transformed—of the way we represent to ourselves, in language, language's refusal to be a mere instrument of transcendent intentions or desires.

Milesi reminds us of an anecdote of Budgen's which is worth quoting in full:

> Joyce once told me (it was during the composition of *Finnegans Wake*) that he thought he had found the meaning of the Tower of Babel story. If I had done my bounden duty I should have been ready with "what?" and "how?" and "tell," but, slow of wit and more apt to ruminate than to ask, I let the occasion slide, so that what Joyce thought was the true inwardness of the Biblical story is anybody's guess. ("Resurrection" 12)

It is perhaps just as well that Budgen's inquisitiveness failed him at this point, since *Finnegans Wake* itself stands as a much richer exegesis of the story of Babel than could have been communicated by even the most meticulous biographer.

NOTE

1. Tim Finnegan's upward mobility is also related to both language and bricks: the ballad informs us that "He had a tongue both rich and sweet, / An' to rise in the world he carried a hod."

WORKS CITED

Budgen, Frank. "Resurrection." In *Twelve and a Tilly: Essays on the Twenty-Fifth Anniversary of* Finnegans Wake, edited by Jack P. Dalton and Clive Hart, 11-15. London: Faber & Faber, 1966.

Derrida, Jacques, et al. "Table ronde sur la traduction." In *L/oreille de l'autre: otobiographies, transferts, traductions: textes et débats avec Jacques Derrida*, edited by Claude Lévesque and Christie V. McDonald, 123–212. Montreal: VLB Editeur, 1982.

———. "Des Tours de Babel," translated by Joseph F. Graham. In *Difference in Translation*, edited by Joseph F. Graham, 165–207. Ithaca: Cornell University Press, 1985.

———. "Two Words for Joyce." In *Post-structuralist Joyce: Essays from the French*, edited by Derek Attridge and Daniel Ferrer, 145–59. Cambridge: Cambridge University Press, 1984.

Jameson, Fredric. *The Political Unconscious: Narrative as a Socially Symbolic Act.* Ithaca: Cornell University Press, 1981.

Milesi, Laurent. "L'Idiome babélien de *Finnegans Wake*." In *Genèse de Babel: Joyce et la création*, edited by Claude Jacquet, 155–215. Paris: Editions du CNRS, 1985.

CONTRIBUTORS

DEREK ATTRIDGE holds a chair in English Studies at the University of Strathclyde, Glasgow. He has written or coedited a number of books on literary language, literary theory, and Joyce, including *Post-structuralist Joyce: Essays from the French* (1984) and the forthcoming *Peculiar Language: Literature as Difference from the Renaissance to James Joyce.* He is currently editing *The Cambridge Companion to James Joyce.*

MORRIS BEJA, President of the James Joyce Foundation, is professor of English and chair of the department at the Ohio State University. He is the author of *Epiphany in the Modern Novel* (1971), *Film and Literature* (1979), and many articles on British, Irish, and American fiction. He has edited volumes of essays on Joyce, Virginia Woolf, and Samuel Beckett. He and Shari Benstock coordinated the academic program for the Copenhagen Symposium.

BERNARD BENSTOCK is professor of English at the University of Miami, Coral Gables. His most recent books are *Critical Essays on James Joyce* and *James Joyce* (both 1985). He has served on the Board of Trustees of the James Joyce Foundation since its inception in 1967, as President from 1971 to 1977, and has been director or program coordinator for the first nine International Joyce Symposia. His forthcoming volume of papers from the Zurich Symposium in 1984 is entitled *James Joyce: The Augmented Ninth.*

SHARI BENSTOCK teaches in the English Department at the University of Miami, Coral Gables. She has written many articles on Joyce, and is the coauthor (with Bernard Benstock) of *Who's He When He's At Home: A James Joyce Directory* (1980). In addition to Joyce, her research has centered on numerous feminist topics, and she is the author of *Women of the Left Bank: Paris, 1900–1940.* She and Morris Beja coordinated the academic program for the Copenhagen Symposium.

ZACK BOWEN is professor of English and chair of the department at the University of Miami, Coral Gables. He is the author of *Musical*

269

Allusions in the works of James Joyce (1974) and coeditor of the *Companion to Joyce Studies* (1984), as well as the author of many articles on Joyce and of *Padraic Colum* (1970) and *Mary Lavin* (1975).

AUSTIN BRIGGS was educated at Harvard and Columbia. The author of *The Novels of Harold Frederic* (1969), he is Hamilton B. Tompkins Professor of English at Hamilton College, where he teaches courses in the Gothic tradition in British and American literature, Dickens, modern British literature, and the language of cinema.

SHELDON BRIVIC, the author of *Joyce between Freud and Jung* (1980) and *Joyce the Creator* (1985), teaches English at Temple University. He has written a novel, *Stealing,* and is now completing a critical study, *Interceptions: Joyce, Lacan, and Perception.*

KIMBERLY DEVLIN teaches English at the University of California, Riverside. She has written several articles on Joyce and is currently working on a larger study of *Finnegans Wake* which explores its connections to Joyce's earlier fiction.

CLIVE HART teaches at the University of Essex. He is the author of many books and articles on Joyce, including *Structure and Motif in Finnegans Wake* (1962), *A Concordance to Finnegans Wake* (1963), and *James Joyce's Ulysses* (1968). He is coeditor (with David Hayman) of *James Joyce's Ulysses: Critical Essays* (1974) and (with C. George Sandulescu) of *Assessing the 1984 Ulysses* (1986). He has also written extensively on the early history of flight. His current research focuses on erotic tension in the poetry and visual arts of the Middle Ages and the Renaissance.

ELLEN CAROL JONES teaches at Purdue University, where she is also Managing Editor of *Modern Fiction Studies.* She is completing her dissertation on Joyce at Cornell University. She has chaired panels at the Dublin Centennial and Frankfurt Symposia, and has also published on Joyce and on Virginia Woolf.

COLBERT KEARNEY studied at University College Dublin and at King's College, Cambridge, and now teaches at University College Cork. He is the author of *The Writings of Brendan Behan* and of the script for the RTE television documentary on Joyce, *Is there one who understands me?;* he has also published articles on various aspects of Irish literature.

JULES DAVID LAW, who teaches at Northwestern University, received his Ph.D. from the Johns Hopkins University in 1983. He is currently completing a book entitled *Reflections on Surface and Depth from Berkeley to Dickens.* He has contributed to several collected volumes on Joyce.

PATRICK McGEE teaches at Louisiana State University. He is the author of articles on Joyce and Faulkner, and of the forthcoming *Paperspace: Style and Ideology in Joyce's Ulysses.* His work in progress includes a book on language and ideology.

MARGOT NORRIS is professor of English at the University of California, Irvine. She is the author of *The Decentered Universe of Finnegans Wake* (1976) and *Beasts of the Modern Imagination: Darwin, Nietzsche, Kafka, Ernst, and Lawrence* (1985).

HENRIETTE LAZARIDIS POWER is writing a dissertation on Dickens, Joyce, and the *Arabian Nights* at the University of Pennsylvania. She received her B.A. from Middlebury College and her M.Phil. from Oxford; she has presented papers at conferences on Joyce, Dickens, and Edith Wharton.

ROBERT SCHOLES is professor of English at Brown University. He is the author of many studies in modern literature and critical theory, including *The Nature of Narrative* (1966, coauthored with Robert Kellogg), *Fabulation and Metafiction* (1979), *Semiotics and Interpretation* (1982), and *Textual Power: Literary Theory and the Teaching of English* (1985). He coedited, with Richard M. Kain, *The Workshop of Daedalus: James Joyce and the Raw Materials for* A Portrait of the Artist as a Young Man (1965).

BONNIE KIME SCOTT is professor of English at the University of Delaware. She is the author of *Joyce and Feminism* (1984), and of *James Joyce* (1987) in the Harvester Feminist Readings series. She is editor of the forthcoming *New Alliances in Joyce Studies,* featuring papers from a 1985 Joyce conference in Philadelphia.

FRITZ SENN is director of the Research Centre of the Zurich James Joyce Foundation (set up in 1985), which he hopes to make truly international. He is the author of numerous articles on Joyce, and of *Nichts gegen Joyce: Joyce Versus Nothing* (1983) and *Joyce's Dislocutions* (1984). One of those who began the James Joyce Foundation, he is currently working on varieties of interdynamism within Joyce's works (such as the narrative treatment of time) or with writers such as Ovid or Homer.

LORRAINE WEIR teaches at the University of British Columbia, where she is also chair of the Program in Comparative Literature and director of the Tenth International Summer Institute for Semiotic and Structural Studies. She has published several articles on Joyce, and is currently completing a book on the poetics of the Joyce system.

INDEX

Absalom, Absalom!, 74
Adorno, Theodor, 98, 203n
Alleyne, Mr., 111, 113–21
ALP, 232–46
Althusser, Louis, 204n
American Mutoscope-Biograph Co., 148
Aquinas, St. Thomas, 207
Arabian Nights, 248–54, 259
Aristotle, 170, 183, 207
Arliss, George, 152
Atherton, James, 4, 47, 54n,
Attridge, Derek, 22n, 262–68, 269
Auden, W.H., 92
Avanti!, 95

Balabanoff, Angelica, 94
Balzac, Honore, 98
Barnacle, Nora, 185
Barnes, Djuna, 83, 178
Barrow, Craig Wallace, 154n
Barsacq, Léon, 148
Barthes, Roland, 76, 225
"Bartleby the Scrivener: A Story of Wall Street," 111–21
Baudelaire, Charles Pierre, 104
Baudrillard, Jean, 199, 200
Bauerle, Ruth, 6, 125
Bazargan, Susan, 154n
Beaujour, Michel, 225, 230n
Beja, Morris, 111–22, 269
Bell, Clive, 175
Benjamin, Walter, 106, 195, 203n
Benstock, Bernard, 23n, 53n, 73–90, 120, 230n, 269
Benstock, Shari, 53n, 230n, 232, 233, 269
Benveniste, Emile, 227
Bergman, Ingmar, 149
Between the Acts, 178
Beyond the Pleasure Principle, 13
Blake, William, 214
Bloom, Leopold, 5, 9, 10, 11, 13, 14, 15, 17, 18, 19, 22, 41, 42, 43, 44, 49, 74, 75, 77, 78, 79, 81, 84, 85, 89, 101, 140, 141, 146, 147, 148, 151, 152, 153, 154n, 157, 160, 162, 163, 164, 165, 195, 196, 197, 198, 199, 222, 223, 226, 235, 236,
Bloom, Molly, 8, 9, 15, 17, 18, 22, 23n, 26, 43, 160, 162, 163, 169, 185, 186, 196, 222, 226, 233, 235
Boardman, Edy, 14
Boheemen, Christine van, 185

Bowen, Zack, 137–44, 269–70
Boylan, Blazes, 41, 42, 79, 160
Brahmin and the Butterfly, The, 150
Brecht, Bertolt, 203n
Briggs, Austin, 145–56, 270
Brivic, Sheldon, 157–67, 270
Brown, Richard, 5
Browning, Robert, 195, 197, 200
Budgen, Frank, 166
Buñuel, Luis, 150
Burke, Carolyn, 192n
Burke, Kenneth, 221, 223, 225, 226

Caffrey, Cissy, 11, 12, 148
Caffrey, Tommy, 11, 12
Campbell, Joseph, 6
Campbell, Thomas, 75
Carroll, Lewis, 233
Ceram, C.W., 154n
Chamber Music, 29, 76
Cheng, Vincent, 22n
Cixous, Hélène, 181, 251, 257
Clair, René, 148, 153
Clement, Catherine, 182
Clifford, Martha, 10
Cohen, Bella, 151, 154n
Connolly, Thomas E., 154n
Conroy, Gabriel, 14, 16, 17, 68
"Counterparts," 111, 113–21
Cowley, Father, 138
Curran, C.P., 57, 119

"Dead, The," 8, 56, 67
Deconstruction, 180–92
Dedalus, Simon, 15, 57, 81, 138, 239
Dedalus, Stephen, 5, 8, 17, 19, 20, 21, 22, 30, 32, 38, 40, 41, 43, 44, 53n, 57,
    65, 67, 80, 81, 86, 88, 90n, 101, 141, 153, 157, 159, 160, 161, 162, 163,
    164, 165, 170, 172, 173, 174, 186, 188, 189, 190, 191, 206, 207, 208, 209,
    210, 213, 221, 222, 223
Deleuze, Gilles, 225
de Man, Paul, 180, 191n, 211, 212
Dennany, Thomas M., 75, 77
Derrida, Jacques, 180, 181, 182, 184, 185, 186, 187, 188, 191, 192n, 207, 211,
    212, 214, 217, 220, 228, 264
Descombes, Vincent, 225
Devlin, Kimberly, 6, 232–47, 270
Dignam, Paddy, 169
Dillon, Mat, 18
Dollard, Ben, 138
Doll's House, A, 246
Doyle, Arthur Conan, 77

Dubliners, 14, 16, 29, 31, 39, 56, 97, 98, 102, 119, 128, 170, 239, 240, 242, 243

Eckley, Grace, 22n
Eco, Umberto, 220, 221, 225
Eglinton, John: *see* Magee, W.K.
Egoist, The, 169
Eisenstein, Sergei, 147, 154n
"Elegy Written in a Country Churchyard," 75
Elliot, T.S., 73, 168, 181, 203n
Ellmann, Richard, 53, 92, 97, 98, 99, 100, 119, 150, 192n, 246n
Emmet, Robert, 89
Epstein, Edward, 141
Eskind, Andrew, 154n
"Essay on Epitaphs," 75
"Eveline," 239, 240, 242, 243, 245, 246
Exile, 87, 117, 123–36

Famous Box Trick, The, 150
Farrington, 29, 111–21
Faulkner, Peter, 168
Faulkner, William, 74
Fell, L. John, 149
Fellini, Federico, 149
Ferrero, Guglielmo, 91, 98, 99, 100, 101, 102
Finnegans Wake, 3, 4, 5, 6, 7, 12, 13, 14, 15, 17, 21, 23n, 25, 29, 30, 32, 33, 35, 36, 37, 38, 42, 43, 47, 48, 50, 51, 52, 74, 77, 79, 83, 85, 86, 88, 89, 90, 117, 124, 145, 149, 153, 154n, 171, 176, 177, 178, 178n, 181, 182, 187, 190, 192n, 206–18, 212, 213, 214, 216, 217, 218, 220, 221, 222, 226, 227, 228, 229, 230n, 232–46, 248–60, 262–68
Flaubert, Gustave, 99
Flying Dutchman, The, 239
Foucault, Michel, 249, 252
Frazer, John, 150, 153
Freud, Sigmund, 8, 13, 191n, 192n, 198, 201, 202, 228, 239
Furey, Michael, 17

Gabler, Hans Walter, 36, 53n, 153
Gallaher, Ignatius, 29
Gallop, Jane, 191n
Garland edition of *Ulysses,* 33–35, 53n, 88, 145, 146, 147, 148, 151, 153, 158, 169, 186, 187, 188, 189, 190, 209, 210, 221, 222, 223, 225, 226, 227
Gay Shoe Clerk, 146
Genesis, Book of, 28, 30, 262, 263
Ghazoul, Ferial Jabouri, 254
Gilbert, Sandra, 168, 186
Gillet, Louis, 74
Gissing, George, 102, 103
Goldberg, S.L., 221
Gordon, John, 22n
Gorki, Maxim, 152
Goulding, May, 15

Gray, Thomas, 75
Great Train Robbery, The, 146
Griffith, Arthur, 96
Groden, Michael, 221
Gubar, Susan, 168, 186

Hamlet, 20, 22n, 38, 40, 188, 210
Hand, Robert, 123–36
Hart, Clive, 89, 123–36, 217, 233, 239, 270
Hastings, Beatrice, 168
Hauptmann, Gerhard, 102, 103, 104
Heath, Stephen, 185, 190, 191n, 192n
Heidegger, 105, 257
Hemingway, Ernest, 103
Henke, Suzette, 170, 260n
Hepworth, Cecil, 147
Herr, Cheryl, 149
Heston, Charlton, 151
Hodgart, Matthew, 4
Horace, 228

Ibsen, Henrik, 102, 103, 104, 124, 207, 245, 246
Industrial Light and Magic, 149
"In the Penal Colony," 85
Irigaray, Luce, 180, 183, 184, 192n
Irish Free State, 181
Iser, Wolfgang, 230n

Jakobson, Roman, 191n
James, Henry, 99
Jameson, Frederic, 203n, 204n, 265
Jardine, Alice, 6
Jolas, Eugene, 180
Jones, Ellen Carol, 180–94, 270
Jones, Rosalind, 185
Jousee, Marcel, 4, 224, 230n
Joyce, Ellen, 56, 64
Joyce, John, 56, 57, 58, 61, 63, 64, 65, 67, 68, 69, 70, 72n
Joyce, Nora, 87, 97, 152, 246n
Joyce, Stanislaus, 58, 61, 62, 72n, 99, 100, 119, 153, 181
Jung, Carl, 185
Justice, Beatrice, 123–36

Kafka, Franz, 85
Kain, Richard M., 182
Kearney, Colbert, 55–72, 270–71
Kenner, Hugh, 124, 134, 168
Keppler, C. F., 121n
Kiss in the Tunnel, The, 147
Krieger, Murray, 230n
Kristeva, Julia, 181, 182, 184, 191n, 255

Labriola, Arturo, 95, 96

Lacan, Jacques, 157–67, 187, 191n, 192n, 212, 215, 217
Lady from the Sea, 245
Law, Jules David, 195–205, 271
Lawrence, D. H. 103
Le Coat, Gerald, 230n
Lefebvre, Henri, 197, 199
Lenehan, 29, 43
Letters, Vol. I, 151
Letters, Vol. II, 91, 95–96, 98, 102, 119, 152, 153
L'Europa giovane, 91, 98, 100
Levenson, Michael, 170
Lewis, C. Day, 92
Lewis, Windham, 105, 167–78, 206, 213
Lidderdale, Jane, 169
Linder, Max, 151
Lindsay, Vachel, 149
Lucie and Paul Léon / James Joyce Collection, 77
Lukács, Georg, 98, 105, 106, 203n
Lumière Brothers, 152

MacCabe, Colin, 170, 192n, 248
MacDowell, Gerty, 9, 10, 11, 17, 42, 44, 45, 84, 146, 147, 148, 160, 161
Mack Smith, Denis, 93, 94
MacNicholas, John, 135, 136n
Magee, W. K. (John Eglinton), 189, 191, 210
Magnetic Mountain, 92
Manganiello, Dominic, 98, 101
Mann, Thomas, 106
Marcus, Jane, 83
Marcus, Mordecai, 121n
Marin, Louis, 224, 230n
Márquez, Gabriel García, 84
Marsden, Dora, 169
Marx, Karl, 98, 100
Mast, Gerald, 146
Maupassant, Guy de, 102
Mayer, David, III, 154n, 261n
McCarthy, Patrick, 23n
McGee, Patrick, 206–19, 271
McHugh, Roland, 11, 12, 21, 229n, 239, 251, 260n
Méliès, Georges, 149, 150
Melville, Herman, 85, 111–21
Men Without Art, 175, 176
Menton, John Henry, 19
Merivale, Patricia, 229n
Meyers, Jeffrey, 175
Milesi, Laurent, 267, 268
Minnis, A. J., 230n
Moby Dick, 85
Moi, Toril, 192n
Montrelay, Michele, 182, 192n
Mooney, Polly, 39

More, St. Thomas, 95
Moretti, Franco, 196, 202n
Mulligan, Buck, 31, 40, 42, 45, 49, 53n, 85, 149, 154n, 161
Murray, Edward, 154n
Murray, William, 119
Mussolini, Benito, 94, 95

Name of the Rose, The, 220
New Country, 92
Nicholson, Mary, 169
Nietzsche, Friedrich, 76, 170, 180, 191n
Nightwood, 83–84, 178
Niver, Kemp R., 148, 154n
Norris, Margot, 3–24, 232, 249, 257, 271

O'Hanlon, John, 12, 23n
O'Hara, Frank, 140
O'Molloy, J. J., 153, 197
One Hundred Years of Solitude, 84
One Man Band, 150
Ortega y Gasset, José, 201
O'Shea, Kitty, 26

Palmer, R. Barton, 154n
Panofsky, Erwin, 151
Parsifal, 4, 20
Paul, Robert W., 154n
Pearce, Richard, 154n
Peeping Tom, 147
Pericles, 88
Plato, 187, 188
Porter, Edwin S., 146
Portrait of the Artist as a Young Man, A, 8, 18, 23n, 29, 30, 39, 41, 48, 58, 60, 65, 66, 67–8, 69, 70, 71, 81, 82, 85, 86, 90n, 97, 117, 124, 128, 133, 168–74, 206, 207, 220, 228
Potts, Willard, 101
Pound, Ezra, 73, 168, 169, 181
Power, Henriette Lazaridis, 248–61, 271
Pratt, George C., 148, 154n
"Preludes, The," 73
Princeton Encyclopedia of Poetry and Poetics, 228

Quinet, Edgar, 21, 22

Ramsaye, Terry, 150
Random House edition of *Ulysses,* 153
Ring and the Book, The, 195
Riquelme, John Paul, 230n
Robbe-Grillet, Alain, 198
Robinson, Henry Morton, 6
Roche, Nasty, 65
Rogers, Robert, 121n

Rooney, William, 99
Rosa Bernd, 102, 103
Rose, Danis, 12, 23n
Rose, Jacqueline, 166n
Roudiez, Leon S., 191n
Rowan, Bertha, 123–36
Rowan, Richard, 125–36
Russell, George, 81
Ryder, 178

Sargent, Cyril, 209, 210
Sarris, Andrew, 145
Sartre, Jean-Paul, 204n
Saussure, Ferdinand de, 191n
Scholes, Robert, 91–107, 182, 271
Scott, Bonnie Kime, 168-79, 271
Senn, Fritz, 25–54, 272
Shakespeare, William, 38, 79, 88, 151, 188, 189, 190, 210
Shaw, George Bernard, 172
Sheridan, Alan, 191n, 192n
Shipman, David, 147
Sinbad the Sailor, 20
Skeat, Walter W., 26, 54n
Smaragdine Tablet, 79
Socrates, 191
Sollers, Phillipe, 181, 183
Solomon, Margaret, 5, 23n
Spiegel, Alan, 154n
Spielberg, Steven, 149
Spivak, Gayatri Chakravorty, 6
Stein, Gertrude, 73, 168, 178
Stephen Hero, 22n, 87, 158, 172, 173
Sternberg, Joseph von, 154n
Swift, Jonathan, 126
Swinburne, 104
Synge, J. M., 67

Tannhäuser, 134
Tarr, 168-75
Temptation of St. Anthony, 150
Things Seen Through a Telescope, 147
Thoreau, Henry David, 118
Thousand and One Nights, The, 248
Three Lives, 178
Through the Looking Glass, 233
Time and Western Man, 176, 177
Tolstoy, Leo, 102, 104
Trismesgistus, Hermes, 79
Turnadot, 4, 20
Tysdahl, B. J., 245

Ulysses, 5, 11, 18, 19, 20, 25, 26, 27, 29, 31, 32, 33 34, 35, 36, 37, 38, 39, 40, 42, 43, 44, 45, 46, 47, 49, 50, 54n, 71, 74, 75, 76, 77, 78, 79, 80, 81,

82, 83, 84, 85, 86, 87, 88, 89, 91, 97, 106, 117, 125, 128, 135, 137–144, 145–54, 157–66, 176, 186, 196, 197, 198, 199, 200, 201, 206–18, 220, 221, 224, 226, 236, 243, 251
Underworld, 154n
Utopia, 95

Verdi, Guiseppe, 93
Verlaine, Paul, 104
Vico, Giambattista, 51, 52, 228, 229
Vinar, E., 221

Wagner, Richard, 134, 136n, 239
Weaver, Harriet Shaw, 4, 55, 168, 169
Weavers, The, 103
Weir, Lorraine, 4, 220–31, 272
Wells, H. G., 172
West, Rebecca, 168, 172
Whitman, Walt, 39,
Widmer, Kingsley, 121n
Wild Duck, The, 104
Wilde, Oscar, 177
Willie's Hat, 148
Winter's Tale, The, 128
Wittgenstein, Ludwig, 203n, 205
Woman of No Importance, A, 177
Woolf, Virginia, 168, 175, 176, 178
Woolsey, John M., 4
Wordsworth, William, 75

Yeats, William Butler, 67, 158

Zecca, Ferdinand, 151
Zola, Émile, 98, 104